THE MIDDLE AGES SERIES

Ruth Mazo Karras, Series Editor
Edward Peters, Founding Editor

A complete list of books in the series
is available from the publisher.

Lyric Tactics

Poetry, Genre, and Practice
in Later Medieval England

Ingrid Nelson

PENN

UNIVERSITY OF PENNSYLVANIA PRESS

PHILADELPHIA

Published by
University of Pennsylvania Press
Philadelphia, Pennsylvania 19104-4112
www.upenn.edu/pennpress

Printed in the United States of America on acid-free paper
1 3 5 7 9 10 8 6 4 2

A Cataloging-in-Publication record is available from the
Library of Congress
ISBN 978-0-8122-4879-1

Lillian

In memoriam

CONTENTS

Introduction

The "boat song" of King Cnut survives in the twelfth-century monastic chronicle of Ely, making it the earliest post-Conquest evidence of an English lyric.[1] The chronicle preserves the song's first quatrain, along with an account of its composition and performance:

> When they were approaching the land, the king rose up in the middle of his men and directed the boatmen to make for the little port at full speed, and then ordered them to pull the boat forward more slowly as it came in. He raised his eyes towards the church which stood out at a distance, situated as it was at the top of a rocky eminence; he heard the sound of sweet music echoing on all sides, and, with ears alert, began to drink in the melody more fully the closer he approached. For he realized that it was the monks singing psalms in the monastery and chanting clearly the Divine Hours. He urged the others who were present in the boats to come round about him and sing, joining him in jubilation. Expressing with his own mouth his joyfulness of heart, he composed aloud a song in English the beginning of which runs as follows:

Merie sungen the munekes binnen Ely	*monks*
Tha Cnut king rew ther-by	*When; rowed*
Roweth, cnihtes, ner the land,	*knights*
And here we thes munekes sang. . . .	

> This and the remaining parts that follow are up to this day sung publicly by choirs and remembered in proverbs.
> The king, while tossing this around in his mind, did not rest from singing piously and decorously in concert with the venerable confraternity, until he reached land.[2]

The chronicle's description of the composition and performance of Cnut's song suggests certain features of the survival, composition, reception, and adaptations of vernacular lyrics in later medieval England. Hearing the liturgical singing by chance, Cnut first joins and then departs from it. Liturgical formulae frequently occasioned new Anglo-Saxon and Middle English verses, in the form of tropes or sequences that amplified the original Latin text.[3] Yet Cnut's song differs from these kinds of adaptations in the oblique relationship it poses between the liturgical source and the new poem, which does not cite or embellish the liturgical text. Rather, it narrates its own inspiration and situation of composition as at once aleatory and somatic. According to the prose account, Cnut's inspiration occurs by chance, and his response to the liturgical song engages multiple senses: sight ("he raised his eyes towards the church"), hearing ("he heard the sound of sweet music"), and, metaphorically, taste ("and . . . began to drink in the melody").[4] By describing Cnut's response to the song in this way, the chronicler suggests features of vernacular lyric that at once identify it with and distinguish it from the monks' song. Such songs were central to regulated institutional practices, from their liturgical use to their function in early education, as children learned them in cathedral "song schools."[5] Yet, as the chronicler's account shows, even these songs can have an element of chance in their reception. Cnut's sensory response to the song emphasizes the somatic and sensual aspects of all music, produced and heard by the body, notwithstanding medieval theories of music that foregrounded its abstraction as a branch of mathematics.[6] Although emanating from the architecturally and symbolically fixed point of the church, the monks' song seems, to the rowers, to have no single point of origin but "echo[es] on all sides." It inspires both a communal performance of the original song ("He urged the others who were present in the boats to come round about him and sing") and a new, spontaneous, vernacular composition. The performances are simultaneous and multiple, as Cnut sings his song over (and with) a chorus of the monks' and knights' liturgical song and continues either aloud or mentally, by "tossing [it] around in his mind."[7]

The surviving quatrain, too, takes as its subject its own composition and in particular its debts to, and differences from, its inspiration. The lyric first describes the occasion of its composition in the third person ("Merie sungen the munekes binnen Ely / Tha Cnut king rew ther-by"). It then shifts tense (from past to present), point of view (from third person to first person), and mood (from indicative to imperative): "Roweth, cnihtes, ner the land, / And here we thes munekes sang." Who speaks the final two lines? The first-person plural at once suggests that Cnut's voice is speaking and invites other singers, past and present, into the voice of the lyric. The combination of all three grammatical shifts marks a distinction between the temporalities of the song and the chronicle. Where the chronicle narrates a linear and completed history, the song continuously re-performs itself as an ongoing event. All of the lyric's singers and audiences—past, present, and future—are invited to "here . . . thes munekes sang." The chronicler represents Cnut's song as a kind of *contrafactum*, or lyric written to fit existing music, which can be sung along with the liturgical offices, recalling the original even as it transforms it. As Sarah Kay remarks, a medieval person would ask of these lyrics not "who is speaking?" but "what am I hearing?" (i.e., what is the musical referent?).[8] Thus, the line, "here we thes munekes sang," alludes at once to an irrecoverable, singular past event and to a recurrent one, the daily singing of the Divine Hours; it is commemorative but also generative. The monks' singing is vigorously present in the line's deixis ("thes munekes"), in the melody of the immediate performance, and in the acknowledgment of the synchronic liturgical performance. And while the lyric's inspiration is affective (Cnut "[e]xpress[es] with his own mouth his joyfulness of heart"), its content is practical: "here we thes munekes sang." Following its composition, Cnut's song persists as a lyric ("sung publicly by choirs") and also migrates to other textual forms ("remembered in proverbs"). Indeed, the song survives for modern readers because of its inclusion in the more robustly attested textual form of the chronicle.

Cnut's boat song merits a place of distinction in English literary history as the first post-Conquest record of an English lyric and thus, in some sense, the first "later medieval" (if not perhaps "Middle English") lyric. Yet this quatrain is also in many ways representative of much of the surviving corpus of insular lyrics between 1100 and 1500. It takes as its subject its own composition and projects its future reception, as many of these lyrics do. Its emphasis is somatic and yet the lyric itself is rhetorically and formally undistinguished by modern standards. Finally, it is incomplete. Far from the "verbal icon" of a complex and totalized poetic object, as the influential twentieth-century critics W. K. Wimsatt and Monroe Beardsley described the lyric poem, Cnut's boat song is permeated by its own history of composition, reception, and transmission.[9]

The song thus raises many questions. Is this a lyric? What does it mean to use as a generic descriptor a word that only enters English in the sixteenth century and comes in the twentieth century to designate a genre whose ascendency is tied to the associated critical practice of "close reading"? Given these anachronisms, does the corpus we call "Middle English lyrics" indeed represent a coherent genre? Do these short poems share features that organize and distinguish them from other medieval literary, didactic, or practical texts? Does identifying them as a genre suggest specific critical reading practices? These questions have come to concern many readers of medieval and later lyric poetry, and they apply equally to most Middle English short poems, as well as to many of those in French and Latin that circulated in later medieval England. Further, examining the generic properties of these poems promises to contribute to broader concerns in literary studies, such as historical poetics (the study of how historical circumstances influence poetic forms and practices) and New Formalism (the integration of formalist and historicist methodologies for literary study), that have motivated scholars across periods to return to questions of literary form, poetry, and the genre of lyric.[10] Some provocative essays and book chapters on medieval English lyrics, notably by Ardis Butterfield, Nicolette Zeeman, and Jessica Brantley, have sought to answer the above questions by considering lyrics as lateral clusters of texts, as implicit literary theory, and as multimedia objects.[11] Yet the last influential book-length study on the medieval lyrics of England, Rosemary Woolf's *The English Religious Lyric in the Middle Ages*, appeared in 1968.

This book undertakes such a study. My central claim is that in later medieval England, the lyric genre is defined as much by its cultural *practices* as by its poetic forms. As Cnut's song shows, plural practices (whether actual or imagined) are attested in the texts of medieval lyrics themselves, as well as in the apparatus and contexts of their survival. Further, lyrics' constellation of practices emerges indirectly and obliquely from regulated institutional forms, such as liturgical performance and ecclesiastical chronicles. They are propagated within and outside these institutions, as singers, audiences, readers, and writers follow and depart from their norms in varying degrees. In short, these lyric practices are *tactical*, in the sense defined by twentieth-century social theorist Michel de Certeau. In tactical practices, subjects find unauthorized, spontaneous, and makeshift pathways among institutional structures (just as Cnut's new song uses and departs from the liturgical offices). By contrast, strategic practices follow defined and normative uses of those structures (e.g., the monks singing the Hours). The tactical reliance on and departure from the institutional forms of textual production define the genre of later medieval English lyric, which draws on other literary and cultural norms both to shape itself as a distinct kind of literary object and to reform the structures that shaped it. And while other medieval genres, such as drama and romance, enjoyed vigorous performance practices and written forms throughout the later Middle Ages, I will argue that the vernacular lyrics that circulated in later medieval England had a unique place within this textual culture because of their particular formal features.[12]

While this study centers on Middle English lyric, it also includes Anglo-French and macaronic poems in its analysis. As several scholars have recently observed, the multilingual environment of England during this period and its situation within a regionally rather than nationally organized Europe invite the expansion of our understanding of medieval "English" literature to include texts in other languages.[13] Lyrics, in particular, are vibrant participants in this multilingual landscape. Their brevity allows for their frequent inclusion in multilingual compilations. Their participation in oral-performative as well as written practices (discussed in greater detail below) allows them to draw on the different registers of each of these languages, which limned a range of "microliteracies" and sociolinguistic practices.[14]

Nonetheless, as Ardis Butterfield has recently observed, insular lyric texts and practices differ markedly from those of their Continental neighbors. In France, Germany, and Italy, lyric poetry is more coherently anthologized and theorized beginning in the thirteenth century.[15] Perhaps because of this coherence, Continental medieval lyrics have been more greatly admired and more extensively theorized than their insular counterparts. While English lyrics bear some marks of the influence of mainland poetry, their practices and forms are largely unique. Thus, while I often situate English lyrics in relation to Continental contexts, and where appropriate draw on critical approaches developed for mainland lyrics, more often the study of insular lyrics demands a departure from these ways of thinking. While the French tradition, in particular, greatly influences English lyric, critical models developed for French lyrics do not completely account for insular practices. To cite just one influential example, while the insular corpus offers examples of the kind of textual lability that Paul Zumthor called *mouvance*, whereby performed texts undergo linguistic changes that defy the determination of a stable "best text," this concept does not account for the kind of transformation witnessed in the relationship between the sung liturgical offices and Cnut's composition.[16] Rather, this is an essentially social relationship of tactics, as a regulated textual performance is transformed by occasional practice. In short, while Continental and especially French lyric traditions will frequently provide contexts for my readings of English and Anglo-French lyrics, this book will focus on insular texts and practices as constituting a distinct medieval literary tradition.

Examining lyric tactics further promises to advance our understanding of medieval literary culture, integrating written texts, performance practices, and poetic forms as central and interdependent features of medieval literature. This book thus defines the medieval lyric genre as much by what it *does* (its cultural work) as by what it *is* (its formal features). Indeed, these two aspects of lyric constitute and influence each other. The episode recording Cnut's song demonstrates many of the features of lyric tactics, both as a practice and as a poetics, in post-Conquest England. This lyric is inspired by an institutionally regulated text but departs from it; it relies on a communal act of singing to facilitate individual composition, and it survives by means of the plural channels of repeated performance, migration into other forms, and inscription in a well-defined textual form. This genre distinguishes itself from its Continental peers by its development, navigation, and theorization of this unique constellation of practices, which emerge from specific aspects of later medieval England's textual and performative cultures.

The next section of this chapter gives an account of the features of these cultures that are most relevant to this study. I then develop a theory of lyric tactics, with reference to Certeau's work, by way of a reading of the thirteenth-century English lyric "Fowls in the Frith." While this book is most interested in examining the short poems of medieval England as a cultural production specific to a time and place, it also is cognizant of the provocative and fraught history of the term "lyric" within the discipline of literary studies and the anachronism of using this term to describe medieval poetry. This chapter thus concludes with a discussion of the difficulties of placing medieval English lyrics in the long history of the lyric genre and suggests how lyric tactics might offer an alternate literary history in which the medieval lyric is paradigmatic rather than marginal.

Text and Practice in Later Medieval England

The modes of textual transmission in later medieval England were diverse. An increase in the production of written texts, by scholastic and legal institutions, occurred within and alongside vibrant cultures of performance. Michael Clanchy's landmark study, *From Memory to Written Record: England 1066–1307*, describes the sweeping post-Conquest changes in English legal culture as it shifts from a performative to a documentary system. Earlier legal culture was event based, centering on performances like the trothplight ceremony, in which symbolic clothing and objects as well as oaths spoken in the presence of witnesses confirmed a legally binding contract.[17] The thirteenth century saw the rise of a documentary bureaucracy, energized by Henry II's legal reforms and Edward I's *quo warranto* proceedings, which asked the nobility to document "by what warrant" they held their franchises.[18] When it appeared, Clanchy's work formed part of a body of transdisciplinary scholarship evaluating the differences between oral and literate cultures, particularly the impact of written textuality on culture.[19] The tone of this work oscillated between the elegiac and the triumphal. By some accounts, once supplanted by literacy, a lost oral culture survived only in fragments or performance practice quickly succumbing to the "technologizing of the word," in Walter Ong's evocative phrase. Yet literacy also drove the creation and adoption of new ways of organizing experience and cognition that drew on the conventions and structures of written texts.[20]

Lyrics circulate within and across these contexts in distinct and often partially attested forms. Yet when considered as one part of the multimodal practices of lyric performance, reception, and recording, we can think of these fragments not as relics of an extinct oral culture but as positive evidence of a comprehensive network of lyric practice, in which partial texts serve as records of and cues for a vibrant culture of performance and dissemination.[21] What are described elegiacally as "lost" lyrics by R. M. Wilson often appear in a form similar to Cnut's boat song: a verse or stanza quoted in another context, such as the partial English lyrics composed by St. Godric, or the single refrain line, "Swete lamman dhin are" (Sweet lover, your favor), recorded in a tale of a priest who misspeaks the mass after being kept awake by churchyard revelers.[22] Flyleaves, margins, and unfilled folios of longer works often preserve lyrics or lyric fragments. Four haunting poems on a flyleaf of Oxford, Bodleian Library MS Rawlinson D 913, including "Maiden in the Moor Lay" and "Ich am of Irlaunde," appear to be the lyrics of danced carols. In a collection of scientific treatises, an enigmatic verse appears following an account of the constellations: "Simenel hornes [horn-shaped loaves] ber non thornes Alleluya."[23] Lyrics and lyric fragments appear as pen trials or as appendages to longer works.[24] They also survive in manuscript miscellanies or anthologies among nonlyric texts. As Julia Boffey puts it, "These poems were recorded unsystematically and often simply accidentally."[25] In other words, the written records of lyrics are unlike those of other medieval texts.

Whereas a scientific treatise, theological summa, or even a long literary work is copied for preservation, with the expectation of consistency and completeness, written lyrics often bear witness in their very incompleteness to their survival in other contexts: in the popular memory, for instance, and in performance.

Even when complete lyrics survive, they tend to appear among diverse collections of texts. Clusters of English lyrics appear in both religious and secular commonplace books; two of these are discussed in later chapters.[26] During the thirteenth and fourteenth centuries, English lyrics often appeared in sermons or in preachers' handbooks. Such lyrics frequently served as summaries of the structure of a sermon (the *distinctio*) or as mnemonics to drive home important themes.[27] What we seldom find in England, especially before the fifteenth century, are dedicated lyric "anthologies," or single-genre codices. By comparison, England's closest neighbor, France, produced many *chansonniers* of troubadour lyrics beginning in the thirteenth century.[28] These "songbooks" canonized lyrics and their composers. They frequently arranged their contents by individual authors, with any anonymous lyrics clustered at the end; others were organized by subgenre (*sirvente*, *jeu-parti*, etc.). Features particular to the medieval manuscript further developed the identity of each poet, from portraits in illuminated initials, to rubrics naming the poet, to prefatory *vidas* describing the poet's life. The first surviving single-author *chansonnier*, comprising the works of Adam de la Halle, dates from the early thirteenth century.[29] These collections also gained generic force in Continental Europe, as the anthologizing of short poems gave rise to "poetry existing for and because of the book": a lyric genre forged in writing rather than in performance, created as much by compilers and readers as by poets.[30] Although later medieval England was not without its own "songbooks," they are distinctly different from the French *chansonniers*. One of the best-known examples, British Library MS Harley 2253 (1330–40; the subject of the next chapter), includes no authorial attributions, and its lyrics appear among a trilingual collection of saints' lives, verse sermons, and fabliaux. The preacher's handbook of John of Grimestone, compiled in 1372, contains lyrics organized according to possible sermon themes. Richard Rolle's lyrics were collected in single-author manuscripts, and collections of liturgical songs in Latin, French, and English, such as we find in the thirteenth-century manuscript British Library MS Arundel 248, are not uncommon. Yet English lyric manuscripts tend to be plain and unadorned by comparison with the lavishly illuminated *chansonniers*, indicating that lyrics occupied a different place in

English culture than in French. Further, these recognizably anthologistic collections from England form only a small part of the material textual history of medieval English lyric, with lyrics more frequently found among diverse texts without recognizable generic organization. On the whole, the kind of authorizing and generic work that the *chansonniers* do for French lyric does not apply in England.

However, it is important to note that while the material forms of lyric texts in England and France differ significantly, English books frequently record French lyrics, reflecting the multilingualism of the English "vernacular." French is an insular language in medieval England, less a foreign and colonizing tongue than a "common possession," an idiom used in a broad array of cultural, social, or institutional contexts.[31] Lyrics especially bear witness to England's linguistic landscape. Many English lyric manuscripts (including the two studied in subsequent chapters) contain French and Latin texts. We find versions of the same lyric in French, English and Latin, such as the lyric beginning "Love is a selkud wodenesse [strange madness]," in Oxford, Bodleian MS Douce 139, where it is copied with Latin and French versions of the same quatrain.[32] And we even find all three languages in the same lyric, as in the lyric beginning "Dum Ludis Floribus," whose final stanza reads,

Scripsi hec carmina in tabulis;
Mon ostel est enmi la vile de Paris;
May Y sugge namore, so wel me is;
Yef Hi deye for love of hire, duel hit ys!

[I've written these songs on a tablet. My lodging's amid the city of Paris. I may say no more, as seems best; should I die for love of her, sad it is!][33]

Further, the relationship between a written text and its medieval performance contexts is necessarily attenuated. As a category of medieval culture, "performance" is less a distinctly demarcated event than a mode or habitus that was available within a range of medieval activities, from socializing in the town center to private reading.[34] As befits their name, many lyrics were sung, but it is often unclear whether surviving lyric manuscripts are directly connected to performance. Some lyric collections that have been dubbed "minstrel manuscripts" have potential institutional affiliations and may be as well suited to private reading as to singing.[35] Lyrics were also sung by nonprofessionals. The performance instructions for the thirteenth-century lyric "Sumer is icumen in," found in a manuscript associated with Reading Abbey and accompanied by music and the parallel Latin text "Perspice Christicola," describe the round form for singing its verses and chorus and suggest that "this canon may be sung by four companions."[36] A handful of other medieval English lyrics also survive with musical accompaniment.[37] The absence of music does not necessarily mean a poem went unsung; many lyrics may have been adapted to well-known tunes contrafactually.[38] For instance, the Latin lyric "Flos pudicitie," which appears with music alongside its French analogue, "Flur de virginite," in British Library MS Arundel 248, bears the rubric "Cantus de Domina post cantum Aaliz." Its editor speculates that this refers to a troubadour or secular song based on the romance connotations of the name "Aaliz."[39] In two manuscripts, the lyric "Man mai longe lives weene [expect]" appears with musical notation, where it is followed immediately by a *contrafactum* (without notation), "On hir is mi life ilong" (My life belongs to her).[40]

While music is perhaps the most obvious indicator of lyric performance, other performance structures also influenced lyric practice. A significant part of the surviving corpus of Middle English lyrics appears in the form of carols, refrain-driven poems that once accompanied a round dance but in the later Middle Ages had an existence independent of the dance form. Guests at fifteenth-century banquets were often asked to sing carols.[41] Other lyrics also have their origins in dance songs, especially those taking the French forms of the *balade, roundel,* or *virelai* that started to appear in England in the second half of the fourteenth century. The sermon lyrics mentioned above were, of course, influenced by a rhetorical tradition that placed as much emphasis on performance as on the composition of the written text.[42] Preachers sometimes drew on the very popularity of performed lyrics, taking them as the texts of their sermons and explicating their moral meanings. In the thirteenth century, one friar built his sermon around an English carol, "Atte wrastlinge my lemman I chese." Another, Stephen Langton, took the French carol "Bele Aelis" as his theme.[43] Evidence of lyric performance, possibly apocryphal, also survives in chronicles like the *Liber Eliensis* that records Cnut's boat song, as well as in Pierre Langtoft's *Chronicle,* later translated by Robert Mannyng of Brunne, which records invective lyrics of Scottish "flyting."[44]

The plural forms of lyric survival and transmission have implications for the widely discussed concept of *auctorite,* the idea that material textual apparatus confers or reifies authorship and authority in medieval English literature.[45] While some critics have argued that particular poets—Chaucer,

Gower, and Richard Rolle—developed a kind of authority based on the lyric form, medieval English lyrics more often tend to be, as Rosemary Woolf says, "genuinely anonymous": authors' names were lost not through the vagaries of archival survival but rather because of their unimportance to contemporary scribes and readers.[46] Indeed, practices of lyric composition—from the *mouvance* and *variance* of a lyric's multiple versions, to the citation of known lyrics in new poems, to the composition of *contrafacta*—meant that it was often meaningless to speak of a single lyric author.[47] Further, the legal and scholastic institutions that produced the written texts of the *auctores* seldom copied vernacular literature, and in England, short poems were even less likely than longer works to be framed with the apparatus of *auctorite*.[48] And while the scholastic prologue's well-defined taxonomy of forms offers a structure for reifying *auctorite* that was deployed by some vernacular authors, if we survey a broad range of vernacular prologues, we discover a more expansive and open-ended literary theory.[49] As Emily Steiner points out, "Authority is something that one is always in relation to, that one is never absolutely identical to, and that one can only provisionally be said to possess."[50] The editors of a collection of English literary prologues note, "Latin theorizing is often too far removed from the situation in which vernacular texts came into being to provide a satisfactory governing template for understanding these prologues or the texts they introduce."[51] With their diverse material contexts and performance practices, insular lyrics require reorienting our "governing template" for literary analysis away from Latinate models, which are too often taken as foundational in the study of medieval English literature, and also away from the hegemonic authority presumed to be the aim of this literature and its composers. What these lyrics demonstrate, instead, is a vital tradition of the literary as a component of community, in which a text's range of potential practices defines and shapes its social and literary existence and importance.

The written records and performance contexts of medieval English lyrics reveal their distinct constellation of practices across the institutions of documentary production and cultures of performance. Further, these lyrics' formal features, especially their (relative) brevity, their mutability (via *mouvance*, *variance*, citation, and contrafacture), and their reliance on rhetorical *topoi*, which I discuss in the next section, differentiate them from other performed texts like romances or plays. These formal features distinguish lyrics as a particularly nimble and modular group of texts, able to insinuate themselves into and around longer narrative or didactic texts, or into the literal blank spaces of the manuscript page, as marginalia or filler. Lyrics also traverse the distinct yet not isolated categories of French and English vernacularity, of writing and performance, of official and popular practices. In sum, what unites these shorter poems as a genre is not only their formal features but also the ways in which these features permit and encourage a set of practices that navigate later medieval England's specific textual and performative cultures.

Lyric Tactics

The brief survey of lyric survival above reflects the complexity of textual and performative cultures in later medieval England. What has been described as a culture in "transition" from orality to literacy can be understood instead as a culture of generative hybridity, in which written texts and performance practices intersect in the corpus of short poems we now call lyrics. Such poems are deeply implicated in, but not entirely of, a range of institutional forms and practices. Yet, by and large, they are not characterized by their resistance to or subversion of such forms and practices; indeed, lyrics frequently emerge from and circulate within institutional contexts. Thus, a participatory and interdependent account of the encounters between lyrics and the institutions of textuality is needed. In particular, the social theorist Michel de Certeau's admittedly speculative and incomplete concept of "tactics" offers a way to describe the practices surrounding medieval lyrics. In *The Practice of Everyday Life*, Certeau makes a distinction between the strategic and tactical uses of institutional forms. A strategy is "the calculus of force-relationships which becomes possible when a subject of will and power (a proprietor, an enterprise, a city, a scientific institution) can be isolated from an 'environment.'" Such a strategy defines an "other" by defining an institutionally controlled space, which Certeau calls a "proper," and generating a set of authorized relations between subjects within and without the proper. By contrast, a tactic is a practice of this "other" subject, a "way of operating" within the structures of power that does not necessarily obey the determinate relationships of strategy. Tacticians seize "opportunities" in order to manipulate events to their advantage, follow "wandering paths" (*lignes d'erre*) through and around the defined trajectories of the proper, and are alert to changing circumstances that might alter their operations. Tactics are, then, the "practices of everyday life," the mundane and irreducible actions of the

"others" that are informed by without conforming to institutional procedures.[52] In Certeau's most famous example, from the essay "Walking in the
City," strategies and tactics are illustrated with the example of an urban
pedestrian. Certeau's walker, a tactician, navigates the fixed forms of an urban
landscape to create "pathways" that elude the disciplinary force of the power
structures that created them. The walker's itinerary is a creative practice
whose map is, we might say, a kind of text composed from the forms and
structures of the city. Most important, for this study, tactics, like strategies,
are relationships to structures of power. But unlike strategies, they are ad
hoc, improvisatory, and unregulated. These relationships are responsive and
adaptive rather than proscribed and determinate, everywhere shaped by structures without being subordinate to them.

"Lyric tactics" refer to the practices by which lyrics are composed, modified, performed, transmitted, and circulated among institutional forms of
textuality. Describing these practices as "tactical" emphasizes the *relationships*
between them and the existing structures with which they interact. These
structures may be literary forms, scribal or compilational conventions, or
cultural or institutional norms. Certeau's conceptual tools and the plurality
of practices and subject positions they describe are in many ways more appropriate to medieval culture than those premised on the more totalizing reach
of discourses in modernity, such as Foucauldian discourse theory. Where
Foucault studies practices ("procedures") that, by their repetition, develop
into a governing apparatus, Certeau seeks a complementary theory that
would account for the manifold practices that are not governed by procedural
relationships. The difference is subtle: while both theorists begin with practice, Certeau critiques Foucault for focusing on procedures that produce a
systematic discourse and overlooking others that "have not given rise to a
discursive configuration."[53] Certeau seeks to describe the outliers, the eccentricities, and the singularities that lend vibrance and spontaneity to everyday
life. These practices do not necessarily oppose or resist the dominant order;
rather, they operate *within* the structures created by them.

As Certeau scholars have observed, *The Practice of Everyday Life* is in
many ways an unfinished work, more a "blueprint" of the parameters of a
cultural studies methodology than a "map" of a complete theory.[54] His dominant metaphor of the tactical is spatial; a strategy "assumes a place," whereas
a tactic has no distinct "localization" and therefore no recognizable "border-
line" that totalizes it with respect to the other.[55] This metaphor seems
to anticipate recent work on mobility and networks emerging from social

theory. Inspired by the actor-network theory of sociologist Bruno Latour, a new model of textuality and cultural transmission sees texts as assemblages created by multiple actors working in a network. These distributed models of textual production and dissemination describe many premodern practices, especially the diverse modes of mobility affecting medieval texts, bodies, and objects. As Jacques Le Goff put it, "The mobility of men in the Middle Ages was extreme."[56] From the itineraries that offer a new perspective on medieval literary history to the decentering and recursive journeys of literary characters, nonlinear and distributed mobilities inform a variety of medieval texts and practices.[57] The most trenchant application of such network theories to the medieval lyric has been put forth in some recent essays by Ardis Butterfield. Butterfield notes that English and Anglo-French lyrics tend to reuse and circulate set phrases—in fact, clichés—that may come from lyric or nonlyric contexts, such as sermons. This aspect of medieval lyric was once derided under a twentieth-century critical paradigm that privileged originality and uniqueness in its assessment of literary value. Yet as Butterfield points out, these clichés are generative and creative; they are an important component of medieval lyric form that encourages a model of reading that differs from the New Formalist paradigm of close reading. Instead, Butterfield proposes "lateral" reading, which would take into account the contexts (social and textual) in which these set phrases circulate, and the Latourian networks of lyrics that together constitute the literary object.[58]

Latour's theories are in many ways more complex and complete than Certeau's, and Butterfield's applications of them are helpful in understanding how medieval lyric form uses and reuses common language in creative rather than derivative ways. Yet exploring medieval lyrics with respect to tactics allows us to extend these theories in two important ways. First, it broadens our definition of the genre from one based on form to one based on practice. Framing it in this way creates a largely false dichotomy; of course, practice is integral to both Latourian network theory and Butterfield's lyric theory. Yet because tactics apply explicitly to practices or modes of operation, considering medieval lyrics in this light shifts our focus from verbal patterning to social practice. Second, Certeau's theory invites us to consider the relationships between lyrics and the normative textual, literary, or performative conventions in a way that refuses to set up a hierarchy or opposition between them. The lyric is a tactical text that relies on and emerges from these standards without being disciplined by them. In this model, rather than appropriating institutional textual practices to gain legitimacy (in the form of authority, for example), lyrics deploy them tactically, exploiting their potentialities, multiplicities, and ambiguities that strategic proscriptions attempt to unify, streamline, and regulate.

Further, lyrics are tactical not only in their practices but also in their implicit theorization of their own genre. Nicolette Zeeman has suggested that lyrics offer one example of how literary genres can, if situated or flagged in a certain way, act as forms of self-theorization that emerge from literature rather than treatises.[59] Throughout this book, studies of lyrics will elaborate how this implicit genre theory takes shape when poetic forms are understood within the contexts of their practices. To begin to understand how this works, I will examine how a pervasive rhetorical figure, the topos or commonplace, demonstrates and develops lyric tactics in a thirteenth-century poem, "Fowls in the Frith." Ernst Robert Curtius, in his magisterial study, *European Literature and the Latin Middle Ages*, identifies the topos as a foundational form of medieval literature. In classical rhetoric, these conventional figures served to locate an audience in a common rhetorical place. Topoi evolved in the Middle Ages as cross-textual motifs: the "book of nature," the *locus amoenus* or ideal landscape, or the world upside-down.[60] For Curtius, topoi are the rhetorical matrix from which medieval literature is generated. While contemporary readers often associate the study of topoi with conservative philological methods, Michelle Warren has recently argued that it can promote ethical humanist modes of reading. In her words, topoi can be understood "not as fixed points but rather as nodes in dynamic global relations, anchored in specific landscapes while claiming vast proportions."[61] With their anonymity and mobility, lyrics perhaps best illustrate how topoi are essentially relational rather than totalizing.

"Fowls in the Frith" not only exemplifies the lyric's reliance on topoi but also unites rhetoric and practice to theorize lyric tactics. Surviving with musical notation in a thirteenth-century cartulary, this poem consists of five short lines.

Foweles in the frith,	*woods*
The fisses in the flod,	*river*
And I mon waxe wod.	*must; mad*
Mulch sorw I walke with	
For beste of bon and blod.[62]	

The poem's frame of reference is ambiguous; it could be a sacred or a profane work.[63] The "birds in the woods, fish in the river" formula was both a secular and a religious topos in the Middle Ages. It has an extensive tradition in Christian writing, beginning in Genesis 1:20, when both birds and fish were created on the fifth day, and continuing in medieval religious literature. The placement of the birds and fish in their natural habitats refers to the cosmic hierarchy created by God, from which man is alienated due to original sin. (Passus 11 of the B-text of *Piers Plowman*, to cite one example, offers an extended meditation on this topos.) Further, the language of the poem appears in other lyrics of the later Middle Ages, such as a lullaby that survives in autonomous copies and in sermons.[64] In the religious or secular context, the final line of the poem is ambiguous. In one reading, the speaker feels sorrow on account of Christ, who was the "best of bone and blood," and of the suffering of his Passion: "I walk with much sorrow *that I feel for* the best of bone and blood." (If secular, "the best of bone and blood" can equally describe the beloved.) Alternately, the speaker himself or herself is the "best (*or* beast) of bone and blood"—the highest order of being in God's earthly creation—who nonetheless feels sorrow: "I walk with much sorrow *despite being* the best/a beast of bone and blood." Even the musical accompaniment to "Fowls in the Frith," which some readers have believed to be liturgical, might have been used for secular purposes.[65]

The poem's topoi locate it within a network of lyric forms while also pointing to the expansiveness of lyric practice. They demonstrate how this particular form creates mobile relations rather than totalizing and isolating the lyric text. Like the rest of the poem, the opening topos works across sacred and secular meanings. Birdsong frequently opens love lyrics, especially in a springtime setting, or *reverdie*. This season excites carnal love but can also heighten a rejected lover's feelings of dissatisfaction. In a secular reading of the poem, the birds and the fish are in their proper places in nature, enjoying the satisfaction of their carnal desires, while the speaker is out of place, experiencing sorrow on account of the "best" woman "of bone and blood." The poem's economical language does not reveal whether the cause of the speaker's sorrow is Christ or a woman.

Further, "Fowls in the Frith" uses its topoi, the rhetorical common places, to thematize place as a poetic and metaphysical construct. The first two lines locate animals in their habitats with isocolons that hinge on the word "in." The preposition replaces the verb in these lines, substituting location for action, and evokes a classical definition of place that was well known in the Middle Ages. In the *Physics*, Aristotle describes eight different uses of "in": the part in the whole, the species in the genus, and so forth. The two opening lines of "Fowls in the Frith" demonstrate Aristotle's final use of "in," when "something is *contained in* a vessel, and, in general, in a place."[66] These lines thus thematize place by using this preposition in lieu of a verb. They suggest stasis but also motion, evoking the micromovements of each animal within its habitat. And indeed, Aristotle conceives place and motion as interdependent concepts: "[I]t would never occur to us to make place a topic for investigation if there were no such thing as change of place. That is the main reason that we think that even the heavens are in place—because they are in constant motion. This kind of change may be either movement or increase and decrease."[67] Aristotle here identifies two kinds of motion, what he calls "movement," or locomotion, and "increase and decrease," or change. Place itself, however, is motionless; it is "the limit of the containing body, [where] the container makes contact with what it contains." Further, the "contents" of such a container must be "a body which is capable of movement."[68] In other words, it is the potentiality of motion that defines the boundary of place, and of form.[69] The first two lines of "Fowls in the Frith" announce this theme, locating mobile entities (birds, fish) in their respective places.

Following the assertion of place and in-place-ness of the first two lines of "Fowls in the Frith," we have an image of Aristotle's second kind of motion, change: "And I mon waxe wod." The verb "waxen," to grow, alludes to an affective state, which the next line connects to Aristotle's first kind of motion, locomotion: "Mulch sorw I walke with." The alliteration of "waxe" and "walke" and the parallel affective terms "wod" and "sorwe" suggest a relationship between the two kinds of motion, change and locomotion, that makes explicit the potential mobility of the birds and fishes invoked in the first two lines. Change and locomotion enter the poem concurrent with its affective content: "I mon waxe wod." As Curtius points out, the topics of medieval poetry, even though they reflect "timeless" emotional states and human relationships, are also figures of change: they generate more topoi, and they describe changes in affect.[70] In other words, this poem's concern with motion is multiply valenced: rhetorical, affective, and hermeneutic.

We have seen how the poem's rhetoric thematizes tactics as situational movements, both human and poetic, across determinate structures (natural, poetic, and metaphysical). But what of this lyric as an object of practice? We have already noted that its musical accompaniment is similarly tactical, with both secular and religious potential. Further, the material form of the lyric is itself displaced in its unique manuscript witness, Oxford, Bodleian MS Douce 139. Largely a collection of thirteenth-century legal documents relating to the town of Coventry, the codex also includes copies of a reissue of the Magna Carta from 1253 and a French verse rendition of the Statute of Gloucester from 1278. "Fowls in the Frith" and its music appear on folio 5r. The poem shares a hand, which appears nowhere else in the manuscript, with the Anglo-French lyric "Ay queer ay un maus," also set to music.[71] These lyrics, copied around 1270, were inserted in the manuscript as quire endpapers after the rest of its contents were compiled. The lyric copies were essentially scrap paper used to protect the more valuable legal material within the book.

In other words, not only does the text of "Fowls in the Frith" thematize displacement, the material text of the poem is itself displaced from a literary context. The vernacular songs have been located in a context of documentary place, among the legal records of an English town. MS Douce 139 owes its existence to an increasing emphasis on the documentary construction of place (in this case, Coventry) arising from the bureaucratic expansion of thirteenth-century England. As the presence of "Fowls in the Frith" shows, the lyrics of medieval England rely on such literary and textual structures but navigate them tactically. This navigation is at once "internal," within the form and rhetoric of the poem, and "external," in the material and performative contexts of its transmission. Yet tactical practice inherently belies the distinction between interiors and exteriors, as the mobility of the one displaces and reshapes the other.

Most vernacular texts of later medieval England are influenced by its particular cultures of textual production and performance. As the example of "Fowls in the Frith" demonstrates, certain formal features of the lyric—its brevity, its rhetoric of the commonplace—make it more amenable to tactical inclusion among other texts and, indeed, to the implicit theorization of the tactical. This conjunction of forms and practices unites these short poems as a genre specific to the culture of later medieval England. How, then, can we understand the relationship between what I am calling the medieval English lyric and the transhistorically defined literary genre of "lyric"? To address this question, I briefly examine the modern emergence of theories of the lyric and of the definition of the Middle English lyric corpus.

Medieval English Lyrics and "the Lyric"

Middle English lyrics have entered modern literary criticism through the highly mediated apparatus of modern genre making, which has been informed as much by post-Romantic aesthetic expectations of lyric poetry as by the philological methods central to medieval studies. Thus, it is worth considering what is at stake in using the word "lyric" to describe this corpus and to what extent the integration of medieval short poems into modern genealogies of lyric can inform and revise transhistorical lyric theory. As many critics of lyric and nonlyric poetry seek to integrate formalist methodologies with their political and historicist critiques, the medieval lyric's difference from the post-Romantic genre promises to make it paradigmatic rather than marginal, as it has frequently been conceived in literary histories of English poetry. This premodern corpus offers a lyric theory that precedes the early modern appropriations of Classical poetics that defined lyric poetry as a genre, as well as Enlightenment concepts of subjectivity that influenced modern poetics.[72] In order to begin to locate medieval short poems in this longer history of lyric genre, I describe below how this corpus came to be identified with the genre, despite the lack of a generic name or poetic theory in the Middle Ages. I then briefly discuss the post-Romantic aesthetic theories that defined and privileged the lyric genre, as well as their more recent critiques, suggesting how medieval lyric can advance culturally and historically inflected formalisms and poetics.

If individual medieval lyrics take shape by means of rhetorical and material tactics, so too does imagining this corpus as a genre—within its own cultural context as well as transhistorically—require tactical thinking. For a medieval person, there was no such thing as a lyric. The Latin *lyricus* seldom appeared in the Middle Ages, and the word "lyric" entered the English language only in the sixteenth century, when it was used to translate Horace's *Ars Poetica* and in the neoclassical treatises on poetics of Sir Philip Sidney and others.[73] In one of its few medieval appearances, in Isidore of Seville's *Etymologies* (615–30), *lyricus* is affiliated with song: "Lyric poets are named after the Greek term ληρεῖν (lit. 'speak trifles'), that is, from the variety of their songs. Hence also the lyre is named."[74] Indeed, of the lyre's etymology, Isidore says, "The lyre is so called from the word ληρεῖν, that is, from 'variety of voices,' because it renders diverse sounds."[75] For the Benedictine schoolmaster Conrad of Hirsau (c. 1070–1150), lyric is merely one of eleven poetic forms (including pastoral, comic, tragic, elegiac, etc.). According to Conrad, "The verse-form in which drinking-parties with their accompanying amusements are described is lyric. It gets its name from *apo to lirin*, that is from variation, hence *delirus* ('crazy') is he who alters from what he was."[76] Of course, the short poems of which Isidore and Conrad speak are Latin compositions whose forms vary greatly over the five centuries separating the two writers and further bear only an attenuated relationship to the poems we now think of as medieval English lyrics.[77] Yet it is worth noting that "variety" seems to be a defining feature of *lyricus*, suggesting at once its plurality and variability. The variety of medieval songs is also evident in the array of vernacular terms that described short poems in later medieval England. These include "*all-purpose* terms like *song, dite*, and *tretys*, . . . *function-related* titles such as *complaint* and *supplication*, and the formal terms (usually French-derived) like *ballade* and *roundel*."[78] Thomas Duncan suggests that the term "song," with its implications of musical accompaniment, best names this corpus, since many of these poems were either composed for singing or took their verse forms from music.[79]

If the names for short poems are diverse, medieval poetic theory also tends to separate them by type. Manuals of lyric forms generally focus on Latin or Continental vernacular poetry. John of Garland's *Parisiana Poetria* (1220–35) includes a section on the *ars rithmica* that describes rhyming and rhythmic Latin poetry, including lyrics.[80] Dante's polemic on vernacular literature, *De vulgari eloquentia*, comes closest to unifying diverse forms of lyric poetry (the sonnet, *ballata*, and any "arrangement of words that are based on harmony") under a single term, *canzone* or "song," which privileges the words rather than the music of these compositions and emphasizes authorship.[81] The French produced manuals on troubadour poetry and anthologies of lyric quotation in the thirteenth century and treatises on the newly popular fixed forms (*rondeaux, balades, virelais*, etc.) in the fourteenth century.[82] However, the most influential poetic treatises focus on narrative poetry: Geoffrey of Vinsauf's *Poetria Nova* (1208–13), Matthew of Vendôme's *Ars Versificatoria* (1175), and the anonymous *Tria Sunt* (1256–1400).[83]

Most medieval English lyrics demonstrate only patchy or limited awareness of Continental treatises, and as we have seen, they survive in very different material forms from their Continental analogues. Thus, our current conceptions of the corpus and theorization of "Middle English lyrics" emerge largely from twentieth- and twenty-first-century editorial and critical work. The pioneering editions of Carleton Brown and Rossell Hope Robbins, published between 1924 and 1952, created a broadly conceived corpus from the short poems scattered across a diverse collection of manuscripts and made it visible to readers.[84] The *Index of Middle English Verse* and its permutations cast an even wider net, including all English verse texts, making possible the comparison of versions and analogues of the short poems. If this kind of editorial work tends toward broad inclusivity, contemporary criticism generally subdivides the corpus thematically or formally. Religious lyrics have been most comprehensively studied.[85] Rosemary Woolf described these poems as "meditative" and traced their motifs across the Latin tradition.[86] Peter Dronke's *Medieval Latin and the Rise of the European Love-Lyric* takes a similar approach to secular lyric, locating Continental and English courtly love lyrics in relation to Latin literary rhetorics. Manuscript contexts also reveal localized meanings and functions of lyrics, from verses that act as *distinctiones* in thematic sermons to the regional politics of the poems of MS Harley 2253.[87]

Yet medieval lyric practice, whether sacred or secular, was not only textual but also read, heard, spoken, and sung—in short, embodied, as a growing critical literature demonstrates. As Emma Dillon points out, the implicit theory of song that emerges from Occitan troubadour lyrics links verbal expression with sound: in these songs, "there are no words which do not have voices."[88] Private devotional reading can also invite performative "habits of thought" into the monastic practice of *lectio*, as Jessica Brantley shows in her discussion of a fourteenth-century Carthusian manuscript containing illustrated lyrics of Richard Rolle.[89] And the poetics of devotional lyrics affect audiences cognitively and psychologically: figurative language mirrors the union of human and divine in the incarnation, for example, and lyric texts can "script emotional performance" in order to instruct readers and speakers in particular modes of feeling.[90] At the same time, secular love lyrics are as much indebted to embodied performance—especially in song and dance—as to conventional textual figures, tropes, and idioms. And like their modern counterparts, medieval lyrics have been studied according to formalisms old and new, from R. L. Greene's magisterial study and compilation of English carols to Nicolette Zeeman's suggestive readings of the "imaginative theory" implicit in English *chansons d'aventure*.[91]

Given the difficulties of working with this corpus, this body of scholarship represents a relatively vigorous critical literature. But while medievalists embrace lyric readings, they are less forthcoming with lyric theories that would unite these diverse texts under a single and comprehensive generic identity.[92] It is perhaps this scarcity that accounts for the elision of the premodern short poem in the broader transhistorical reassessment of English lyric and poetic form.[93] For if medieval English lyrics have been undertheorized in their own time and in ours, they differ starkly from the post-Romantic lyric, whose generic identity is central to the development of modern literary criticism. For Hegel, the three primary literary genres—lyric, epic, and drama—were determined by the relationships they presented between the inner and outer worlds, or "subjectivity" and "objectivity." In this theory, lyric is subjective, epic objective, and drama at once subjective and objective.[94] His theory had a long afterlife: to cite one example, Stephen Dedalus paraphrases it in James Joyce's *Portrait of the Artist as a Young Man*.[95] But while this tripartite theory of genres claims to descend from Aristotle and Horace, its modern permutations elide the modal system on which Classical aesthetics is based, which is less dialectical and more tabular in its structure. That is, Classical aesthetics separated rhetoric from content, implicitly constructing a matrix of genres that permit combinations of each. Indeed, the modern capacious sense of "lyric" is absent from most classical poetics, which, like the later work of Isidore and Conrad, divides short poems into iambics, satires, praise poems, and so forth.[96]

Hegel's dialectic privileges the dramatic genre for its capacity to unite internal and external experience. Yet for many post-Enlightenment thinkers, lyric's ability to express the inner experience of the solitary and autonomous subject lent it a special interest. Lyric poetry was thought to be the language of a contemplative solitude (Latin *otio*) untouched by the compromises and negotiations (*neg-otio*) of intercourse with the world. This understanding of lyric led to its definition as a particular kind of private speech. John Stuart Mill's dictum, "Eloquence is *heard*, poetry is *over*heard," was taken up by Northrop Frye, who remarks that lyric is "preeminently the utterance that is overheard."[97] It is expanded in M. H. Abrams's description of a subgenre, the "greater Romantic lyric," which "present[s] a determinate speaker in a particularized, and usually a localized, outdoor setting, whom we overhear as he carries on, in a fluent vernacular which rises easily to a more formal speech, a sustained colloquy, sometimes with himself or with the outer scene, but more frequently with a silent human auditor, present or absent."[98]

The expression of interiority that characterizes this model of lyric poetry made it an apt object of study for twentieth-century humanist critics, who saw the psyche as transcultural and transhistorical. The creator of "practical criticism," I. A. Richards (a psychologist by training), claimed that reading poetry existed on a continuum with other experiences that develop a person's selfhood: "It is impossible to divide a reader into so many men—an aesthetic man, a moral man, a practical man, a political man, an intellectual man, and so on. It cannot be done. In any genuine experience all these elements inevitably enter."[99] A good critic "must be an adept at experiencing, without eccentricities, the state of mind relevant to the work of art he is judging."[100] For other critics, the primary subjectivity constituting the lyric poem is that of the poet himself. Eliot identifies "three voices of poetry" that depend as much on who speaks as on who listens. The three voices are the poet talking to himself or to no one (lyric), the poet addressing an audience of any size (epic or, Eliot asserts, dramatic monologue), and the voice or voices of distinct dramatic characters addressing an audience (drama). Eliot prizes the "first voice" of lyric, which he prefers to call "meditative verse," as fulfilling the primary function of poetry: "The first effort of a poet should be to achieve clarity for himself."[101] Likewise, in an analysis of Herrick's "Corinna's going a-Maying," Cleanth Brooks remarks, "The poet is a maker, not a communicator. He explores, consolidates, and 'forms' the total experience that is the poem. I do not mean that he fashions a replica of his particular experience of a certain May morning like a detective making a moulage of a footprint in wet clay. But rather, out of the experiences of many May mornings, and out of his experience of Catullus, and possibly out of a hundred other experiences, he fashions, probably through a process akin to exploration, the total experience which is the poem."[102] Rejecting mimesis, Brooks posits poetry as the linguistic "vehicle," to use his term, of the poet's complex subjectivity.

W. K. Wimsatt and Monroe Beardsley expunge both poet's and reader's subjectivities from the reading of lyric, replacing it with a "speaker": "[E]ven a short lyric poem is dramatic, the response of a speaker (no matter how abstractly conceived) to a situation (no matter how universalized). We ought to impute the thoughts and attitudes of the poem immediately to the dramatic *speaker*, and if to the author at all, only by an act of biographical inference."[103] This at once anonymizes and universalizes the complex, experiential subjectivity that generates a lyric poem. This view of lyric persists, notably in the work of Helen Vendler, for whom modern lyric poetry expresses the common "soul" divested of attributes such as race, gender, or social class.[104]

Most recently, Jonathan Culler's aptly titled *Theory of the Lyric* puts forward a model of the genre that identifies the distinctive language of lyric poetry as the defining feature of the genre. Culler identifies four qualities of language specific to lyric poetry: (1) its mode of address to another person or object, which constitutes an indirect address to the reader; (2) its nonmimetic language "events"; (3) its "ritualistic" sound patterns (rhyme, rhythm, etc.); and (4) its use of hyperbole.[105] Just as post-Enlightenment poetic theorists found lyric's transhistorical genre identity in its capacity for subjective utterance, Culler identifies these verbal and rhetorical features as the basis for defining a unified lyric genre across time and space. As he puts it, genres "have the singular property of being potentially resistant to unidirectional historical evolution, in that generic possibilities once exploited remain possible, potentially available, while political, social, and economic systems have moved on in ways we think of as irreversible."[106]

Critiques of such universalizing claims frequently situate both lyric and nonlyric verse in its plural, contingent, and social contexts.[107] In his 1957 radio address, "Lyric Poetry and Society" (translated into English in 1974), Theodor Adorno observed that the concept of the solitary speaker of lyric has ideological underpinnings, since this figure emerges from the alienation produced by capitalist social structures.[108] Adorno and other Marxist critics articulate ways in which qualities of the lyric genre, such as Hegel's durable assertion that it is "subjective," emerge from specific structural and ideological features of culture, such as the alienation produced by capitalism. When applied to modern lyric, Marxist critique tends to be oppositional: the private self is in necessary conflict with a postindustrial society; what Charles Bernstein calls "official verse culture" is antagonistic toward the eccentric poetry of the avant-garde.[109] The group of poet-theorists that identify as the Language poets assert that their writing "places its attention primarily on language and ways of making meaning that takes for granted neither vocabulary, grammar, process, shape, syntax, program, or subject matter. All of these remain at issue."[110] Language poetry attempts to extend the boundaries of linguistic expression beyond reference, rhetoric, or ritual, drawing into the ambit of poetry (if not of lyric) abstract sound, discourses from the colloquial to the bureaucratic, and the layout of the printed page. This school largely subscribes to a Marxist politics of lyric, in that it understands uses of language to express "the social determination of consciousness," especially, for the twentieth and twenty-first centuries, by capitalist economic and cultural forces.[111] As Marjorie Perloff notes, however, the protesters against "official verse culture," too, adhere to particular lyric canons that, even as they claim expansiveness, elide a great deal of poetry that could productively enter into and alter their lyric theories.[112] Recognizing marginal voices and difference as constitutive of the plural identities within cultures, many readers have turned away from lyric to focus on forms that more apparently express these heteroglossic voices: novels, autobiographical narratives, and other writings not conventionally considered literary.[113]

Yet lyric in particular and poetry more generally are far more diverse and flexible than conventional post-Enlightenment aesthetics allow. As so-called New Formalist analyses, especially those pertaining to lyric and poetics, demonstrate, rhetorical and material poetic forms are themselves historically contingent, and expanding our study of verse beyond the traditional definitions of "lyric" promises to reveal a different literary history.[114] Yet many critics also find lyric's formal and practical qualities compelling enough to retain its status as a distinct object of study. For every call to "let 'lyric' dissolve into literature and 'literature' into culture," there is a plea to preserve lyric as a distinct genre.[115] Defenders of lyric cite many qualities that distinguish it as an object of study: its special ability to suspend temporality, its difference from narrative, the particularities of its voice, and its verbal music, to name a few.[116] Further, the pedagogical usefulness of lyric that I. A. Richards recognized—it is a text short enough to be read, digested, and discussed in a single classroom session—remains for many a compelling reason for its study. Another is doubtless the unique pleasure of reading lyrics: their gem-like intricacies, their verbal music, their rhetorical richness, and the intimacy of lyric voices.

Medieval lyrics, it must be said, have often been accused of falling short of these marks. For every "Alisoun," with its earthy eroticism and intricate stanza form, there are ten monorhymed didactic lyrics prodding their readers toward renunciation and contrition. For this reason (among others), medieval English lyrics have often been omitted from or superficially treated in transhistorical accounts of the genre.[117] But it is precisely because these poems resist the formal paradigms and aesthetic models that have determined much lyric criticism in the past century that a new examination of this corpus promises to generate a critical paradigm that might productively enter into and enrich transhistorical lyric theories. Conversely, features of multiple contemporary poetic theories that present themselves as oppositional can productively inform a study of medieval English lyric, which at once participates in the kind of rhetorical ritual language that Culler identifies and draws widely on the kinds of linguistic and material resources championed by the Language poets. Yet none of these modern poetic theories offers an entirely adequate lens for understanding the premodern genre. While the theory of tactics that I have outlined above is essentially Marxist (in its concern with practice, use, and structures of power), it differs from existing Marxist lyric criticism in an important way. The theory of tactics is not oppositional with respect to the structures of power; it is relational, recombinative, and generative. As such, while specific tactics may be subversive in effect, they are as a whole dependent on existing structures. Further, while medieval English lyrics share some commonalities with lyrics of other times and places, their specific cultural contexts influence and even produce their forms, material witnesses, and performances. Thus, understanding that all of these features of medieval lyrics are governed by ad hoc tactics allows us to recognize how a particular approach to practice can do as much to define a genre as its rhetorical forms. Shifting the emphasis from form to practice in the study of this genre suggests that for medieval people, as for us, the lyric genre performs a distinct kind of cultural work. And while it is outside of the scope of this book to explore fully the implications of the model of medieval lyric tactics for the long history of the genre, it is my hope that this study will provide an entry point for thinking about the place of the medieval insular corpus in this history. It is for this reason that, in this book, I call these poems "lyrics" despite the lack of historical justification for the term, in order to assert that this corpus deserves a place within the broader history of this English genre. It is precisely the lack of generic definition that allows the cultural object we now call "medieval lyric" to work tactically on institutional forms of textuality and, conversely, to define itself as the genre that does this tactical work. The very looseness of this medieval corpus suggests its extension to post-medieval poetry within and outside of traditional definitions of "lyric."

*   *   *

Tactics are above all *modes of relation*. Thus, this book focuses on lyrics in contexts where their relations—to the manuscript page, to a compilation, to longer or distinct literary forms—help to define the genre's practices. Of particular interest are those poems and contexts that emphasize and theorize lyric practice, especially when it encounters more standardized or normative forms. Taken together, these textual relationships suggest an implicit lyric theory centered on tactical practice and demonstrate particular aspects of lyrics that facilitate these practices. Each chapter of this study thus considers a larger structure that contains lyrics, whether a manuscript compilation or a long literary work, and each begins with a lyric from its text or manuscript that exemplifies its implicit lyric theory. Although it is not comprehensive, this study attempts to be expansive in its corpus, including sacred and secular, anonymous and authored, compiled and interpolated lyrics. By integrating poetry that is usually separated by theme or context in critical discourse, I seek to demonstrate the persistence of tactics across the significant formal changes to the lyric during the later Middle Ages in England. If tactics define the practices of a genre, then they should flexibly adapt to new forms the genre takes. Thus, conceiving broadly of lyrics in relation to other textual forms (within miscellanies as well as in longer poetic works) demonstrates how tactics persist as lyric forms change.

The core chapters of the book focus on compilations and literary texts of the fourteenth century (although their lyrics, in many cases, record or adapt earlier compositions), while this introduction and the conclusion extend my findings to the longer later medieval period. I have chosen this temporal frame for a few reasons. First, the textual cultures I discussed earlier were still taking shape during the fourteenth century, inviting a sense of freedom and experimentation with their conventions. Second, many lyrics survive in fourteenth-century texts and manuscripts (even when they were composed earlier), offering a significant corpus that is unavailable in earlier post-Conquest England. My final reason is literary-historical. The fourteenth century, once central to Middle English literary criticism, is now rarely considered in its entirety: the newly vital rubric "early Middle English," the significant cultural changes of post-Plague England, and the sense that a disproportionate focus on what were once called the "Ricardian poets" led to overlooking important medieval literature and culture, especially in the fifteenth century, have all served to expand medieval literary studies in productive ways.[118] In this study, though, I suggest that the fourteenth century is an identifiable and distinct epoch in the history of English lyric, whose tactics bear on earlier and later lyrics. Examining this century in its entirety additionally suggests a new reading of a primarily narrative poet who was deeply interested in lyrics and lyricism: Geoffrey Chaucer. Rather than an originary figure who transforms Continental lyrics into a new English form, Chaucer emerges in this study as a transitional figure in the history of English lyric with ties to an existing insular genre based not on influence or sources but on practice.

This book falls roughly into two parts that both show how lyric tactics emerge in and as relations to established medieval forms. The first two chapters focus on manuscript compilations containing significant groups of lyrics. My decision to emphasize the material contexts of lyrics in the first half of this book has to do, in part, with the lack of a comprehensive critical edition of medieval English lyric poetry. Anthologies of Middle English lyrics have long been available, but these largely neglect the multilingual and multigeneric contexts in which these poems tend to survive. As I was completing this book, Susanna Fein and David Raybin's enormously helpful edition of the complete manuscript of British Library MS Harley 2253 became available, as did the digital edition of the Vernon manuscript. Such manuscript editions promise to illuminate the contexts of English lyrics; my own chapter on Harley 2253 contributes, I hope, to an understanding of the place of lyrics in medieval English books. Yet any single compilation is also necessarily idiosyncratic; thus, I have chosen to examine two very different, near-contemporary books containing lyrics. My final reason for emphasizing material contexts in the first part of this book has to do with understanding medieval written texts as a kind of practice. Like lyric poems, medieval English manuscripts are governed by conventional forms that their creators, transmitters, and audiences improvise on, elaborate, and modify. The manuscript compilations discussed in the next two chapters navigate such forms tactically in order to render and theorize the performative and textual practices of lyrics.

Chapter 1, "The Voices of Harley 2253," focuses on the Herefordshire household book containing the well-known "Harley lyrics," British Library MS Harley 2253 (1330–40). The compilation and layout of this lyric's texts demonstrate an attention to a concept of voice that can productively replace our modern idea of a lyric "speaker." Medieval scholastic philosophy, grammatical and rhetorical theory, and the Derridean phenomenology of voice all theorize it as a tactical practice. The Harley manuscript's inclusion of lyric dialogues, poems with nested speakers, and even the scribe's deployment of parchment holes to influence the voices that might perform his texts suggest that lyric voices are important tactics for a diverse range of writing and performance practices.

A tactical lyric voice probably seemed productive and inclusive to the secular household that produced Harley 2253. Yet its moral implications could be troubling for the major producers and disseminators of liturgical or sacred lyrics: friars. To understand how friars relied on lyric tactics for what are ultimately strategic ends, Chapter 2 studies William Herebert's commonplace book (1314–33), a collection of practical and preaching texts that includes the friar's own English hymn translations. This chapter demonstrates that for Herebert, the tactical practices encouraged by lyric language, with its tendency to adopt different meaning according to circumstances, pose a doctrinal problem. How can the popularity of lyrics be deployed in the service of pastoral care while preserving their doctrinal consistency, especially in a literary form whose tactics make it morally ambiguous? A little known Anglo-French lyric in Herebert's compilation, "Amours m'ount si enchanté," poses (and resolves) this problem thematically and formally. Herebert's hymn translations draw on the tactics suggested by this poem to separate song's affective power in performance from its doctrinal regulation in written texts. Lyric tactics thus permit Herebert to reconcile its performance practices with the more strategic forms of scholastic textual conventions.

Whereas manuscript miscellanies use tactics to navigate between the performative and the written aspects of lyric practice, later insular lyrics increasingly explore relationships among literary forms. The second half of this book thus considers how these tactical relationships continue to inform the development of the medieval English lyric. Putting the lyrics in Geoffrey Chaucer's longer works in dialogue with their literary and practical contexts, I demonstrate how later fourteenth-century lyrics continue the tactical practices that shaped earlier lyrics. This is not an argument for direct influence. Rather, my claim is that tactical practice continues to define the insular lyric even as new lyric forms and lyric theories, chiefly those of Continental poetry, influence English literature. Recalling that tactics are modes of relation to existing structures, we can see that these later English lyrics define themselves tactically in relation to other literary forms.

In Chapter 3, "Lyric Negotiations: Continental Forms and *Troilus and Criseyde*," I focus on the relationships between insular lyric practices, new Continental lyric forms, and the political issues raised by Chaucer's historical romance. This chapter takes the social forms and practices of Antigone's song as paradigmatic of Chaucer's understanding of the insular lyric genre, even as it draws on French and Italian poetic sources. The poetics, performance context, and reception of the song present a tactics of negotiation, which speaks to *Troilus and Criseyde*'s political concern with reconciling individual and communal desires. Subsequently reading the *cantici Troili* and the palinode through the model of lyric developed from Antigone's song, I demonstrate how Chaucer's adaptations of Petrarch diminish the kind of panoptic authorial control that the original texts generated and, further, resist (even if they ultimately succumb to) totalizing Petrarchan models of poetics and governance. The lyric tactics of Antigone's song permeate the poem's formal and political concerns, as Chaucer uses the insular lyric's practices to challenge Petrarchan absolutism.

If the lyric tactics of *Troilus and Criseyde* motivate considerations that are essentially political, those of *The Legend of Good Women* (1385–96) are more ethically focused. Largely a collection of exempla, or short narratives that teach a moral lesson, *The Legend of Good Women* purports to act as a further palinode to *Troilus and Criseyde* by telling stories of faithful women. Chapter 4, "Form and Ethics in *Handlynge Synne* and *The Legend of Good Women*," locates the *Legend*'s lyricism within an English tradition of practical ethical lyric: in particular, the use of lyric within exemplum. This chapter reads the lyric interludes in the *Legend* alongside those of Robert Mannyng's *Handlyng Synne* (1303), a collection of verse exempla. For both authors, lyric interpolations expose and reform the exemplum's formal and ethical disjunction: its conflicting drives toward narrative contingency and moral closure that challenge a practice of moral reasoning based on cases. By contrast, lyric practices suspend exemplary narrative's drive toward closure, encouraging an ethics that consists of recursion and attentiveness to contingency rather than telos. While all of the lyric interludes in these narrative poems draw on medieval and proto-modern lyric forms, ultimately their practices remain central not only to the definition of the genre but also to its ethical and cultural work. As the "father of English literature," Chaucer has often figured in stories of origin: the "first" English poet, for instance, to appropriate and reform Latin theories of authorship.[119] My reading of Chaucer is rather as a transitional figure, between the tactics of earlier English lyric and the increasingly vernacularized forms of textual authority.

The lyric tactics described in these chapters suggest an alternate narrative of English lyric history, in which a distinct insular genre not only informs Chaucer's lyrics but also continues to influence the development of lyric in the fifteenth century and beyond. By way of conclusion, I suggest that the tactical cultural work of lyric continues into the late medieval and early modern periods, even as they anticipate features of modern lyric. I discuss how the medieval Orphic myth of the verse romance "Sir Orfeo" offers an alternative to the classical Ovidian narrative of loss that can inform our reading of the relationship between medieval and modern lyricism, as well as read two later lyrics, the fifteenth-century "Adam lay y-bounden" and Thomas Wyatt's "Whoso list to hunt," through this alternate Orphic lens.

To understand genre as a conjunction of practices rather than forms recovers the social and cultural existences of texts. Literature, in particular, offers audiences outside of institutions and their protocols flexibility in their adaptations of and responses to these texts. The forms of lyric poetry especially invite tactical practice. Their brevity, performativity, and stylistic features make them nimble and modular with respect to larger textual structures, both material and rhetorical. Even as lyric texts change forms, the practices they initiated continue to teach us to read, respond, and adapt poetry to our world and our world to poetry.

CHAPTER I

The Voices of Harley 2253

Each of the next two chapters explores how a manuscript compilation draws on and theorizes lyric tactics and demonstrates the ways in which medieval English records of lyrics articulate relations of practice. Because tactics are modes of relation, I examine multiple relationships within these compilations, from the broad compilational logic of the whole manuscript to more local interactions between a text, its page, and its surrounding texts. This approach has a natural affinity with studies of the so-called manuscript matrix, the method of philology that considers the place of individual texts within their books.[1] It also serves to elucidate an insular approach to lyric compilations that distinguishes them from their French counterparts, even as many of these English codices record French texts. Further, like much medieval literature, lyrics had a dual existence as performance and text. Yet where text is durable, persistent, and transtemporal, performance is transient, localized, and only partially documentable. Nonetheless, the marks of performance everywhere inflect written texts.[2] This chapter focuses on how tactical relationships between medieval performative and writing practices shape and are shaped by the lyric and nonlyric texts of one of the most important surviving collections of pre-Chaucerian lyric, British Library MS Harley 2253.

In particular, I explore how these texts represent and theorize voice, a feature of lyric that illuminates the tactical relationships between the performative and the textual. Voice is central to lyric, which is frequently characterized by modern critics as an "utterance," yet medieval lyrics use voice in ways that confound post-Romantic models of the genre. While many of these poems do present a single lyric "I" that represents, in the words of Rosemary Woolf, "one-half of a dialogue" with an absent interlocutor, others thematize and exemplify the tactical qualities of lyric voices.[3] Medieval theories of voice engage both its abstract and practical aspects, attending to both its textual (in the work of medieval grammarians) and its performative (in the work of medieval philosophers and rhetoricians) functions. As my discussion of these theories will reveal, there are institutional contexts and norms intended to govern both of these aspects of voice. But when the biological, performative, and literary features of voice converge in lyric texts, they navigate these norms erratically. This is not to say that voice is equivalent to tactics. Rather, inasmuch as theories of voice prescribe normative vocalizing practices, the ways in which lyrics move among writing and performance encourages, even necessitates, a tactical approach to these prescriptions. The rhetorical figure known as "ethopoeia," which went under several different names in the Middle Ages, is helpful for understanding these tactics. As we shall see, this figure unites the affective, social, and circumstantial particulars of a speaker in literary voice.

The scribe-compiler of MS Harley 2253 interleaves prayers, dialogue poems, refrain poems, and single-voice poems in ways that draw on features of medieval and proto-modern theories of voice. Although not anthologized by genre, lyrics constitute an important class of texts within this compilation. As critics have increasingly noted, the relationship between the Harley lyrics and the other texts of this manuscript is less that of figure to ground than of tile to mosaic.[4] Yet, as we shall see, these lyrics exemplify medieval theories of the relationship between voice and speaking subject that at once resonate with the manuscript's nonlyric texts and distinguish lyric as a specific class of texts among them. The social, performative, and textual qualities of this kind of voice create not a single lyric "speaker" but rather voices for lyric readers, performers, and audiences that express tactical relationships to normative structures.

Most critics have agreed that the speaker of a medieval lyric is a chimera, less a definitive subject than a placeholder for successive writers, readers, or performers of the text.[5] As we have seen in the previous chapter, the idea of a lyric speaker derives largely from post-Romantic definitions of the genre. If instead we consider lyric in terms of voice, we can draw on a rich body of medieval philosophical and scholastic theory. As the lyrics of MS Harley 2253 demonstrate, voice inheres in both performance and text in medieval theory and practice. To begin to understand how this works, consider the well-known Harley lyric, "When the Nightingale Sings":

When the nyhtegale singes, the wodes waxen grene;	*grow*
Lef ant gras ant blosme springes in Averyl, Y wene,	*burst forth*
Ant love is to myn herte gon with one spere so kene!	
Nyht ant day my blod hit drynkes. Myn herte deth me tene.	*grieve*

Ich have loved al this yer that Y may love namore;	
Ich have siked moni syk, lemmon, for thin ore.	*favor*
Me nis love never the ner, ant that me reweth sore.	*regret deeply*
Suete lemmon, thench on me—Ich have loved the yore!	*for a long time*

Suete lemmon, Y preye the of love one speche;	*word*
Whil Y lyve in world so wyde, other nulle Y seche.	*seek*
With thy love, my suete leof, mi blis thou mihtes eche;	*increase*
A suete cos of thy mouth mihte be my leche.	*kiss; medicine*

Suete lemmon, Y preye the of a love-bene:	*love-token*
Yef thou me lovest ase men says, lemmon, as Y wene,	*believe*
Ant yef hit thi wille be, thou loke that hit be sene.	
So muchel Y thenke upon the that al Y waxe grene.	

Bituene Lyncolne ant Lyndeseye, Norhamptoun ant Lounde,	*London*
Ne wot Y non so fayr a may as Y go fore ybounde.	*bound to*
Suete lemmon, Y preye the, thou lovie me a stounde!	*soon*
Y wole mone my song	
On wham that hit ys on ylong.[6]	*the one who caused it*

This lyric interleaves the conventions of the solitary love lament and the performative and petitionary love complaint. Beginning with the conventional *reverdie* opening, it situates itself within a tradition of erotic poetry: "When the nyhtegale singes, the wodes waxen grene." Nature's *eros* makes a poignant, if conventional, contrast to the lover's pain: "Love is to myn herte gon with one spere so kene." The lover's sighs in the second stanza demonstrate how voice is a tactic of both performance and text. Sarah McNamer remarks that the devotional lyric, "I syke when y singe," "script[s] sorrowful sighs for the reader to perform"; saying "I syke" compels the speaker to perform the sigh that the song describes.[7] However, in its use of the past tense, "When the Nightingale Sings" textualizes this performance: "Ich have siked

moni syk, lemmon, for thin ore." The immediate performance context of
this verse, then, is not that of pain but of petition: "Suete lemmon, thench
on me." As a complaint, this lyric "negotiates between feeling and form," in
the words of Lee Patterson.[8] The lyric's perpetuation of the textual voice—its
knowing participation within the traditions of *reverdie*, love lament, and
complaint—depends on the lover's consent to its performance, as suggested
in the final stanza. The direct address to the "suete lemmon," prominent at
the beginning of two stanzas, anticipates an audience that is at once present
(as the addressee of these lines) and absent (as the audience of the deferred
performance). As heartfelt as it seems, the voice of the love petition is not
private but invokes a wider community ("Yef thou me lovest ase men says";
"loke that hit be sene").

Although the poem's final stanza has generally been understood as simply
another quatrain, on stylistic grounds I would speculate that this stanza acts
as an envoy, perhaps even a later addition, to the first four quatrains. The
final line of the fourth stanza ends "al Y waxe grene," an ironic echo of the
first line's "the wodes waxen grene." "Grene" works as a pun in the fourth
stanza, suggesting that the lover grows ill or lustful—or both—with thoughts
of his beloved. Ending the poem here gives it stylistic closure that is of a piece
with the use of repetition elsewhere in these stanzas, such as the anaphora of
"suete lemmon." The final stanza amplifies or transforms earlier lines, for
instance, giving "world so wyde" the geographic specificity of "Bituene Lyncolne ant Lyndesey, Norhamptoun ant Lounde" and offering another "suete
lemmon" line. The last line of the poem as it stands opens up a new frame,
shifting from the implied immediate presence of the beloved (the "suete lemmon" addressed in the imperative) to the deferral of her presence ("Y wole
mone my song"). This shift calls our attention to a second lyric voice (even
if it is that of the same speaker). This stanza's change in voice recalls the
envoys or *tornadas* of French medieval poetry, from troubadour lyrics to
motets, which often employed such a shift.[9] As Judith Peraino puts it, French
lyricists often used the final stanza to "graft" multiple voices into a single
lyric, whether these were the voices of lover and beloved, master and minstrel,
or even the public and private personae of the poet himself.[10]

The final stanza of "When the Nightingale Sings" is in many ways similar to the French envoy tradition, but certain differences are worth noting.
Many of the French envoys name or encode the identity of the poet, and the
irony or humor in their vocal shifts is dependent on recognizing this identity.
This poet, while firmly anonymous, is by no means what Leo Spitzer, in a

seminal essay, calls an "everyman" whose words are completely fungible. Spitzer's categorization relies on texts where a known author appropriates language that cannot possibly apply to him or her, usually by direct quotation or literal translation. In one example, he cites a passage from Marie de France where she claims personal experience of a story's teller in an echo of the original but elsewhere acknowledges her use of a written source.[11] The final stanza of "When the Nightingale Sings" uses voice differently. While drawing on the French envoy tradition, it neither directly appropriates its language nor relies on the poet's identity for its effect. Instead, this stanza transforms the French convention tactically, suggesting an expansive but not limitless range of possibilities for its speaker, who would be familiar with the women and terrain "Bituene Lyncolne ant Lyndeseye, Norhamptoun ant Lounde." In other words, while much of the poem consists of an arrangement of conventional lyric language (though beautifully executed), the final stanza locates this conventional language within a specific horizon of practices. As we will see, this poem's compilation and layout in MS Harley 2253 amplifies how its voice mediates between such textual and performative practices, which in turn informs the arrangement of the larger miscellany.

To understand how this works in the manuscript as a whole, it is helpful to consider how medieval theories of voice express its multimodal capacities and how these can be put in dialogue with modern discussions of lyric voice. This discussion occupies the first half of this chapter. The second half of the chapter provides an overview of the manuscript's contents and social context and reads a selection of English and French lyrics from the manuscript, both well known and lesser known, as well as some of the manuscript's Latin devotional texts.

Voice and the Lyric

Voice is where sound meets language, a grammatically vexed and poetically fertile medium fundamental to human communication. In this section, I show that in medieval theory, voice—particularly literary voice—is inherently tactical, articulating relationships between writing and performance and between a subject's interiority and his external world. In medieval philosophy, grammar, and music theory, theories of voice rely on and elucidate ontological distinctions. Aristotle says that *vox*—here meaning voice or even "vocal sound"—consists of "a certain kind of sound belonging to what has a

soul" that has signifying power.[12] While musical instruments produce a
sound similar to voice, only living beings—including animals—have voices.
In Aquinas's commentary on this passage, voice is what turns meaning into
sound: "Not every sound belonging to an animal is a vocal sound. For the
tongue may make some sounds that are nevertheless not instances of vocal
sound—just as those who cough make a sound that is not a vocal sound. For
if there is to be vocal sound, what forces the air [against the windpipe] must
be something with a soul, along with some imagination intended to signify
something. For a vocal sound must be a certain significant sound, either
naturally or by convention."[13]

For Aristotle and Aquinas, voice is produced by, yet distinct from, a
speaking subject. It is the medium through which a subject's internal
image—stored in the imaginative faculty—encounters the external world.
Because voice in these definitions is not only a linguistic medium, medieval
grammarians further distinguished types of voice by their semantic potential.
According to Donatus, "Every sound [vox] is either articulate or confused.
Articulate sound can be captured in letters, confused sound cannot be written."[14] Priscian describes four different types of vox based on two binary pairs:
articulate or inarticulate (depending on whether the sound has intentional
meaning) and literate or illiterate (depending on whether it is writable). He
acknowledges that unwritable sounds (such as a human groan) may have
meaning, and writable sounds (such as a nonsense word or transcribed animal
noise) may lack signification.[15] Later grammarians drew on these four types
to classify sounds ranging from human spoken language, applause, and whis-
tling to animal noises and the sounds of natural phenomena like crashing
waves.[16]

The difference between Donatus's and Aristotle's definitions of vox cap-
tures a medieval concern with the relationship between voice and speaker.
Whereas for Aristotle, the ontological status of the producer of sound determined whether or not it was a "voice," for Donatus and the early grammarians, a sound's resolution into the phonetic alphabet was central. This
association between writing and voice not only speaks to grammar's close
relationship to performed oratory in the early period (it was a foundational
discipline for the study of rhetoric) but also reveals how writing and voice are
co-constitutive in premodern culture. Their interdependence is particularly
evident in drama: the multivocal drama of ancient Greece owes its conception to a phonetic alphabet that weds sound to letters, for example, and
medieval drama borrows many of its conventions from legal rhetoric.[17]

But while access to writing was controlled, in the Middle Ages, by institutions of literacy like the schools and the church, voice is a biological attribute shared by humans and animals. As poets have long recognized, human language draws on both aspects of voice, its grammatical and systematic principles and its nonrepresentative sounds. Ezra Pound described these, respectively, as *logopoeia* (meaning) and *melopoeia* (sound).[18] Later medieval grammarians like John of Garland recognized both aspects of language. In addition to his better-known *Poetria Parisiana* (discussed in the next chapter), John composed an "equivocal" grammar, a medieval genre of long poem that distinguishes and contextualizes like-sounding words.[19] As he puts it in the prologue to this poem, "equivocum celat sub eadem plurima voce, / quorum nomen idem" (an *equivocum* hides under a voice [word] these many [meanings], which have the same name).[20] The treatise (like others in the genre) distinguishes among like-sounding words in a mnemonic verse:

Augustus, -ti, -to Cesar vel mensis habeto,

Augustus, -tus, -ui vult divinacio dici

Mobile si fiat, *augustus* nobile signat,

Augeo dat primum, dant gustus avisque secundum.

[*Augustus*, -ti, -to means Caesar or the month (of August); *Augustus*, -tus, -ui means divination. If it becomes an adjective, *augustus* means noble. The verb "augeo" (to grow) gives us the first meaning; "gustus" (taste) and "auis" (bird/omen) give us the second.][21]

Just as equivocal grammars unite the melodic and grammatical qualities of voice, rhetorical treatises also give primacy of place to voice, an essential component of the rhetorical canon of *actio*, or delivery. Quintilian acknowledges that a "good voice" is among the natural gifts necessary for success in oratory[22] and devotes part of his discussion of delivery to the correction of vocal infelicities: "Again our teacher must not tolerate the affected pronunciation of the *s*, with which we are so familiar, nor suffer words to be uttered from the depth of the throat or rolled out hollow-mouthed, or permit the natural sound of the voice to be over-laid with a fuller sound, a fault fatal to the purity of speech."[23] The ethics of oratory are implicit in the privileged faculty of speech: "If therefore we have received no fairer gift from heaven than speech, what shall we regard as so worthy of laborious cultivation, or in what should we sooner desire to excel our fellow-men, than that in which mankind excels all other living things?"[24]

Following the newfound popularity of the pseudo-Ciceronian *Rhetorica ad Herennium* in the twelfth century, delivery became a subject of serious rhetorical discourse in the later Middle Ages, as well as an influence on the broader culture, permeating scholastic treatises and performative practice.[25] The *Herennium* describes tones of voice appropriate for different kinds of material: "Conversational tone comprises four kinds: the Dignified, the Explicative, the Narrative, and the Facetious. The Dignified, or Serious, Tone of Conversation is marked by some degree of impressiveness and by vocal restraint. The Explicative in a calm voice explains how something could or could not have been brought to pass. The Narrative sets forth events that have occurred or might have occurred. The Facetious can on the basis of some circumstance elicit a laugh which is modest and refined."[26] The author then proceeds to describe the physical qualities of each tone. For example: "For the Dignified Conversational Tone it will be proper to use the full throat but the calmest and most subdued voice possible, yet not in such a fashion that we pass from the practice of the orator to that of the tragedian. For the Explicative Conversational Tone one ought to use a rather thin-toned voice, and frequent pauses and intermissions, so that we seem by means of the delivery itself to implant and engrave in the hearer's mind the points we are making in our explanation."[27] To a later medieval audience, the *Herennium*'s distinctions among oratorical voices might well have recalled Isidore of Seville's discussion of song and its varieties of voice: "A song (*cantus*) is the voice changing pitch, for sound is even-pitched; and sound precedes song. Arsis (*arsis*) is elevation of the voice, that is, the beginning. Thesis (*thesis*) is lowering the voice, that is, the end. Sweet (*suavis*) voices are refined and compact, distinct and high. Clear (*perspicuus*) voices are those that are drawn out further, so that they continually fill whole spaces, like the blaring of trumpets."[28]

In short, the concept of voice integrates theory and practice in several medieval liberal arts. The qualities of vocal expression were understood to be artful, in rhetorical delivery and in singing, as well as meaningful. Thus, discussions of voice in these treatises reveal the performative foundations of medieval knowledge practice. The alliance of knowledge and its delivery is perhaps best expressed in John of Salisbury's introduction to the *Metalogicon*:

> Just as eloquence, unenlightened by reason, is rash and blind, so wisdom, without the power of expression, is feeble and maimed. Speechless wisdom may sometimes increase one's personal satisfaction, but it rarely and only slightly contributes to the welfare of human society. Reason, the mother, nurse, and

guardian of knowledge, as well as of virtue, frequently conceives from speech, and by this same means bears more abundant and richer fruit. Reason would remain utterly barren, or at least would fail to yield a plenteous harvest, if the faculty of speech did not bring to light its feeble conceptions, and communicate the perceptions of the prudent exercise of the human mind.[29]

Far from a transparent medium of knowledge, voice here is generative and productive, "fecund." Indeed, in the twelfth century, *eloquentia* (communication) came to be regarded as half of knowledge, complementing *philosophia* (content). Despite detractors who criticized the tendency toward garrulity in the champions of eloquence, voiced language was increasingly recognized as the medium of social negotiation, "an important part of a corpus of attitudes, behaviors, skills and science that kept civil society alive."[30]

For lyric poets and audiences, the relationship between physical voice and literary or textual voice is codified in the rhetorical device of *ethopoeia*. The earliest known description of the figure appears in Aphthonius's fourth-century *Progymnasmata*, a late antique rhetorical handbook: "Ethopoeia is imitation of the character of a proposed speaker. There are three different forms of it: apparition-making (*eidolopoeia*), personification (*prosopopoeia*) and characterization (*ethopoeia*). Ethopoeia has a known person as a speaker and only invents the characterization, which is why it is called 'character-making'; for example, what words Heracles would say when Eurystheus gave his commands. Here Heracles is known, but we invent the character in which he speaks."[31] In Aphthonius's definition, ethopoeia is the umbrella figure for all invented speech, with distinctions for the ontological status of the speaker. The ethopoetic speaker is "known" (a historical or literary figure) and alive, the eidolopoetic speaker is known and dead, and the prosopopoetic speaker is invented. There are further three modes of ethopoetic speech: affective, circumstantial, or a mixture of the two.[32]

The *Progymnasmata* gained new popularity in the early modern period following its 1572 translation by Reinhard Lorich, and no evidence exists of its use during the medieval period.[33] Yet grammatical and rhetorical treatises popular in medieval schoolrooms discuss the composition of ethopoetic speeches, often under one of the following figures: *adlocutio, conformatio, sermocinatio, fictio personae, prosopopoeia*.[34] In a rare medieval use of Aphthonius's term, Isidore of Seville offers the following definition:

We call that 'ethopoeia' whereby we represent the character of a person in such a way as to express traits related to age, occupation, fortune, happiness, gender, grief, boldness. Thus when the character of a pirate is taken up, the speech will be bold, abrupt, rash; when the speech of a woman is imitated, the oration ought to fit her sex. A distinct way of speaking ought to be used for young and old, soldier and general, parasite and rustic and philosopher. One caught up in joy speaks one way, one wounded, another. In this genre of speech these things should be most fully thought out: who speaks and with whom, about whom, where, and when, what one has done or will do, or what one can suffer if one neglects these decrees.[35]

Isidore's definition expresses the idea that written representations of speech can vary according to both affective and social factors: status, occupation, gender, mood, and situation of address. The *Rhetorica ad Herennium* describes, under the figure of *conformatio*, "making a mute thing or one lacking form articulate, and attributing to it a definite form and a language or a certain behavior appropriate to its character."[36] Priscian's definition of *adlocutio* ("impersonation") is ethopoetic:

> Impersonation is the imitation of speech accommodated to imaginary situations and persons. . . . Speeches of impersonation can be addressed either to particular persons or to indefinite ones. . . . There are simple forms of impersonation, as when one creates a speech as though he were speaking to himself; and there are double impersonations, as though he were speaking to others. . . . Always, however, be careful to preserve the character of the persons and times being imagined: some words are appropriate to the young, some to the old, some to the joyful, some to the sad. Moreover, some impersonations have to do with manners, some with passions, and some with a mixture of the two.[37]

Geoffrey of Vinsauf provides an example of the speech of a pope as a kind of "refining by dialogue" (*expolitio per sermocinationem*): "Oh how marvelous the virtue of God! How mighty his power! How great I now am! How insignificant I once was! From a small stock I have grown in a trice to a mighty cedar."[38] Elsewhere in the *Poetria Nova*, Geoffrey parodies the figure. The discarded tablecloth grieves, "I was once the pride of the table, while my youth was in its first flower and my face knew no blemish. But since I am old, and my visage is marred, I do not wish to appear."[39] With its focus on the particularity of experience, ethopoeia had a natural affinity for the rhetorical study of personal "attributes," elaborated in Matthew of Vendôme's *Ars Versificatoria* (1175) and the anonymous *Tria Sunt* (1256–1400).[40]

Schoolroom exercises in ethopoeia and related figures were practiced from late antiquity (Augustine won a contest for his speech voicing Juno's rage at her powerlessness to keep Aeneas out of Italy) to the early modern period.[41] In antiquity and the early Middle Ages, the figure was used to teach letter writing, and a few examples, in which ethopoeia appears among a broader range of rhetorical figures, survive from the later Middle Ages.[42] This practice encouraged students, some of whom became poets, to think about evoking a character with a voice that conveys his or her particular experience of emotions, social codes, and mores. It is perhaps difficult for us, who largely expect literary voices to do these very things, to appreciate how specific a use of voice this is and, further, how it establishes a literary convention that synthesizes a character's inner and outer life by means of his or her voice. Some of the most poignant passages in Chaucer's long poems are ethopoetic interludes, from Criseyde's lament for her lost reputation ("Thorughout the world my belle shal be ronge") to Dido's lament in the *House of Fame*.[43] (This figure was considered particularly suitable for the representation of female grief.) Further, to a medieval rhetorician, the soliloquy and the dialogue existed on an ethopoetic continuum, the dialogue being a juxtaposition of alternating ethopoetic utterances.[44]

Ethopoeia, then, is a figure of represented speech that is at once subjective and objective, affective and circumstantial. It is inherently tactical because it improvises rhetorically on a set of known circumstances from myth or history. Moreover, the ethopoetic voice of medieval lyric is distinct from the voice of the "speaking subject" that characterizes post-Romantic lyric theory. As I discussed in the introduction, Hegel defined lyric as the genre that takes as its content "not the object but the subject, the inner world, the mind that considers and feels, that instead of proceeding to action, remains alone with itself as inwardness, and that therefore can take as its sole form and final aim the self-expression of the subjective life."[45] This model of voice was most cogently critiqued by structuralist and poststructuralist thought. In *Voice and Phenomenon*, Derrida critiques the Western metaphysics that identifies an "inner voice" of thought with self-presence. For Derrida, the figure of the inner voice creates the fiction of self-presence, but the very fact of figuring it as a voice puts thought into the realm of signification. That is, an "inner voice" of thought is subject to the *différance* and the fundamental instability of representation that Derrida would more famously attribute to writing.[46] Yet as David Lawton has recently discussed, literary voice, especially in medieval literature, is qualitatively different. It creates what he calls "public interiorities," which project subjective expression into the public, or social, realm. These voices are characterized by "unstable reproducibility"; they can be endlessly iterated but without any presumption of fidelity to an original.[47]

Scholars of medieval literature have long recognized the slippery relationship between lyric voice and speaking subject. Who is it who says "I"? Anglo-American critics have frequently answered this question with recourse to Leo Spitzer's classic essay on the "I" as an "everyman": "in the Middle Ages, the 'poetic I' had more freedom and more breadth than it has today: at that time the concept of intellectual property did not exist because literature dealt not with the individual but with mankind: the 'ut in pluribus' was an accepted standard."[48] Spitzer's model accounts for what he sees as the free substitution of one "I" for another, especially in prefaces and poetry. This suggestion was later developed by Rosemary Woolf, in her description of the "genuinely anonymous" religious meditative lyrics whose plain style willfully resists the development of an individual poetic voice in favor of universality, and by Judson Boyce Allen, who describes certain medieval English lyrics as "sublimat[ing]" the individual ego in the lyric ego.[49] Most recently, A. C. Spearing has argued that in medieval literature, the poetic "I" inheres not in the speaker but in the text. In lyrics in particular, "the 'I' is little more than an empty space, waiting to be occupied by any reader." For Spearing, what this text ultimately represents is the written word, whose point of origin is the poet, not a lyric speaker. In one poem, "the inner life evoked as the medium for the trivial outward incidents recalled seems to me to be specifically that of the writer . . . the 'I' as writer, rather than the 'I' to whom the events recorded originally occurred."[50] While Spearing's critique of a critical tendency to see the "speaker" of a medieval poem as a literary character (an approach deriving ultimately from Wimsatt's and Beardsley's idea of lyric poetry as dramatic monologue) is a welcome and necessary correction to an overly simplistic reading practice, in rejecting the totalizing of the speaker, he ends up totalizing the text. Although it draws on Derrida's critique of the voice as self-presence, Spearing's analysis more directly recalls older New Critical reading practices that evacuate historical particularity from a text.

The French critical tradition has tended toward structuralist and post-structuralist analyses of the "I" as a purely linguistic and grammatical phenomenon (most notably in the work of Paul Zumthor). Yet in response to the influence of structuralism on French medieval lyric criticism, some scholars have argued for the centrality of subjectivity to poetic and particularly lyric texts. Michel Zink traces the affiliation of lyric with affective subjective expression as a result of a literary history in which other medieval genres—satire, drama, and prose narrative—carve out distinct formal and thematic areas that by comparison mark lyric as the genre of individual expression.[51] Further, as Sarah Kay notes, social and historical circumstances inflect such signifying lyric voices: "historical factors such as gender and economic status, relationships with authors and patrons, leave perceptible traces on the subjective voice. . . . The 'individual' need not be conceived of contrastively, as differing in some essential way from others. The historical influences which combine with different discourses to construct the sense of self necessarily contribute features which are held in common with other selves."[52]

Ethopoeia figures the structural, circumstantial, and public aspects of the first-person pronoun, acknowledging its own rhetorical artifice within a trope that accommodates social circumstance and difference. Some of this has to do with the historically specific conceptions of subjectivity and interiority that inhered in medieval thought. It has been amply demonstrated that a turn toward interiority, beginning in the twelfth century and elaborated, especially, in medieval religious writings, penitential discourse, and secular literature, marked the later Middle Ages. Yet scholars of the Middle Ages remain divided on whether premodern subjectivity is marked by an opposition, even an antagonism, between the inner self and the outer world or whether these are contiguous.[53] Medieval uses of ethopoeia demonstrate that voice expresses a relationship between internal and external, between self and world. Ultimately, though, ethopoeia is premised on the inherent performativity of all utterances, as a figure for speech that integrates affect and circumstance in order to communicate to a public.[54] Ethopoeia bears some relationship to the idea of a lyric "persona," but it also differs in important ways from this modern concept. Chiefly, where a poetic persona is presumed to represent a complex, total subject, an ethopoetic voice is an utterance specific to both a speaker *and* his or her local and contingent circumstances: the words of Andromache over Hector's corpse or of the tablecloth once discarded. My emphasis on an ethopoetic lyric voice that integrates text and performance also has some affinity with recent work on the performativity of medieval lyric reading practices.[55] However, these tend to locate the lyric's performativity in the inner experience of the reader or performer, whereas my account emphasizes the full spectrum of transmission practice of medieval lyrics, comprising interiority, performance, grammatical and rhetorical conventions, and material witnesses.

What I am proposing, in short, is that the ethopoetic voice of the medieval lyric "I" is a tactic in the practice of the genre. As we have seen, the medieval concept of voice engages both its performative and textual qualities. Ethopoeia, in some sense, *makes* lyrics with ad hoc improvisations on the conventions of both textual and performative voices. We have seen one instance of this in our analysis of the vocal shift in the envoy of "When the Nightingale Sings"; the next section will demonstrate how ethopoetic tactics inform the compilation and layout of lyric and nonlyric texts throughout MS Harley 2253. It is helpful at this point to refer to Michel de Certeau's description of the interaction between orality and the written text in contemporary culture, which offers a surprisingly apt way of understanding the voices of Harley 2253. In his discussion of the modern "scriptural economy," Certeau describes writing as an essentially strategic practice that produces a text on the regulated blank space of the page.[56] Although often presented as oppositional to writing, orality is implicated in such a scriptural economy, since like writing, it is not unitary but plural and historically determined. To escape the power structures produced by the scriptural economy, Certeau concludes his discussion with an impassioned if vague call for "transformations" as a tactical alternative to writing: "Henceforth the important thing is neither *what is said* (a content) nor the *saying* itself (an act), but rather the *transformation*, and the invention of still unsuspected mechanisms that will allow us to multiply the transformations."[57]

Certeau's scriptural economy is a product of capitalism and as such not directly applicable to premodern textual culture. However, the blank space of the medieval manuscript page is equally as regulated as the modern printed page, and its texts are equally reliant on practices of orality and writing. What the figure of ethopoeia suggests is a rhetoric that navigates these practices tactically, drawing on the conventions of each mode to produce lyric poetry. The ethopoetic voice makes its texts from the contingent relations between composer and audience, scribe and poet and reader.

The Tactics of Voice

Texts with tactical voices are predominant in Harley 2253, in part because of the circumstances of its production and its larger social and cultural milieu. Compiled between 1330 and 1340, the codex is a trilingual collection of devotional, practical, and profane texts. It begins with four quires, on folios 1 to 48v, of biblical stories in Anglo-Norman, copied in a thirteenth-century hand conventionally assigned to "Scribe A." A new quire begins on folio 49, where we first see the hand of the principal scribe (the "Harley scribe") who copied, with a few exceptions, the remainder of the manuscript and compiled it with the work of Scribe A. Of the 106 texts that the Harley scribe copied, 47 are in English verse, which dominates this part of the manuscript. French verse accounts for twenty-five items, French prose for seventeen items, and Latin prose for twelve. There are four macaronic items, three of these in verse. The vernacular verse in the manuscript includes devotional verse, secular love lyrics, and political and social satires. Two verse items are written in the form of "interludes," with cues for performance by different speakers. Prose is primarily reserved for devotional texts, such as hagiographies, instructions for pilgrimage, biblical material, and prayers or other devotional instructions.[58]

The "Harley lyrics"—that is, the English shorter poems of the manuscript —have been read as a unique medieval archive and as a forerunner of modern lyric. Their poetic art earned them a place in the transhistorical lyric canon denied to most Middle English lyrics before Chaucer. While some of the manuscript's secular love lyrics draw on the conventions of the French courtly love lyric tradition, many of their readers agree that their style and sentiments are earthier and more direct than their Continental analogues.[59] The concrete qualities of the Middle English language and the social context of a manuscript produced at a distance from the London courts intersect with the rarefied themes and sentiments of French courtly poetry to produce a corpus at once elevated and earthy. Primarily appearing in the manuscript's fifth booklet, the love poems represent women with a particularity that veers toward the explicitly sexual.[60] To their admirers, the lyrics' uniqueness resides in their artistry in synthesizing the refined and the quotidian, as well as the fragility of survival of what appears to be a fully sophisticated English lyric corpus that emerges from the West Midlands with scant evidence of a prior tradition.

Scholars have also considered the place of these lyrics within their larger manuscript context, among the rich collection of devotional and political lyrics, not to mention prose saints' lives, interludes, and prayer instructions that comprise MS Harley 2253.[61] Such analyses read the secular and devotional love lyrics in relation to the book's other contents, including political poems and devotional prose, and to its geographical significance.[62] The devotional lyrics, for example, take up the idioms and topoi of the love lyrics, a conjunction made explicit by the Harley scribe's copying of two *contrafacta*, one profane and one sacred, beginning "Lutel wot hit any mon" in sequence on folio 128.[63] Although once considered a haphazardly assembled "miscellany," the manuscript's compilation by a primary scribe and its relatively coherent selection and arrangement of its texts have more recently invited consideration of the book as a deliberately arranged "anthology."[64] In this view, the Harley scribe exercised a near-authorial degree of control over the selection and layout of his texts, from global concerns, such as what Carter Revard calls the "oppositional thematics" of the dialectical arrangement of texts in the manuscript, to local particulars, such as the scribe's arrangement of devotional texts around holes in the parchment to encourage the reader to meditate on Christ's wounds.[65]

Harley 2253 also displays a geographical coherence, both in the conditions of its production and the world represented in the poems. The manuscript was produced near Ludlow, in Herefordshire, by a secular clerk who also copied many surviving legal documents in the area.[66] The codex has a regional flavor; the three saints whose lives it records (Ethelbert, Edfrid, and Wistan) are affiliated with Hereford and Leominster, and its flyleaves contain portions of the Hereford Cathedral Ordinal.[67] The Harley scribe's hand appears in two other codices with ties to the area, British Library MS Harley 273 (1314–15) and MS Royal 12.C.12 (1316–40), containing the romance *Foulke le FitzWarin*. This scribe also copied forty-one legal documents from Herefordshire, suggesting that he was a resident of the region. The imagined geography that emerges from the lyrics of Harley 2253, with their frequent use of place names from within and outside Herefordshire and their fetishization of both the "lond" and its local women, reveals a sensibility "fundamentally regionalist but also intrinsically cosmopolitan."[68] The manuscript's collection of texts from across England displays an awareness of the larger world in which the western province is an active participant.[69] Its contents reveal Celtic influences in their allusions, prosody, and rhetoric.[70] The sense of what we might call "Herefordshire exceptionalism," the idea that this county constituted a unique and distinct place in the larger world, grew as the region saw increased travel during the first half of the fourteenth century. Pilgrims visited Herefordshire following the canonization of Thomas Cantilupe (1320), and Adam Orleton (bishop of Hereford, 1317–27; of Worcester, 1327–33; and of Winchester, 1333–45) sent his clerical *familia* on administrative trips within England and beyond.[71]

Within this at once proudly provincial and cosmopolitan context (akin to what modern social theorists call a "glocal" sensibility), texts traveled by multiple channels: institutional and informal, written and performed. One poem in particular, a largely unnoticed French poem beginning "Quant fu en ma iuvente," demonstrates how lyric voice can express these multimodal practices.

Quant fu en ma juvente
E en ma volenté
Molt mis ma entente
Certe a jolifté.
Molt fu pesaunt e lent
A chescune bounté,
Ne pensoi de la rente
Que me serroit demaundé.

Tut fut mon cuer mis
Certe a folour;
Molt fu en verglis—
Alas, a icel jour!
Que trop en ay pris
De terrien honour,
Jour e nuit ma pensé mis
En trop fol amour.

Certes, molt desirroi
Aver lel amisté,
Mes nule ne trovoi
Quant je le oy prové;
Quant je bien regardoi,
Ne vi qe vanité.
Sovent dis "weylowoi"
De quoi ai je pensé.

Un jour m'en aloi deduyre,
Mon solas querant;
Avynt par aventure
Qe je oy un chaunt.
A ce mis ma cure,
Si estois escotaunt—
Certes, bone e pure
La dite fut del chaunt!

La dite du chaunt
Vus dirroi, come je say;
Touz ceus qe vont pensant
Pur quere amour verray,
Attendent a mon chaunt!
Je lur enseigneray
De un ami, fyn amaunt,
Bon, bel, e verray.

"Flur de tote bounté,
E de pureté auxi,
Fluret de tote leauté
E de clareté, vous dy,
Chescun manere de bounté
Puet um trover en ly.
Flur de tote pieté
Molt est tresdouz amy."

[When I was in my youth and at my will, I eagerly pursued my desire wholly for amusement. I was quite lethargic and slow regarding any virtue, nor did I think of the cost that would be exacted of me. All my heart was set entirely on folly; truly, I was on slippery ice—alas, for that day! When I was overconcerned with earthly honor, day and night I set my mind on extremely foolish love. Indeed, I deeply desired to have true friendship, but I found none when I had tried it; when I looked closely, I saw only vanity. Often I said "weilowoi" about what I desired. One day I went to be amused, seeking my comfort; it happened by chance that I heard a song. To this I paid attention, and I stood listening—indeed, good and pure were the words of the song! The words of the song I will tell you as I can; all those who go wishing to seek out true love, listen to my song! I will instruct them about a friend, a pure lover, good, beautiful, and true. "Flower of all goodness, and of purity as well, little flower of all faithfulness and brightness, I tell you, every sort of goodness may one discover in him. Flower of all mercy, truly he's a most kind friend."][72]

This poem is as much about lyric transmission as it is about conversion, as the first-person voice of the poem learns both the affective states of proper devotion and their text and performance. The poem's representation of lyric practice and its deft deployment of commonplaces at once employs and comments on the tactics of voice. It begins in the idiom of the *pastourelle*: the speaker of the first stanza seeks "jolifté" (mirth), but the pursuit of profane pleasure only makes him say "weylowoi." (Because this English word is a rhyme word in the poem, it is likely that the poem, or at least its introduction, was composed in England.) The speaker converts upon hearing a devotional song, which teaches him to transfer his desires from earthly to spiritual objects. As it is presented here, the nested song both performs the speaker's conversion *in* singing and converts his audience *by* singing.

Further, the transition to the nested song is blurry, as the poem's initial "I" gradually transforms from audience to speaker. "The words of the song, I will tell you as I can." The listener replicates his own experience, becoming the singer in this moment. But where does the song begin? It may begin immediately after the declaration, "I will tell you as I can" with the lines, "All those who go wishing to seek out true love, listen to my song," an address to the audience that is common among medieval lyrics (including many in this manuscript). It is equally possible that the song begins in the following stanza, as it is punctuated above, with the lyric commonplace "Flower of all goodness," which originated in the courtly love lyrics of the troubadours but soon migrated to devotional poetry.[73] Although it more commonly refers to Mary, here the "flower" is Jesus. If the nested song begins here, it draws our attention to the way in which rhetoric—the commonplace—is mediated through multiple voices of performance, the two within the poem and perhaps a third in live performance. The two possibilities are not mutually exclusive; the very ambiguity of this lyric reveals a network of mediating voices of listener, singer, and text. Lacking a single subject position for the first-person voice, the speaker's identity as a penitent or spiritual authority is tactical. He advises his audience to "Go to him [Jesus] running! Put to the test whether what I sing to you be true" (Alez a ly coraunt! / Metez en asay /Si ce seit veir qe vous chaunt).[74] The performer-speaker (the "I" of the opening lines) is a penitent within the poem but an agent of conversion in its performance. The performer-speaker is thus a surrogate figure for the audience of the poem in its moment of performance. This marks an important distinction from the common model of the medieval "I" as an "everyman" first put forth by Spitzer. Spitzer and others who have extended his work tend to see this first-person pronoun as originating with a single author whom other writers then "plagiarize," or an ego that "subsumes" (to use Judson Boyce Allen's term) those of its audience—in short, as a linear process that tends toward degradation and dilution.[75] Yet here and in other poems in the manuscript, the fiction of oral performance demonstrates the ad hoc and improvisatory shifts

within the poem's voice that characterize its ethopoetic tactics. As new speakers embody the poem's voice, it transforms, proliferates, and adapts to local
contingencies.

These shifts have implications for ideas of textual and institutional
authority. The authority of the embedded song comes not from the identity
of the person who composed the text but from its transmission by a fellow
penitent. In other words, the mediating voice both gains its authority from
the prior text and tactically authorizes the text in the situation of performance. Other texts in Harley 2253 thematize tactical authority more directly.
The Anglo-Norman poem beginning "Cyl qe vodra oyr mes chauns" (The
one who wishes to hear my songs) poses the authority of song via its mediations in texts and emotions:

Cyl qe vodra oyr mes chauns,
En soun cuer se remyre:
Si il, en fet ou en semblauns,
Rien touche a la matire
De un chaunçon en romauns
Ou la en orrez descrire
La lessoun a leals amantz,
Vous y comencez a lyre!

[He who would hear my songs, let him examine his heart: if it should, in deed or likeness,
touch at all upon the subject of a song in plain French in which you'll hear described the
lesson for true lovers, begin to read there!][76]

The poem offers a series of maxims on how to advise, praise, and sympathize
with one's friend. At the conclusion of the poem, the speaker invites his
audience to evaluate his advice:

Ore pri a tous lais e clers,
Si ne me chaut qe l'oye,
Qe nul ne prenge le travers
De fyn amour verroie,
Car leal cuer n'est pas divers;
Eynz ayme droite voie.
Ly "Tu autem" est en ce vers;
Ly respounz soit de joye!
Amen.

[Now I pray of all laity and clergy, and I don't care who hears it, that no one go against pure true love, for a loyal heart is not fickle; instead it loves correctly. The "Tu autem" is in this poem; let the response be joyful! Amen.][77]

The speaker asks the entire audience ("tous lais e clers"), not only the educated members, to follow the poem's advice. Auditors are acknowledged as participants in the creation of love and friendship and indeed of the text itself. The final two lines, "the 'Tu autem' is in this poem; let the response be joyful!" refer to a common liturgical element, the phrase "Tu autem Domine miserere nobis" (But you, Lord, have mercy on us), which concluded readings and preceded the congregants' response.[78] The poem's metaphorical use of this antiphonal text locates authority as much in the audience's responsive (but also rote) performance as in the written text.

Indeed, many of Harley 2253's lyrics represent performance—especially of poetic tropes and genres—as a kind of authority. Among the manuscript's many texts in dialogue form (including the interludes "The Harrowing of Hell" and "Gilote et Johan," the debate poems "De l'yver et de l'esté" and the "Debate between Body and Soul," and other lyrics), the verse dialogue commonly titled "De clerico et puella," which I will call "Clerk and Girl," suggests how performing voices negotiate authority. The poem appears to begin with a soliloquy of lament:

My deth Y love, my lif Ich hate, for a levedy shene;	*bright*
Heo is brith so daies liht, that is on me well sene.	*She; as; I see clearly*
All Y falewe so doth the lef in somer when hit is grene,	*wither*
Yef mi thoht helpeth me noht, to wham shal Y me mene?	*complain*
Sorewe and syke and drery mod byndeth me so faste	
That Y wene to walke wod yef hit me lengore laste;	*expect to go mad*
My serewe, my care, al with a word he myhte awey caste.	*she*
Whet helpeth the, my suete lemmon, my lyf thus forte gaste?[79]	*to destroy*

On a first reading (or hearing), one might assume that the poem will continue in the voice of the lamenting lover. But in the third stanza, the woman speaks, answering the question of the previous line:

Do wey, thou clerc! Thou art a fol! With the bidde Y noht chyde.	*Go away; wish; argue*
Shalt thou never lyve that day mi love that thou shalt byde.	*enjoy*

Yef thou in my boure art take, shame the may bityde;   *bedroom*
The is bettere on fote gon then wycked hors to ryde.[80]   *You are better off*

The interruption and abrupt shift in tone comments implicitly on the genre and rhetoric of the love lament. It is a genre that slips easily into fabliau, when the assumption of solitude that lends pathos to the lover's lament is located in its performance context. The apparently rhetorical question that concludes the second stanza—"Whet helpeth the, my suete lemmon, my lyf thus forte gaste?"—in fact initiates a dialogue. As we saw in other poems in the manuscript, such as "Quant fu en ma juvente," the situation of transmission is part of the text. Further, the text comments on its own rhetoric. Yielding at last to her lover, the lady says, "Thou semest wel to ben a clerc, for thou spekest so scille [well]." The performance of the poem's rhetoric assumes its own authority, as the lady gives the clerk permission to "don al thy wille."[81]

The poem that follows "Clerk and Girl" in the manuscript is "When the Nightingale Sings," the extended love lament in the first person that I discussed at the beginning of the chapter. The compiler's juxtaposition of these poems encourages us to read the latter poem as an amplification of the first two stanzas of "Clerk and Girl," its petitionary language (discussed in the opening section) heightened by this compilational choice. As it is presented here, then, "When the Nightingale Sings" appears as the opening salvo of an erotic negotiation, rather than as a solitary meditation. Further, scribal choices suggest that as much as voice can tactically navigate a written text, features of the material text can suggest tactics to the voice of performance, too. The poem appears on folios 80v to 81r, with the first stanza following "Clerk and Girl" on folio 80v. There is a hole in the parchment at the top of folio 81r, and the scribe uses it to subtly influence the performance of the text (see Figure 1). Nancy Durling has suggested that this scribe uses holes in the parchment on which he copies some devotional poems to remind the reader of Christ's wounds.[82] I suggest that Scribe B was similarly intentional in his use of this parchment defect in his copy of "When the Nightingale Sings." In every line that has a "the" ("you") in the middle, the scribe copies "the" on the right side of the hole, even though such a short word could easily fit on the left (see lines 3, 5, and 9 in Figure 1). The scribe thus conveys materially the pain of lovers' separation. Likewise, he separates "world" from "so wyde," again conveying distance. Further, the location of the hole could influence the voice of performance. The first line across the hole is "Ich have

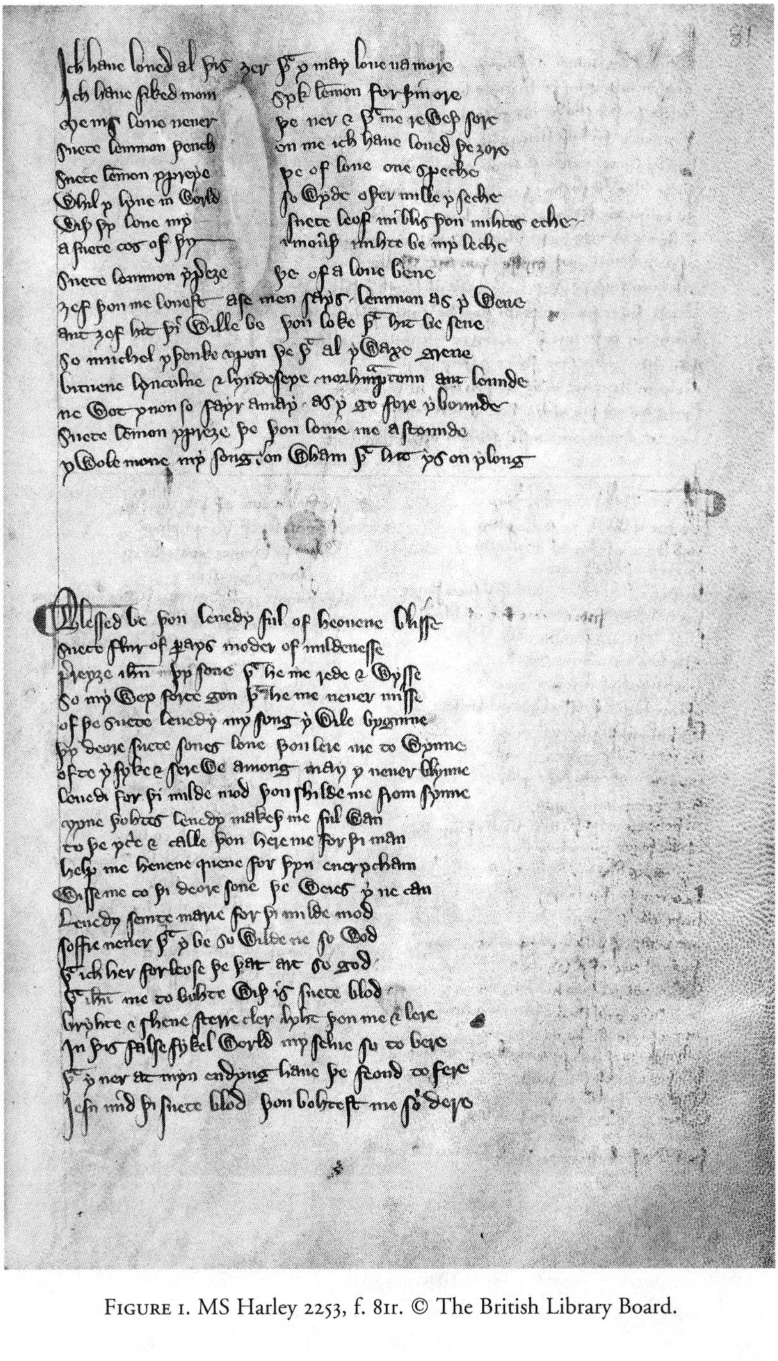

Figure 1. MS Harley 2253, f. 81r. © The British Library Board.

siked moni syk, lemmon, for thin ore," with the hole between "moni" and "syk." The reader's or singer's voice catches between these two words, imitating a sigh. Since the hole rarely separates the line into its two halves, that is, by the caesura, it creates a labored breathing when read aloud as a reader naturally pauses as his eyes traverse the hole and again at the caesura.

The copy of "When the Nightingale Sings" demonstrates the multiple tactics of poetic voice with respect to both the written text and its performance. Another poem in the manuscript, "Annot and John," also draws on vocal tactics to emphasize how poetic voice can integrate fixed discursive structures with ad hoc performance practices. The opening stanza of this poem adapts the language of the medieval lapidary to describe the beloved's peerlessness:

Ichot a burde in a bour ase beryl so bryht,	*I know; lady; bower*
Ase saphyr in selver, semly on syht,	*sapphire; lovely*
Ase jaspe the gentil that lemeth with lyht,	*jasper; gleams*
Ase gernet in golde, ant ruby wel ryht;	*set*
Ase onycle he ys, on yholden on hyht,	*onyx; she*
Ase diamaund the dere in day, when he is dyht;	*she; adorned*
He is coral ycud with cayser ant knyht;	*She; proven by; emperor*
Ase emeraude amorewen this may haveth myht.	*in the morning; maiden; power*
The myht of the margarite haveth this mai mere;	*daisy; splendid*
For charbocle Ich hire ches bi chin ant by chere.[83]	*ruby; countenance*

Subsequent stanzas aggregate images from herbals, aviaries, and romances. The aviary stanza uses its conceit to remind us of the performance context of the poem: "Hire nome is in a note of the nyhtegale, / In an note is hire nome. Nempneth hit non? [Will no one name it?] / Whose ryht redeth, roune to Johon [Whoever reads it correctly, whisper to John]."[84] As the lyric voice rearranges and repurposes the discourses codified in written texts, it also invites a performative multivocality, the plural whispers of the audience as they solve the riddle. The poem's central pun—that the name "Annot" is in "an note"—reminds us of the gap between sound and meaning that motivated the grammarians' distinction between types of voices. Interpreting the wordplay is, the poem tells us, an act of "right reading."[85]

The two *contrafacta* beginning "Lutel wot hit any mon," on folio 128, perhaps most clearly illustrate the difference between voice and speaker. Here is the first stanza of each poem, in the order they appear in the manuscript:

Lutel wot hit any mon	*knows*
Hou love hym haveth ybounde,	
That for us o the rode ron	*cross; bled* [lit. *ran*]
And bohte us with is wounde.	*his*
The love of him us haveth ymaked sounde,	*whole*
Ant ycast the grimly Gost to grounde.	*deadly spirit*
Ever ant oo, nyht and day, he haveth us in is thohte,	*always*
He nul nout leose that he so deore bohte.	
Lutel wot hit any mon	
Hou derne love may stonde,	*secret; survive*
Bote hit were a fre wymmon	*Unless; generous*
That much of love had fonde.	
The love of hire ne lesteth no wyht longe;	*man*
Heo haveth me plyht, ant wyteth me wyth wronge.	*She; pledged; blames*
Ever ant oo, for my leof, Icham in grete thohte,	
Y thenche on hire that Y ne seo nout ofte.[86]	

These two poems make explicit the tactics of lyric commonplaces: "Lutel wot hit any mon" is a rhetorical structure that can express a sacred or profane meaning. We can well imagine the same speaker uttering both lyrics, but the voice of each is distinct. Indeed, both poems describe a vocal petition for mercy: "That we han ydon, Y rede [believe], we reowen sore, / Ant crien ever to Jesu, 'Crist, thyn ore [favor]!' "; "Adoun Y fel to hire anon / Ant crie, 'Ledy, thin ore!' "[87] Although the text is similar, the voices are distinct in their purpose and situation.

The centrality of vocal tactics in Harley 2253 not only applies to the texts that modern critics have identified as lyrics but also proves to be a pervasive organizing principle of the manuscript's compilation. Critics have largely neglected the prose texts in the latter part of the manuscript, on folios 128v to 140v (where the manuscript breaks off).[88] Theo Stemmler believes that the compiler's anthologizing impulse led him to include these texts because they are all religious or didactic prose.[89] In fact, this section of the manuscript is far more specific in its compilation and has much to tell us about the place of texts in the lives of the manuscript's audience. Many of the devotional prose texts present an ethopoetic idea of voice, with prayers, psalms, or other devotional acts recorded alongside descriptions of their performance con-texts.[90] One representative text, item 99, introduces a prayer copied in the manuscript by explaining its potential use-contexts:

[introduction] Quy chescun jour de bon cuer cest oreisoun dirra remissioun de ces pecchiés avera, ne de mal mort morra, mes bon fyn avera. Sy ascun bon chemyn aler volez, cest oreysoun le jour dirrez, e ja en voye desturbé ne serrez mes pees en chemyn averez. E devaunt chescun ou vous vendrez. Honour, amour, e grace troverez. Si vous estes en mer travylé de tempeste, pernez un hanap pleyn de ewe de la mer e dites cest oreysoun outre le ewe. E pus la gittez en la mer, e la tempeste cessera. E quy en bataille vodra aler die cest oreysoun outre la ceynture de son espé, e pus se ceynte de ce, e le myeux ly avendra. Ne ocys ne playe mortel avera. . . . E a chescune foiz e en chescun lu, al comencement diez la Pater Nostre e Ave Maria. . . . Ditez ces trois salmes devant le oreysoun: "Deus misereatur nostri" [Psalm 66], "De profundis" [Psalm 129], "Voce mea ad Dominum clamavi" [Psalm 141].
[the beginning of the prayer] Domine Deus omnipotens, Pater, Filius, et Spiritus Sanctus, da mihi, n[omine], famulo tuo, per virtutem sancte crucis victoriam contra omnes et super omnes inimicos meos ut non possint mihi resistere nec contradicere.

[(introduction) One who says this prayer with good heart each day will have remission for his sins, will not die a bad death, but will have a good end. If you wish to have a good journey, say this prayer on that day, and you will not be disturbed in your passage but will have peace in your journey. And in the presence of each person wherever you arrive, you will find honor, love, and grace. If you are troubled by a storm at sea, take a goblet full of seawater and say this prayer over the water. And then throw it in the sea, and the storm will end. And one who wishes to go into battle should say this prayer over the belt of his sword, and then gird it about himself, and the best will come to him. He'll have neither death nor a mortal wound. . . . And at each time and in each place, in the beginning say the Paternoster and Ave Maria. . . . Say these three psalms before the prayer: "May God have mercy on us" [Psalm 66], "Out of the depths" [Psalm 129], and "I cried to the Lord with my voice" [Psalm 141]. (the beginning of the prayer) Lord God, all-powerful Father, Son, and Holy Spirit, grant me, n[ame], your servant, by the power of the holy cross victory against all and over all my foes so that they be unable to resist me or to speak against me.][91]

The instructions and the prayer petition for both worldly and otherworldly benefits. According to the introduction, the prayer absolves its speaker and also guarantees a good death; it confers wisdom and ensures victory against one's enemies, in battle and perhaps elsewhere. The instructions constitute a program of ethopoetics—a combination of situation and utterance—while also suggesting, in miniature, the compiler's science. Correct use of the prayer ("cest oreysoun") depends on the texts that "surround" it in practice (the three psalms "Deus misereatur nostri," "De profundis," and "Voce mea ad Dominum clamam") and the reader's or penitent's assimilation of the text: "da mihi N [for "nomine," or "your name here"] famulo tuo." But in its proscriptive mode, the introduction also acknowledges the importance of the vocal performance of the prayer and the particular outcomes of each use-context, such as saying the prayer over a goblet of seawater to calm a tempest or saying it over one's sword for protection in battle. This model of prayer invites its readers and speakers to become tacticians, adapting the authorized text to their particular circumstances.

Similarly, several distinct items (101, 109a, 110, and 111) list occasions for specific psalms. For example:

Quy velt que Dieu sovyegne de ly, die troi foiz cest salme: "Usquequo Domine" [Psalm 12]. Qui de rien se doute, die troiz foiz cest salme: "In te Domine speravi" [Psalm 30]. Si vous volez estre deliveré del poer del Deable, ditez le jour trey foiz cest salme: "In te Domine speravi" [Psalm 30].

[One who wishes that God remember him, say this psalm three times: "How long, O Lord" (Psalm 12). One who is fearful of anything, say this psalm three times: "In thee, O Lord, have I hoped" (Psalm 30). If you wish to be freed from the power of the Devil, say this psalm three times in the day: "In thee, O Lord, have I hoped" (Psalm 30)].[92]

More elaborate liturgical instructions are given in other texts in the manuscript. Items 107 and 108 list the masses to be said in particular circumstances. The former provides a week's worth of masses to be said when one "est en tristour, prisone, poverté, ou chiet en maladie" (is in sadness, prison, poverty, or falls in sickness).[93] The latter lists seven masses in honor of God and St. Giles, patron saint of cripples, lepers, and nursing mothers. Item 115 offers detailed instructions, in Anglo-Norman, for contemplation during the daytime hours, including the texts of prayers to recite and the biblical events to contemplate at each hour. As these instructions make clear, each performance of a sacred text constitutes a tactical assumption of the text's authority, which is conversely determined as much by the conditions of performance as the situation of the speaker.

My discussion of the Harley manuscript began with the poem "When the Nightingale Sings," a widely studied love lyric that, when read in isolation, appears to conform to certain features of post-Romantic lyric theory. By itself, this poem reads as the extended utterance of a single subject expressed with formal closure. Yet as we have seen, both the poem's text and its material context demonstrate how its lyric voice results from the situation of its practice, whether read from the page or performed. The prayer instructions with which I have concluded also demonstrate this kind of voice. The compilation and texts of MS Harley 2253 demonstrate how the medieval concept of "voice" is an example of one kind of tactic that creates an ad hoc and improvisatory relationship between a text and its practices. The manuscript's lyrics, in particular, demonstrate a written and performing voice distinct from the "utterance" of a complex and unified subject that has been construed as the hallmark of post-Romantic lyric and also distinct from the totalized poetic voice inhering in the text that has been favored by some medieval literary critics. Because its theorization in medieval philosophy includes both its biological and rational capacities, voice is the common tactic of many texts compiled in MS Harley 2253, both lyric and nonlyric. Yet lyrics in particular demonstrate how this medieval understanding of voice encourages tactical modes of practice, both in oral performance and in scribal copying and layout. As the compilation of Harley 2253 demonstrates, medieval lyrics have voices through which experiences, circumstances, and emotions can speak tactically.

CHAPTER 2

Enchanting Songs and Rhyming Doctrine in William Herebert's Hymns

Although scholars and editors have typically separated sacred and profane lyrics as objects of study, tactical practices define both kinds of lyrics. In fact, the very interdependence of these two thematics in medieval English literature motivates this generic definition. As Barbara Newman has recently demonstrated, secular and sacred meanings "cross over" into each other, mutually influencing structures of interpretation.[1] By their nature, tactics can navigate such separations and distinctions, recombining or integrating them in sometimes surprising ways. In the previous chapter, we have seen how the compilation and texts of Harley 2253 implicitly theorize a concept of voice across these categories, expressing less an "everyman" than what we might call an "anyman," a circumstantially qualified utterance that can nonetheless shift readily among speakers. This model of voice informs both scribal and performative practices. But while a tactical lyric voice may have seemed inclusive to the kinds of secular households responsible for the production and dissemination of Harley 2253, its moral implications could be troubling for the primary producers and disseminators of vernacular sacred lyrics: friars.[2] For members of these orders, who undertook much of the pastoral care of the laity following the mandates of the Fourth Lateran Council in 1215, the relationship between the sacred and secular was of special concern. As they sought to communicate doctrine to lay audiences, friars sometimes found it expeditious to compose vernacular lyrics or to retrofit moral interpretations to popular tales and songs.[3]

Because of the complexity of the fraternal use of lyrics, it may be helpful at this point to recall the distinction between strategies and tactics. Both of these terms refer to modes of relation to institutional forms and standards. A strategic relationship to these forms follows their prescribed usages. By contrast, a tactical relationship to these forms is ad hoc and improvisatory, often involving unauthorized hybridization, recombination, or merging of discrete forms or categories. As representatives of their order, friars often write, translate, and perform a variety of texts in ways more strategic than tactical, since these texts are intended to convey normative and established doctrine. Because of its tactical nature, the genre of lyric could prove intractable to friars' strategic aims; the improvisatory practices central to medieval lyric language, performance, and reception may appear antithetical to the communication of a stable and consistent moral message. Yet in seeking to capitalize on the popularity of these short poems in order to appeal to a lay audience, friars themselves used tactics to adapt and repurpose lyrics. As Claire Waters has discussed, friars had to navigate between their dual identities as ecstatic or charismatic performers, which linked them to divinity, and as representatives of their institutional orders who transmitted authorized doctrine.[4] Thus, perhaps more than any other group of lyric readers, writers, and performers, friars had to reconcile the tactics of the lyric genre with their strategic aims for its usage.

This conflict is extensively explored and theorized in the commonplace book compiled and partially copied by the friar William Herebert, British Library MS Additional 46919 (1314–33). A collection of practical texts, sermons, and didactic lyrics, the codex concludes with Herebert's own English hymn translations. This chapter's central claim is that Herebert uses tactics in his translations in order to draw on song's emotional and popular appeal and to convey doctrine. Herebert accomplishes this by using a combination of academic and popular poetic and rhetorical practices, as well as scholastic conventions for presenting written texts that convey textual authority. Ironically, in Herebert's translations, lyrics' tactics are pressed into the service of strategic aims—expressing normative morality—even as they undergird the popular features of song that make it an effective pastoral instrument. His tactics reside in negotiating among the different modes of doctrine and affectivity available in both learned and popular textual practices of composition, transmission, and reception.

In order to illuminate the conflict surrounding lyric and its tactics for medieval friars in general, and Herebert in particular, my discussion begins with a little-known Anglo-French poem in the manuscript, "Amours m'ount si enchaunté." This poem presents an implicit lyric theory that raises many of these questions of the relationship between doctrine, affect, and lyric. My reading offers a model for the distinction between the performative and affective qualities of lyric (or "song") and its moral rhetoric. "Amours m'ount si enchaunté" suggests that "song" can be understood as an act of performance that, while conducive to transgression for its affective and somatic appeal, can also be inherently and productively tactical in combatting its own sinful tendencies. Nonetheless, the French poem locates doctrinal meaning in the more strategically produced and regulated written text. Its concerns reflect larger discourses of song, performance, and rhetoric that were especially intense within the fraternal community. Following this discussion, I turn to Herebert's hymn translations, which take up and expand the distinction between song and doctrine. The friar uses tactical practices in his translations in order to integrate scholastic textual theories of translation and authority with the affective and popular appeals of performance. Herebert's English hymns unite his scholastic influences with popular preaching and liturgical practices to stabilize song's morality by separating its affective performance from its doctrine.

Equivocation and Enchantment

William Herebert's commonplace book reflects his fraternal and scholastic training. Although records of his life are few, it appears that he was born in the last quarter of the thirteenth century in the west of England or in Wales, with his native convent in Hereford. In the second decade of the fourteenth century, he was at Oxford, where he became a lector at the Franciscan convent in 1317. He subsequently returned to Hereford and died there in the 1330s.[5] As an Oxford friar, Herebert was well acquainted with the problem of the relationship between rhetoric and doctrine that emerges from both scholastic sources and popular preaching practice. He annotated seven known manuscripts, containing works by Roger Bacon, the *Tractatus* attributed to Thomas of Eccleston, and other theological works; his duties as lector and his preaching career in Hereford required charismatic public speaking.

Herebert completed the compilation of his commonplace book, MS Additional 46919, toward the end of his life. The book is the richest source of Herebert's own writings, including six complete Latin sermons, sermon outlines, and twenty-three translations of poems. In addition, the book contains devotional verses and sermons in French by his contemporary, the friar Nicholas Bozon. Yet not all of the material is "preacherly"; the book also

contains the thirteenth-century Anglo-Norman grammar of Walter Bibbesworth known as "Le Tretiz," practical treatises on hunting and falconry, and
a poem on the Crusades.[6] The manuscript has chiefly been studied for its
collection of Herebert's nineteen English hymn translations that he copied
in the final gathering of the manuscript, which will also be the focus of the
second part of this chapter.[7]

Less frequently discussed is the French poem "Amours m'ount si
enchaunté" (Love has so enchanted me), yet I believe that this poem offers
an implicit lyric theory that informs how Herebert understands the pastoral
function (and concomitant generic identity) of short poetry. The main point
I wish to make in the following discussion is that in this poem, the poet
makes tactical use of the aural and intellectual pleasures of its particular formal techniques, at first with reference to love poetry but ultimately turning
them to moral use. As we shall see, "Amours m'ount si enchaunté" differentiates between what it calls "song" and "rhyme," thereby realizing thematically
and formally a contemporary discourse on the moral problems and possibilities of lyric poetry. The poem appears on folios 92r to 93r of the manuscript
under a rubric in Herebert's hand: "Cy comencent les dytees moun syre
Gauter de Bybeswurthe. Regardez, lysez, apernez" (Here begins the poem of
my lord Walter of Bibbesworth. Look at it, read it, learn it).[8] The poem
appears, unattributed, in only one other manuscript, Cambridge Corpus
Christi Coll. MS 450 (which also contains Bibbesworth's grammar). Aside
from Herebert's rubric and the coincidence of the texts in the Corpus Christi
manuscript, there is no other evidence linking this poem to the Walter
Bibbesworth who wrote "Le Tretiz" that begins Additional 46919.[9] Further,
as I shall demonstrate below, this song appears to derive from Gautier de
Coinci's long verse collection, *Les Miracles de Nostre Dame.* Herebert's rubric
does more than simply misattribute the author of the poem, however; it also
marks this poem for special attention. A modern reader, too, might be drawn
to this poem for formal reasons. Its rhetoric is based on "equivocal rhyme,"
wordplay on homonyms or near-homonyms, which became especially popular in later medieval French poetry.[10] At the opening of the poem, the equivoca are "chant/er" (sing, song), "enchant/er" (sing, enchant, charm), and
"deschant/er" (descant, disenchant, sing badly, contradict). The poem's
opening gives us a sense of its playful rhetoric:

Amours m'ount si enchaunté qe jeo ay tut dys deschauntee
Tut qauntke jeo chauntoye, qar touz jours deschauntoye.

Pur ceo tieng mon chaunt a deschaunt qaunt jeo en chauntaunt
Chaunt chaunt par qey j'enchaunte la chaunte qe jeo chaunte,
Chaunçoun ou chaunçounette, qe n'est chaunçoun nette.
Qar la mieuth chauntaunte sy est deschauntaunte
Quaunt ele chaunte tel chaunz qe n'ad en sey ly douz chaunz.
Qar par lour chauns deschaunteez unt les genz si enchaunteez
Q'yl quydent estre chaunteours, mes yl sunt tut deschaunteours,
Qar lour ames deschauntent touz les chaunz q'yl chauntent.

[Love has so enchanted me that I have always sung badly/been disenchanted with/
contradicted everything that I was singing, because I always sang badly/sang the descant.
For this reason, I hold my song as singing badly/disenchanting/descanting when I, in
singing/enchanting, sing a song by which I enchant/sing the song that I sing, one song or
another that is not a clean/moral/refined song. Because the best singing is so
disenchanting/contradicts/descants so much when she sings such songs that she does not
have sweet songs in her. Because with their bad/disenchanting/descanting songs they have
so enchanted people that they suppose themselves singers, but they are all bad singers/
disenchanters/descanters because their souls sing badly/contradict all the songs that they
sing.][11]

As is evident from this short excerpt, the poem is dense and multivalent; each
line has a number of possible translations, and the one above is intended
simply to give the reader a sense of the poem's meaning and wordplay. Its
inclusion in Herebert's book raises a number of questions. First, why was it
marked for special attention by Herebert and misattributed in his rubric?
Second, what does its equivocal form suggest about song as a genre; in particular, what relationships does it create among morality, performance, and
rhetoric?

To address both questions, it is necessary to understand the likely source
of this poem. This appears to be Gautier de Coinci's *Les miracles de Nostre
Dame* (1214–36). In this long poetic work, the monk Gautier rejects the secular aims of courtly literature but co-opts their conventions, especially those
of romance and lyric, to inspire religious devotion in his audience.[12] Gautier
wrote extensively about the correct moral use of song, equivocating on
"chant," "enchant," and "deschant" in a manner similar to the poet of
"Amours m'ount si enchaunté" in the Herebert manuscript. One of the songs
in *Les miracles de Nostre Dame* demonstrates Gautier's use of the technique:

Amors, qui seit bien enchanter,
As pluisors fait tel chant chanter
Dont les ames deschantent.
Je ne veil mais chanter tel chant,
Mais por celi novel chant chant
De cui li angle chantent.

[Love, who knows well how to enchant/sing, you have made many sing such a song which
their souls sing against/contradict. But I do not want to sing such a song, but I sing a
new song for the one the angels sing about.][13]

The uses of these *equivoca* are more clearly moral in Gautier's poetry than
they are in the opening of "Amours m'ount si enchaunté." Yet as the poem
in the Herebert manuscript continues, it soon becomes clear that its primary
intention, too, is moral. Shortly following the opening quoted above, the
Herebert-compiled poem describes the conversion of the singer's affections
from "Maryot" (a commonplace name for a shepherdess) to "Mary":

Ore par une suy sy enchaunté de qy j'ay mes chauns chauntee
Qe ly plusours y vount chauntaunt, mes ore dy en mon chaunt taunt
Qe ja plus ne chaunteray; de Maryot mon chaunt terray
Qar de Marye voyl chaunter.

[Now I am so enchanted by the one about whom I sang my songs that I went about
singing many of them, but now I say this much in my song, that I will sing no more; my
song of Maryot will stop because I wish to sing of Mary.][14]

The poem also invokes a well-known motif of "Ave" reversing "Eva," the
Annunciation redeeming original sin, as a form of song:

Ha! dame Eve, mal chaunt chauntas quant Adam taunt enchauntas
Q'yl manga vos chaunçonz. . . .
Ne fust ly chaunt douz dount chaunta <<Ave>> qe Gabriel chaunta,
. . . .
Adam e tu chaunterez taunke ly faufee enchaunterez.
Car <<Eva>> deschauntames e par <<Ave>> countrechauntames.

[Ha! Dame Eve, you sang a bad song, when you so sang to/charmed Adam that he
swallowed your songs. . . . You didn't sing the sweet song of *Ave* that Gabriel sang. . . .

Adam and you will sing until you've sung to/enchanted the Devil. For we unsang *Eva* and countersang with *Ave*.][15]

Adam "swallowed" Eve's bad song when he committed original sin, suggesting that sin consisted as much in his belief in Eve's false speech as in his consumption of the forbidden fruit.[16] Yet Christ, the word made flesh, is engendered by Mary's bodily absorption of the word of God, "Ave." Indeed, "Ave" is a tactic countering Satan's strategic song of "Eva": "<<Eva>> deschauntames e par <<Ave>> countrechauntames" ("We unsang *Eva* and countersang with *Ave*"). Elsewhere in the poem, "deschaunt" tends to connote sinfulness and error. Here, the poet inverts the implications of the established structures of equivocal rhyme and of the song of "Eva," adapting these forms to quite different ends. In short, this poem's opening deploys lyric tactics for morally strategic ends, foregrounding these special qualities of "song" with its equivoca.

"Amours m'ount si enchaunté" strongly echoes several parts of Gautier's *Miracles*. This suggests the poem in the Herebert manuscript is a redaction of the longer work. Gautier chastises clerks who sing "unclean" songs, which could mean either aesthetically or morally impure: "De Tyebregon et d'Emmelot / Laissons ester les chançonnetes, / Car ne sont pas leurs chanchons netes" (Let be those little songs of Tyebregon and Emmelot, because they are not clean/moral/refined songs").[17] As we have seen, the opening of "Amours m'ount si enchaunté" also equivocates "chaunçounnete" (little song) and "chaunçoun nette" (clean/moral/refined song). And like the poem in Herebert's manuscript, Gautier's poem also warns against abandoning "Mary" for "Maryot."[18] The similarity between "Amours m'ount si enchaunté" and sections of Gautier's work is so pronounced that it suggests that the poem in Herebert's manuscript began its textual existence as one of the Gautier-inspired short texts circulating at the time.[19] In attributing the poem in his manuscript to Walter Bibbesworth, Herebert may simply have been confusing his "Gauters." But it is also likely that he finds the attribution credible on stylistic grounds: Bibbesworth's grammar is written after the style of Latin grammatical poems (discussed in the previous chapter) that demonstrate the proper use of these equivoca.[20] Herebert's sensitivity to the rhetoric of "Amours m'ount si enchaunté" suggests that he is not immune to both its charms and its hazards, its enchantments and disenchantments. Consider these lines from the opening: "Pur ceo tieng mon chaunt a deschaunt qaunt jeo en chauntaunt / Chaunt chaunt par qey j'enchaunte la chaunte qe jeo chaunte" (For this reason, I hold my song as singing badly/disenchanting/ descanting when I, in singing/enchanting, sing a song by which I enchant/ sing the song that I sing). First, we can note that the lines are extremely difficult to comprehend because of their repetitions (and of course, other translations are possible). The equivocal form thus demotes semantic meaning in favor of *melos*, the sheer musicality of the repeated language. If, as the poem states, this is the "deschaunt," the descant or disenchanting song, it is musically seductive. As these lines multiply "song" semantically, its moral valence becomes unstable: "qaunt jeo en chantaunt / chaunt chaunt" can mean "When I, in singing, sing a song" but can also mean (if we combine "en chauntant" into a single word), "When I sing an enchanting song." With all of these enchantments, it is easy to lose sight of the fact that the song in question here "n'est chaunçoun nette" (is not a clean/moral/refined song).

My point here is that the probable source, derived from Gautier de Coinci, is much clearer in the moral valences of its *equivoca* than the poem "Amours m'ount si enchaunté." Especially in its opening, the version in Herebert's book more clearly manifests the tension between song's doctrinal meanings and the range of its performance practices by means of its use of *equivoca*, which must be read with extremely close attention to local and contingent contexts in order to determine whether they connote virtue or vice. We see one attempt to work through this tension in the rubric in Herebert's hand: "Regardez, lysez, apernez" (Look at it, read it, learn it). Here, Herebert privileges the visual and material text over its performance: although the rhymes and wordplay in the poem appeal to the ear, the text as a didactic tool must be consumed with the eye. Herebert instructs the reader to "look at" the text and thereby "read" and "learn" it. His emphasis on the written text of this poem affirms it as a source of knowledge—which will also influence his presentation of his hymn translations—even as the spurious attribution suggests a destabilizing susceptibility to its *melos* in performance.

The poem's evocation of song's enchantment and descanting (i.e., polyphony) also touches on a contemporary controversy over liturgical performance, which was often couched in language particularly damning to members of the fraternal orders. With the thirteenth century's post-Lateran emphasis on pastoral care came debates over the decorum of a range of performance practices, from liturgical singing to excessive rhetorical embellishment, that were, on one hand, thought necessary to appeal to an illiterate or semiliterate laity and, on the other hand, suspect for their potential to distract from the seriousness of doctrine. What Claire Waters has called the preacher's "two bodies," his charismatic humanity and his clerical authority, often came into conflict in performance.[21] Singing the descant, in particular, threatened the physical continence of the singer: "The singer . . . embarking on one of the long passages of discant . . . soon becomes aware of the true spirit of the continuous melodic rhythm; though he may begin with caution, by degrees his utterance becomes involuntarily louder, more and more rapid, and more and more emphatic, and his surrender is at last so complete that he restrains himself with difficulty, or perhaps even does not restrain himself, from sympathetic movements of the feet and contortions of the body."[22] Many ecclesiastics and music theorists heaped scorn upon singers who demonstrated such a lack of self-control. According to some, polyphony was one of a number of degenerate practices enjoyed by the growing class of secular clerics, from gambling to hunting.[23] Robert of Courson's *Summa* (1208–12/13) links embellished liturgical singing with sexual wantonness, and it proscribes "minstrellish" performance styles but permits skillful singing.[24] A carol that survives in a fifteenth-century collection more humorously associates sexual and musical promiscuity. Its female speaker admires the cantor Jankin's melismatic style:

Jankin at the *Sanctus* craked a merie note,	*trilled*
And yet me thinketh it dos me good—I payed for his cote.	
Jankin craked notes an hundred on a knot,	*all together*
And yet he hakked hem smaller than wortes to the pot.[25]	*chopped; roots (vegetables)*

Jankin's song has a potent physical affect: in a perverted annunciation, the speaker finds herself pregnant at the end of the song. Yet even among these aspersions, polyphony gained a kind of cachet in liturgical singing and musicianship more generally. Emerging primarily from Paris, it benefited from its association with this medieval center of learning and culture. And as musical notation became increasingly standardized and nuanced in the thirteenth and fourteenth centuries, the ability to improvise beyond the page in performance became a mark of advanced musicianship.[26] Further, in courtly circles, the pleasures of song, especially polyphonic song, were even deemed moral alternatives to sexual behavior.[27]

The "countersongs" of *Eva* and *Ave* most trenchantly pose the dual nature of song as damning and as redemptive. As we have seen, both of these functions of song are expressed in the multivalent equivoca *chant, enchant,* and *deschant.* Toward the end of the poem, however, a new equivocal rhyme suggests a stable alternative.

S'amour m'aprent de chaunt affere
En novel compas de ryme en la mer la ou jeo ryme
E me fet chaunçoun rymé en la mer myeuth rymer
D'assez q'avaunt ne rymoye qaunt jeo de foles rymoie.

[So love teaches me to put together from my song a new scheme of rhyme, in the sea where I row/steer/rhyme, and a rhymed/steered song makes me row/steer/rhyme better in the sea by far than I rowed/steered/rhymed before, when I rhymed about foolish women.][28]

This section of the poem significantly and productively changes the equivocal rhyme from "chant/enchant/deschant" to "ryme/rymer" (to rhyme, row, or steer). Rhetorically and semantically, this stabilizes song's morality. The "ryme/rymer" equivocation is based on a single word with two meanings rather than a cluster. Even as its rhetoric is dualistic, the meanings of these equivoca are stabilizing: they row, steer, and generally direct the rhyme in a manner that the earlier part of the poem, with the ambiguity of its equivoca, did not. As I have laid it out here (based on the manuscript lineation), the poem appears to have internal rhymes, for example, "E me fet chaunçoun *rymé* en la mer myeuth *rymer*" (my emphasis). However, the poem can equally be understood as composed of shorter end-rhymed couplets: "E me fet chaunçoun *rymé* / en la mer myeuth *rymer*." Most lines in Herebert's copy mark the caesura following the first rhyme with some kind of punctuation (a *punctus*, *virgula*, or *punctus elevatus*). Because the "ryme/rymer" equivocation is based on a single word, it emphasizes the poem's end rhymes more than its equivoca. By contrast, the opening of the poem can also be read as end rhymed, yet its triple equivoca and their overall density structures these verses as much or more than do the end rhymes.

Further, end-rhymed poetry was explicitly theorized as a form that promoted regularity and concord. John of Garland's *Parisiana Poetria*, one of the few medieval treatises to discuss rhymed poetry, describes it as a branch of music, with the medieval understanding of music's capacity to reconcile difference.

> Rhymed poetry is a branch of the art of music. For music is divided into the
> cosmic, which embraces the internal harmony of the elements, the humane,
> which embraces the harmony and concord of the humors, and the instrumental,
> which embraces the concord evoked by instruments. This includes melody,

quantitative verse, and rhymed verse. . . . A rhymed poem is a harmonious arrangement of words with like endings, regulated not by quantity but by number of syllables. "Harmonious arrangement" serves as the genus; for music is a harmonious arrangement of disparate elements and tones—"discordant concord" or "concordant discord." "Words with like endings" distinguishes it from melody. "By number of syllables" refers to the fact that a rhymed poem consists of some precise number of syllables, be it many or few. "Not by quantity" distinguishes it from the art of quantitative verse. "Regulated" indicates that the words in a rhymed poem should fall in a regular cadence.[29]

John's treatise is unusual in explicitly identifying Latin rhymed poetry, which was growing more popular in the later Middle Ages than classical quantitative verse, as a branch of music, which was highly theorized as a regulated mathematical science in medieval liberal arts curricula. He further associates rhyme with syllabic rather than quantitative verse. In this account, the uniform syllable *numbers* of end-rhymed poetic lines (rather than their *lengths*, which characterized quantitative verse) help to create the "discordant concord" or "concordant discord" associated with academic music theory.

Rhyme, then, has the salutary capacity to harmonize discord. Although "Amours m'ount si enchaunté" is both equivocal and rhymed throughout, the shift to the "ryme/rymer" equivoca toward the end of the poem serves to emphasize its end rhymes as a primary poetic structure. The poem's sea change is underscored by the meanings of "ryme": rhyme, row, and steer. Rhyming has the capacity for moral guidance rather than ecstatic "enchantment." The poem concludes by explicitly transforming Gabriel's "song" of *Ave* into such a rhyme.

Gabriel, bone ryme as e ta chaunçoun ben rymé as.
Qar qy la rymera en paradys rymera,
Ou nous tretouz rymeroms par <<Ave>> qe nous cryeroms.
Ore vous ay, dame, rymee, veyez si jeo ay bien rymé.

[Gabriel, you have a good rhyme and your song has steered us well/has rhymed well. Because whoever will rhyme/will steer toward it will rhyme in Paradise, where we all will rhyme/steer by *Ave* what we believe. Now I have rhymed/steered you, Lady, see if I have steered you/have rhymed well.][30]

Significantly, the verb "cryeroms"—"we believe"—takes the place of the expected equivocum in the penultimate line. Rhyme has steered us toward unequivocal faith. As a poetic structure, rhyme can engage with both the performative-aural and the textual-visual: although it has strongly sonic qualities, it is also visibly marked in medieval manuscripts by punctuation, lineation, and/or bracketing. The implicit lyric theory of "Amours m'ount si enchaunté" suggests that while song's rhetoric can dangerously "enchant" audiences, singers, and readers, tactics can invert those dangers by repurposing and reorienting those same forms. Further, those who render songs as written texts can draw on the more strategic rhetoric of stable, unequivocal rhymes.

"Amours m'ount si enchaunté" addresses song's morality formally and thematically, subtly manipulating its balance of equivoca and end rhymes to propose a kind of solution to the potential conflict between fraternal song's popular appeal and its doctrinal mandate. Such concerns form a distinct part of a larger discourse of suspicion of song and rhetoric. In antifraternal discourse, the populism of friars' sermons was lambasted as diluting dogma, and medieval literature frequently portrays friars as sexually wanton. Pope John XXII's papal bull of 1322 famously denounced musical ornamentation in liturgy, complaining of singers who "truncate the melodies with hoquets, . . . deprave them with discants . . . [and] even stuff them with upper parts made out of secular songs."[31] Soon afterward, the Dominican Pierre de Baume compared the populist elements of sermons to the use of descant. "It is the same with sermons today as it is with motets. . . . [N]ow there are discants in the motets, so that only the tune can be followed. It charms the ear and has no other use. Similarly in the old days sermons were such as to profit the people. But now they have rhymes and curious comparisons, and philosophical subtleties are mixed with them; so many sermons do no good; they only please the hearers as oratory."[32] Yet if song threatens to overwhelm orthodoxy with physical pleasure, it can also have a generative, even redemptive power. Other fraternal lyrics and writings address these concerns by discriminating between moral and immoral uses of song and rhetoric. A lyric that appears twice in John of Grimestone's 1372 preaching handbook (under the headings "De Adulacione" and "De Decepcione") singles out song for its corrupting effects:

Thei ben nouth wel for to leuen	*believe*
That with manie wordis wil quemen;	*flatter*
For often deceyued the briddes be	
With sundri songes an loueli gle.[33]	*music*

Yet Grimestone's handbook is itself one of the most significant surviving collections of English religious lyrics, arranged by thematic headings for pastoral use. Indeed, friars relied on song, among other popular texts and performance practices, to communicate doctrine to the laity. For example, the "Love Rune" of friar Thomas of Hales (before 1272), rubricated as a "cantus" in the sole manuscript witness, warns the maiden to whom it is addressed of the fickleness of mortal lovers and the impermanence of riches: "Theyh he were so riche mon / As Henry ure kyng, / . . . Al were sone his prute [pride] agon; / Hit nere on ende wrth on heryng [herring]!" However, the friar idealizes Christ as a lover with reference to his wealth: "He is ricchest mon of londe, / So wide so [As far as] mon speketh with muth; / Alle heo beoth to His honde [at his command], / Est and west, north and suth!"[34] The adaptation of such conventions of popular song was part of a broader preaching practice of using common sayings, proverbs, and exempla drawn from popular romances in sermons.[35]

One rationale for these pastoral adaptations can be found in a thirteenth-century fraternal sermon that takes a popular song, rather than the usual scripture or authoritative text, as its theme. In this sermon from Cambridge MS Trinity 43, the theme "Atte wrastlinge my lemman I ches [choose], / and atte ston-kasting I him for-les [forsake]" is explicitly attributed to a popular source:[36] "My leue frend, wilde [rowdy] wimmen and golme [men] i my contreie, wan he gon o the ring [when they dance in a ring], among manie othere songis, that litil ben wort [worthy] that tei singin, so sein thei thus: 'Atte wrastlinge my lemman etc.'"[37] The preacher justifies his choice of theme, invoking a tension between the authority of the embodied prophet and that of the written text: "And we findin iwritin in a bok, that te maister maude [made], that nevere ne lei [lies], that is i the holy godspel, that suete Jesu Crist spak: 'there is iwritin, that of euery idel word, that men spekin i this werld, men sal giuen andsuere offe [answer for] and raison o domisdai.'"[38] The preacher's introduction of his scriptural source, Matthew 12:36, invokes the relationship between authority and the written text that we have seen in Herebert's rubric to "Amours m'ount si enchaunté."[39] It is "iwritin in a bok, that te maister maude, that nevere ne lei." A production of a "maister," the book is the material witness of truth. Yet the contents of the book are the words "that suete Jesu Crist spak," authorized by his embodied humanity and prophetic status. The preacher's translation locates the text of Matthew 12:36 within a moral authority that relies on both embodied speech and the written word. The dual authority of Christ's speech and the written text justify the preacher's stated intention: "idele wordes tornen to note [benefit] of saule. For liclike [most likely] nis no folie ifundin, that sum wisdom nis bundin [enclosed] inne, who-se kouthe it wel ut-bringin [bring forth]."[40] The sermon explicates the first part of the English verse, "Atte wrastlinge my lemman I ches," to refer to the person who chooses Christ as his lover by wrestling against the three temptations of world, fiend, and flesh. The second line, "Atte ston-kasting I him for-les," refers to those who, through the stone-like hardness of their hearts, lose their love for God.

Fraternal debates about the efficacy and morality of using song to communicate doctrine emerged from larger concerns about the use of elaborate rhetoric in lay preaching. Was it more important to hew closely to doctrine or to appeal to one's audience? Some church authorities advocated simplicity in the language of popular sermons. In the late twelfth century, Cardinal William Durand advised preachers to adapt their speech to their audience's level of learning, lest they be guilty of vanity in displaying their own erudition. Archbishop Pecham's 1281 *Constitutions* state that priests should teach the *pastoralia* in the vernacular, without rhetorical decoration or artifice.[41] The rhetorical manuals that flourished as a result of the increased emphasis on preaching were also divided on the use of verbal embellishments. Thomas Waleys's *De modo componendi sermones cum documentis* (1336–50) discourages rhythmic language in sermons, comparing its dangers to those of song:

> Quid autem valeant isti colores rhythmici, non video, nisi quod delectent aures audientium. . . . [I]mmo, valde offendunt, quia fructum sermonis impediunt, et vanitatem praedicatoris manifeste ostendunt, qui potius videtur praetendere personam joculatoris quam praedicatoris. Impediunt autem fructum sermonis, quia, dum aures exteriores nimis occupantur in suavitate vocis, aures interiores ipsius cordis minus hauriunt de virtute rei et sententiae, sicut et qui multum delectatur in cantu minus attendit ad rem quae canitur.

> [Moreover, I do not see the value of those rhythmic devices, unless to delight the ears of the hearers. . . . On the contrary, they offend more severely because they obstruct the message of the sermon, and clearly display the vanity of the preacher, who is more strongly seen to assume the character of a minstrel than a preacher. Moreover, they obstruct the message of the sermon because while the external ears are too much occupied with sweet voices, the interior ears of the heart itself derive less of the virtue of the meaning and message, just as whoever is delighted greatly in singing attends less to the thing that is sung.][42]

Waleys's warning centers on the perils of minstrelsy and song in their ability to evacuate meaning (*sententia*) and understanding from language. His final simile interestingly elides sermon with song; to be delighted (*delectatur*) by either threatens one's apprehension of semantic and moral meaning.

On the other hand, rhetorical flexibility was sometimes necessary for communicating with the laity. The Bible itself, as some fraternal scholars noted, uses rhetorical colors to reach a catholic audience.[43] Robert of Basevorn's *Form of Preaching* (1322) notably defends the use of rhetoric in sermons: "What some say . . . seems to me altogether reprehensible: that preaching ought not to shine with false verbal embellishments—for in very many sermons of St. Bernard the whole is almost always rich in colors."[44] Robert lists "winning over of the audience" as an element of a successful sermon but admits that an audience's knowledge will limit a preacher's ability to conform to the precepts of sermon composition.

> But, say that one must preach in English and should undertake as his theme: *walk ye* [*ambulate*]. Could he without fault choose as the main authority one in which there would not be *walk ye* [*ambulare*] but its convertible *to go* [*ire*]? For example if one would say: one must walk first, freely, on the way of God because of definite and just reward; hence the Lord also says *Go ye also into my vineyard and I will give you what is just* [*Ite et vos in vineam meam, et quod justum fuerit dabo vobis*]? It seems to me yes. Nor is there any difference in English between one or the other, and I see nothing to prevent this unless there be some learned men who note the authorities in their sermons because in Scripture the difference between *to walk* [*ambulare*] and *to go* [*ire*] is immediately evident but the unlearned do not know how to discern it.[45]

Robert's care in justifying the substitution of "to go" for "to walk" in an English sermon reflects the importance of lexis to the increasingly popular "thematic" sermon form, which emphasized exploring multiple texts associated with a single word.[46] Here, he points out that lexical purity is impossible when a sermon's audience is not acquainted with the language, Latin, of the authoritative text. Thus, when preaching in English, it is permissible to expand a theme on *ambulate* ("walk ye") with texts containing *ite* ("go ye"). In Middle English, *walken* and *gon* are not as distinct as modern English "to walk" and "to go"; rather, both verbs could and did stand in for one another. "To walk" was a primary meaning of *gon*, and *walken* often carries the primary meaning of "to go" or "to become," as in this Harley lyric cited in the previous chapter: "Sorewe ant syke ant drery mod byndeth me so faste / that y wene to walke wod."[47] The first English-to-Latin dictionary, the fifteenth-century *Promptorium Parvulorum*, offers the following definition: "Walkyng abowte, or goyng: Deambulacio."[48]

In summary, fraternal anxieties about the morality of lyric focused a number of debates concerning, on one hand, the rhetorical, affective, and aural appeal of performance and, on the other hand, the relationship between these rhetorical and musical pleasures and the demands of doctrine and moral teaching. Preaching friars bore the dual and at times conflicting responsibilities of performing charismatically in order to appeal to their audiences and imparting the tenets of doctrine approved by the church. If song was effective for the first purpose, its tactical practices made it particularly vulnerable to the corruption of its message. Yet the poem "Amours m'ount si enchaunté" and Herebert's rubric for it suggest a solution that involves these problematic tactics as well as institutional strategies. Its initial equivoca associate "song" with performativity, affect, and moral turpitude. Yet equivocal rhyme is inherently tactical because it relies so heavily on context and circumstance for its interpretation. As the "Eva/Ave" inversion demonstrates, these tactics can overcome our sinful propensities by improvising on and repurposing their forms. The second part of the poem directs such tactics toward more strategic practices, as it aligns a more orthodox poetics and doctrine with end rhyme by means of the rhyme/row/steer equivoca. Combined with Herebert's rubric to "look at, read, and learn" the French poem, the poem's conclusion suggests that the more strategic forms of scholastic textual theory can be productively used in concert with tactics to stabilize lyric morality without sacrificing its affective power. In the next section, we will see how this distinction is reflected in Herebert's compilation, layout, and translations of the hymns that conclude his codex.

Affect, Authority, and Translation in Herebert's Hymns

In his commonplace book, William Herebert frames his hymn translations with the apparatus of scholastic authority. Yet to preserve the affective power of song, he draws on the genre's tactics. That is, for Herebert, the affective and moral dimensions of his translated hymns can both be preserved as long as lyric tactics are put into the service of strategic didactic aims.

Hymns constitute a special category of song. Developed in a liturgical context, the monastic performance of the hours, they were also recognized as pedagogical, affective, and popular texts.[49] Young boys in England learned Latin grammar and religious doctrine by means of liturgical songs in cathedral "song schools," and from the twelfth century onward, the popular book of glosses on the hymns known as the *Liber Hymnorum* was used as a school text.[50] Liturgical song as a means of affective expression is based, in part, on Job 30:31: "My harp is turned to mourning, and my organ into the voice of those that weep," and Isidore says that a hymn is "a song of joy and praise."[51] Hymnody and vernacular song are intimately linked in English literary history. The first English lyric, which today we call Cædmon's "Hymn," emerges from, even as it transforms, liturgical tradition. As Bede tells it, the song was composed by divine inspiration, when Cædmon dreams of an angel who orders him to sing the praise of God and His creation.[52] The origin story places Cædmon outside the center of monastic culture—he has just left the banquet hall where he would have to sing for his supper—yet still within its institutional purview. Cædmon's song, too, represents a point of origin in English literary history that is also materially marginal to Latin liturgical poetry, surviving as it does in glosses to Bede's Latin poem.[53] As Bruce Holsinger has pointed out, the poem's meter, long described as accentual, can also be scanned as accentual-syllabic, a meter that at the time was more common to Latin liturgical poetry, although it came, of course, to dominate modern English lyric.[54]

Although liturgical songs had considerable institutional forces determining their practice, they were nonetheless subject to the tactics of the broader genre of song. Hymns were explicitly understood as sung texts. According to the *Liber Hymnorum*, "If it be praise and praise of God and it is not sung, it is not a hymn."[55] An eleventh-century compilation of the miracles of Saint Foy at first questions the appropriateness of peasants singing secular songs during an all-night vigil. However, in the middle of the night, the doors of the sanctuary at which they wait miraculously unbar themselves, leading the composer of the story to conclude that all of these forms of song are equally sacred. In a discussion of this text, three modern scholars point out that "[t]he miracle narrative thus rehearses a difference between monastic liturgical chant and unauthorized lay singing only to refute such a distinction; clearly a major part of its rhetorical project was to undermine the privileged status of the Latin liturgy controlled by the monks and to authorize lay and vernacular 'liturgies.'"[56]

Hymns were also resources for extra-liturgical vernacular poetry. Christopher Page speculates that the unbeneficed liturgical singers employed by cathedrals might have earned additional income composing vernacular lyrics to hymn music.[57] Some Anglo-French *pastourelles* pair French half-lines with verses from Latin hymns. In one example, "En May quant dait," lines from a Latin hymn are used both for seduction and the defense of virtue by the poem's male and female speakers:

En may quant dait e foil e fruit	*parens natura parere*
E cist oysaus s'aforcent tus	*cantus amenos promere*
Une pucele sanz conduit	*in cultu latens paupere*
Par un matin vet en deduit	*jam lucis orto sidere.*

[In May, when leaf and bud must *appear obeying nature* and all these birds grow louder *to bring forth pleasant songs*, a maiden without escort *concealing herself in poor clothes* went to enjoy herself one morning *just as the sun had risen.*][58]

This poem goes on to demonstrate the abuse and the correct use of hymn language by means of tactics. As the male speaker attempts to seduce a maiden with sensual hymn verses, she repulses him with defensive verses, culminating in an appeal to the Holy Spirit to protect her virginity: "*Veni, Creator Spiritus!*" With less orthodoxy, a jocund drinking song uses hymn language irreverently:

Or hi parra,
La cerveyse nos chauntera
      Alleluia!
Qui que aukes en beyt
Si tel seyt com estre doit,
      res miranda!

[Now it seems the beer will sing us, *Alleluia*! Whoever drinks any of it, if such a one knows how he should be, *a miraculous thing*!][59]

As these examples show, hymns are subject to the kind of tactical practice that characterizes vernacular English lyric; their forms are circumstantially adapted and modified. For a friar like William Herebert, the stakes of preserving hymns' affective appeal as well as their doctrinal meaning were high, central as these songs were to his dual mission to instruct and engage his audience. One way that Herebert imparts doctrinal authority in his manuscript is strategic: he employs the conventions of scholastic texts. As a whole, MS Additional 46919 demonstrates a strong scholastic influence, especially in its adaptations of the *accessus ad auctores* to vernacular texts.[60] Many of the texts in this manuscript begin with an Anglo-Norman or Latin rubric that includes some of the elements of the *accessus*: the title of the work, the name and a brief description of the author, his intention, the "matter" (*materia*) of the text, and the branch of learning to which it pertains. One particularly substantive example is Herebert's rubric to William Twiti's "Art of Hunting": "Ici comence le art de venerie le quel mestre Guyllame Twici venour le Roy dengletere fist en son temps pur aprendre autres" (Here begins the art of hunting which Master William Twiti, hunter for the King of England, made in his time to teach others).[61] Herebert gives the branch of learning, "the art of hunting"; the name of the author, "William Twiti"; a brief description of the author, "hunter for the King of England"; and the intention of the work: "for others to learn from." Less detailed rubrics identify the author, when known, the material, or the intention of the text. For instance, "Cest tretys de la Passion fist frere Nicole boioun del ordre de freres menours" (Nicholas Bozon, of the order of the Friars Minor, made this treatise/poem on the Passion); "Cy comence la descripcion de chiualerie par Hue de Tabarie" (Here begins a description of knighthood by Hue de Tabarie); and "In libro qui intitulatur Sydrac. capitulo 444. De equo dicitur sic" (In the book titled Sydrac chapter 444. Of the horse is said thus).[62] Though briefer than the typical *accessus*, Herebert's rubrics are clearly influenced by the scholastic textual tradition, conferring the apparatus of authority on pastoral and practical texts.

The scholastic conventions of compilation and rubrication carry over to Herebert's hymn translations, where they establish both moral and textual authority. Indeed, Herebert's use of these conventions to demonstrate authority in the codex's final gathering of hymn translations, on folios 205r to 211v, may seem overdetermined. He writes his name in the margin beside all but one of the translations and frequently rubricates them with the Latin title of the sources, as well as marginal Latin incipits for each stanza. The opening of this gathering includes all of these features, in addition to the following note in the lower margin (see Figure 2):

Istos hympnos et Antiphonas quasi omnes et cetera transtulit in Anglicum, non semper de uerbo ad uerbum, sed frequenter sensum, aut non multum

Herodes þou wykked fo / whar of ys þy dredynge · — Hostis Herodes
And why art þou so sore agast / of cristes towmynge · impie ?c
He reueth he nouȝth erthlich god / þat maketh ous heueneкynges ·
þe kynges wenden here way / and foleweden þe sterre · — þat magi
And sothfast lyȝth whych sterre lych souȝten vrom so verre ·
And sheuden wel þat he god / in gold / and stor / and mirre ·
Crist ycleped heuene lomb / so com to seynt Ion · — Lauacra puri ??
And of hym was ywasshe þa sinne nadde non ·
to halewen oure wassouth water / þat sinne hauet worden ·
A newe myȝte he cudde / þer he was at a feste · — Nouum genus potent
he made wille whych his water / six cannes by þe reste ·
Vor þe water turnde into wyn / þorou cristes oune heste ·
We loueþ þe myd þe / þat shewedest þe todai · — Gloria ? ??
wyth þe uader and þe holy gost wythouten endedai ·

·:——: Vexilla regis prodeunt &c:·

þe kynges baneres beth forth ylad ; — ·: Herodes ?
þe rode tokne ys nou to sprad ·
whar he þat wrouȝt hauet al monkunne ;
anhonged was vor oure sunne · —
þer he was wounded and ywronge · — Quo uulnerate mfup ·
wyth sharpe spere to herte ystonge ·
to wasshen ous of sinne clene ·
water and blod þer ronne at ene ·
þis forsuld ys dauuedes sawe · — Impleta ?? ???
þat was prophete of þe olde lawe ·
þat saide men ȝe mowen þ se ·
hou godes trone ys rode tre ·

Istes hympnos & intiphonas est de ? ceta ?ustulit, no ?? de illo
ad ubi? ?? ?rchure senfu aut no wiltu Sechmandos? imanu sua
sepsit ff? willo Herebert. Ol usu ?? ???? Intervr? orer þ aia de sris.

declinando, et in manu sua scripsit frater Willelmus Herebert. Qui usum huius
quaterni habuerit, oret pro anima dicti fratris.

[These hymns and antiphons for the most part Friar William Herebert
translated into English, not always word for word but more often for the sense,
or not departing too much from it, and wrote them in his own hand. Whoever
has the use of this volume, let him pray for the soul of the said friar.][63]

Herebert's phrasing locates his practice in a long tradition of translation
theory, beginning in antiquity, that explores the conflict between translation
for rhetoric and for meaning.[64] Should a translator seek to convey his source's
meaning as accurately as possible, or should he create the most rhetorically
effective text in his target language? In a famous passage from *De optimo
genere oratorum*, Cicero rejects "word-for-word" translation: "And I did not
translate them as an interpreter, but as an orator, keeping the same ideas and
the forms, or as one might say, the 'figures' of thought, but in language which
conforms to our usage. And in so doing, I did not hold it necessary to render
word for word [*non verbum pro verbo*], but I preserved the general style and
force of the language."[65] For Cicero, rejecting "word-for-word" translation
means privileging rhetorical elegance. Similarly, Horace warns in his *Ars Poetica*, "do not seek to render word for word as a slavish translator" ("nec verbum verbo curabis reddere fidus interpres").[66] Jerome, in his Epistle 57 to
Pammachius (*De optimo genere interpretandi*), cites both Cicero and Horace,
and goes on to claim that he translates "not to translate word for word, but
sense for sense" ("non verbum e verbo, sed sensum exprimere de sensu").[67]
As Rita Copeland points out, Jerome's use of the two classical sources in
fact inverts their message: while Cicero and Horace rejected word-for-word
translation in order to make their works more rhetorically pleasing to their
audiences, Jerome uses this translation model to emphasize the moral message
over the rhetorical appeal of a translation. For Oxford friars like William
Herebert, Jerome's translation theory became hugely influential; Roger
Bacon, of whose works Herebert prepared a collection and commentary,
quotes this passage from Jerome.[68] Herebert's own note on translation, then,
follows Jerome, both in its wording and in its intent to transmit meaning
over rhetoric, *sensus* over *verbum*.

But verbal translation is only part of Herebert's project of creating an
English hymnal. In addition to the scholastic features of layout that authorize
the doctrinal meaning, Herebert organizes his collection to promote liturgical

performance. The compilation of the gathering largely follows the ritual time of the liturgical year.[69] It begins with a translation of the Epiphany hymn, "Hostis Herodes impie" (Herod, impious enemy), followed by "Vexilla regis prodeunt" (The banners of the king go forth), sung in the latter part of Lent.[70] Next appears the Palm Sunday hymn, "Gloria laus et honor" (Glory, praise, and honor), followed by a translation of the Good Friday reproaches (the *improperia*) under the heading, "Popule meus, quid feci tibi?" (My people, what have I done to you?).[71] Shortly thereafter, we find two Marian hymns, "Thou wommon boute uere [without equal]," possibly Herebert's original composition, and "Ave maris stella" (Hail, star of the sea), probably sung at the springtime feast of the Annunciation.[72] A Pentecost hymn, "Veni Creator spiritus" (Come, spirit creator) follows, and then a selection of hymns and antiphons for the Christmas season: "Alma redemptoris mater" (Loving mother of the redeemer), "Conditor alme siderum" (Holy maker of the stars), and "Christe redemptor omnium" (Christ, redeemer of all).[73]

While this arrangement facilitates performance, Herebert's translations use lyric tactics in order to distinguish a hymn's moral meaning from its performance practices. Many of them draw on conventions of English lyrics; for instance, two hymns merge the popular carol form, in which a refrain is repeated after each verse, with liturgical performance practices. The hymn "Gloria, laus, et honor" was sung antiphonally at Palm Sunday services, and the Good Friday reproaches were typically performed in procession.[74] Other hymns more directly take on the kinds of tactics used in "Amours m'ount si enchaunté." For example, the Latin poem "Ave maris stella" uses the convention of "Ave" reversing "Eva" that we saw in the French lyric:

Sumens illud Ave
Gabrielis ore,
Funda nos in pace,
Mutans nomen Evae.

[Taking up that Ave from Gabriel's mouth, establish us in peace, changing the name of Eve.][75]

The Latin hymn is a masterpiece of verbal economy in sexsyllabic four-line stanzas. Herebert's translation converts the imagistic style of the original, which contains few finite verbs, into English narrative tetrameter.[76] His second stanza reads,

Thylk "Aue" that thou vonge in spel   *received; the Gospel*
Of the aungeles mouhth kald Gabriel;
In gryht ous sette and shyld vrom shome,   *peace; protect*
That turnst abakward Eues nome.[77]

Herebert's translation of this hymn converts the spare imagery of the song
into syntactic units that follow contemporary preaching style.[78] For instance,
the tetrameter lines offer a more natural unit of breath for speaking than the
sexsyllabic line and also alter the meter so that it cannot be sung to the
original music. Herebert further changes the syntax of the Latin source, using
hypotaxis in his translation to emphasize the logic of its doctrine. The present
participles of the original, "sumens" and "mutans," lend immanence to the
Latin hymn. In the English translation, subordinating and relative pronouns
(Thylk "Aue" *that* thou vonge in spel; *That* turnst abakward Eues nome)
organize the reversal of original sin into logical, progressive units. Strikingly,
Herebert translates "Mutans" (changing) as "turnst abakward," departing
from the literal sense of the original to emphasize the verbal and doctrinal
reversal. Yet Herebert follows his source in failing to render the precise inversion of the words "Ave" and "Eva" that we saw in "Amours m'ount si
enchaunté." Like his source, Herebert uses the genitive form of "Eva" (Evae/
Eues), making the reversal didactic and doctrinal but not rhetorical. However, in "Ave maris stella," "Ave" and "Evae" are end-rhymed. Herebert's
translation of "Ave maris stella," then, radically mutes the *melos* of the original, realizing the "unsinging" of "Eva" described in the French lyric. At the
same time, he transforms the hymn into a workable text of performance,
albeit one that has more in common with the "steering" strategies of an
orthodox preacher than with an affective song of praise.

Herebert elsewhere draws on the rhetorical resources of preaching. His
translation of the Epiphany hymn "Hostis Herodes impie" uses various techniques of amplification, in particular repetition and example, to expand the
economical syntax of the original. The first stanza of the Latin hymn reads,

Hostis Herodes impie,
Christum venire quid times:
Non eripit mortalia
Qui regna dat coelestia.[79]

Herebert's translation expands the octosyllabic lines into a monorhymed
stanza of three long lines:

Herodes, thou wykked fo, wharof ys thy dredinge?   *fear*
And why art thou so sore agast of Cristes tocominge?   *deeply frightened*
Ne reueth he nouth erthlich god that maketh ous heuene kynges.[80]   *take*

Herebert's translation repeats the question of the second verse, "quid times," to emphasize the emotion in these lines: "*wharof* ys thy dredinge"; "*why* art thou so sore agast." He adds specific details to create more memorable images: "Deum fatentur munere" ("[The magi] praised God with gifts") becomes "And sheuden [showed] wel that he ys God in gold and stor and mirre." Although he sacrifices the vividness of "Aquae rubescunt hydriae" ("The waters of the jar redden") for a less dramatic image—"He made vulle [full] wyth shyr [clear] water six cannes by the leste"—the substitution serves to remind his audience of the two miracles at the wedding at Cana, the filling of the jars and the turning of water into wine. "Shyr water" also picks up the doctrinal message of the previous stanza, in which Christ is baptized by St. John "To halewen [consecrate] oure vollouth [befouled] water."[81]

As Domenico Pezzini points out, Herebert's translations frequently privilege the needs of a preacher over conventional poetic *melos* (although I do not share his opinion that the translation of the "Aquae rubescunt hydriae" stanza is a "poetic disaster").[82] As he notes, Herebert's translation of a stanza of the Passion week hymn, Venantius Fortunatus's "Vexilla regis prodeunt," elides the reference to song in the source:

Impleta sunt quae concinit
David fideli carmine
Dicens: in nationibus
Regnavit a ligno Deus.

Yvoluuld ys Davidthes sawe,   *Fulfilled; saying*
That soth was prophete of the olde lawe,
That sayde: "Men, ye mowen yse
Hou Godes trone ys rode tre."[83]   *throne; cross*

Herebert transforms David's song ("carmine") into a "sawe" here, I suggest, because of the way Fortunatus positions the psalm in this verse. The Latin poet summarizes the text of the psalm, reading it typologically as a prophetic insight into the redemption of the crucifixion. While psalms were often understood as affective expressions in the Middle Ages, here David's psalm is a "sawe," a Middle English term emphasizing content and meaning.

Yet elsewhere in his translation of this well-known hymn, Herebert introduces lyric rhetorics to amplify its sense of praise and petition. He adds a first-person pronoun in the first verse:

Vexilla regis prodeunt,
Fulget crucis mysterium,
Quo carne carnis conditor
Suspensus est patibulo.

The kynges baneres beth forth ylad;	*are led forth*
The rode tokne ys nou tosprad	*portentous*
Whar he, that wrouth hauet al monkunne,	
Anhonged was uor oure sunne.	*Hanged; for*

Herebert anticipates the first-person plural of the second verse ("nos lavaret"), making the hymn a direct address from the outset. He continues this pattern in his use of the interjection "ha" when the hymn shifts to a vocative, second-person address:

Arbora decora et fulgida
Ornata regis purpura,
Electa digno stipite
Tam sancta membra tangere.

Ha trœ, that art so vayr ykud,	*O; renowned*
And wyth kynges pourpre yshrud,	*clad*
Of wourthy stok ykore thou were,	*chosen*
That so holy limes opbere.	*limbs; hold up*

Again, Herebert picks up a verbal cue from a later stanza, in this case the explicit vocative interjection of "O crux ave spes unica," which he translates as "Ha croyz, myn hope, onliche my [my only] trust," as well as the concluding petition of "Te summa Deus Trinitas." His translation amplifies the apostrophe that, as we have seen, is characteristic of medieval praise lyrics. In other words, Herebert's translation underscores the presence of both typological doctrine (David's "sawe") and affective lyric rhetorics (apostrophe) in this hymn; the two may coexist, his translation implies, as long as both functions, while distinct, serve didactic ends.

When Herebert does use the term "song," he associates it primarily with affect or praise. His translation of "Christe redemptor omnium" renders "Ob diem natalis tui / Hymnum novum concinimus" as "And wœ, nomliche, that bœth bouht wyth thyn holy blod / Vor [For] thys day singeth a neowe song and maketh blisfol mod [good cheer]."[84] Here, the "hymnus" of the Latin becomes "neowe song," perhaps inspired by the verb "concino" (to sing with) that also appears in this stanza but regardless syntactically and contextually parallel to "maketh blissful mod." His translation of the Palm Sunday hymn, "Gloria, laus et honor," takes as its topic the voicing of praise. Its Latin refrain uses the liturgical response "Hosanna":

Gloria, laus et honor tibi sit rex Christe, redemptor
Cui puerile decus prompsit Hosanna pium.[85]

Herebert translates the Latin "prompsit," to "bring forth," with an English word that suggests effusion, "gradden" ("to cry out").[86]

Wele [Joy], heriyyng [praise], and worshype boe to Crist, that dœre ous bouhte,
To wham gradden [cry out] "Osanna!" chyldren clene of thoute.[87]

In the stanzas of the translation, however, he repeatedly emphasizes how singing constitutes a performance of praise. Consider the following translation:

Plebs Hebraea tibi cum palmis obvia venit,
Cum prece, voto, hymnis adsumus ecce tibi.

The volk of Gywes [Jewish folk], wyth bowes, comen ageynest the,
And wœ wyht bœdes [prayers] and wyth song mœketh [humble] ous to the.[88]

Herebert condenses the translations of "voto" and "hymnis" into "song" and transforms the sense of beholding in "adsumus ecce tibi" into a verb of submission, "mœketh." Song's potential for affective expression is instrumental in devotion, able to reverse the violence and aggression of the Passion ("The volk of Gywes, with bowes, comen ageynest the"). The translations of the next two verses expand this idea of song:

Hi tibi passuro solvebant munia laudis,

Nos tibi regnanti pangimus ecce melos.

Hi placuere tibi, placeat devotio nostra,

Rex bone, rex clemens, cui bona cuncta placent.

Hœ [They] kepten the wyth worsyyping ageynst thou shuldest deyye,

And wœ syngeth to thy worshipe in trone that sittest heyghe.

Hoere [Their] wyl and here mœkynge thou nome tho to thonk;

Queme [May it please] the, thœnne, mylsful [merciful] kyng, oure ofringe of thys song.[89]

Song is a performance of devotion, of worship; an "ofringe" to God that works "ageynst" his adversaries. Its power lies not in conveying doctrine but in practicing the "glory, praise, and honor" of God that the refrain describes.

If song is a practice that primarily engages the emotions, the written text is the source of doctrine, with a moral authority that is undergirded by the conventions of scholastic compilation and rubrication. We saw above how Herebert adapts the forms of the academic *accessus ad auctores* in the rubrics for many texts in the "Commonplace Book." His most extended use of the academic prologue occurs in his own translation of Luke 1:26–38, the Gospel for the Feast of the Annunciation, which is the final item in this codex. The poem that Herebert entitles, "Euangelium: Missus est angelus Gabriel," begins with six lines with the rubric "Prologus":

Seynt Luk, in hys godspel, bryngeth ous to munde	*reminds us*
Hou Godes Sone of hoeuene com tok oure kunde,	*heaven; nature [mortality]*
And sayth who was messager and of whom ysend,	*sent*
Into whuch lond, to what wymman, and yn whuch toun alend.	*went*
Of Luk leche, our leuedy proest, lofsom in aprise,	*priest; excellent in renown*
Lustneth lithe oure leuedy lay that ginth in thisse wise.[90]	*meekly; begins; way*

This prologue names the author ("Seint Luk") and tells us something about him ("Luk leche, our leuedy proest"). He then tells us the contents of the gospel, emphasizing the most important points: "Hou Godes Sone of heovene com tok oure kunde / And saith who was messager and of whom isend, / Into whuch lond, to what wimman, and in whuch toun alend." Finally, he frames the following poem as a kind of song: "oure leuedy lay." Following the prologue, Herebert notes the start of his translation of Luke 1:26–38 with a paraph and the marginal incipit, "Missus est."[91] The text

follows the gospel quite closely, except where rhyme and syntax demand
otherwise. At the conclusion, Herebert reiterates the message of his prologue:

Who so nule nouht lye that maketh trœwe asay,	*proves to be true*
Of our leuedy Marie thys ys seynt Lukes lay,	
To hœuene hœ make ous stye at oure endeday. Amen.[92]	*she; ascend*

Here, the song is explicitly "seynt Lukes lay": both the prologue and the
epilogue are noteworthy for their insistence on Luke's authorship, aided by
the form, in the case of the prologue, of the scholastic *accessus ad auctores*.

Elsewhere, Herebert takes a liturgical text as his starting point but
includes some nonliturgical source material. The poem headed "Quis est iste
qui uenit de Edom, Ysa. 63. Herebert" (Who is he who comes from Edom,
Isaiah 63. Herebert)[93] is a liberal translation of Isaiah 63:1–7, recast as a dialogue between the angels and Christ. Although apparently inspired by the
reading for the Wednesday of Holy Week, the poem does not simply translate
the liturgical text, which excludes the sixth verse of the Scripture. Instead,
Herebert includes a note at the end of his main translation: "In epistola que
legitur feria 4 maioris ebdomade non est plus" (In the epistle that is read on
the fourth day of holy week, there is no more).[94] Then, in the bottom margin
of the page, he copies a translation of Isaiah 63:6, using annotations to indicate the proper place of these verses in the text. Beneath the marginal translation, he writes, "Istud est de integro textu libri, sed non est de Epistola" (This
is from the whole text of the book, but is not in the [liturgical] Epistle).[95]
Perhaps most clearly here we see how Herebert integrates the scholastic conventions of the page with the tactics of lyric rhetorics and performance in
order to achieve his dual and ultimately strategic pastoral aims: to delight
and instruct.

The challenges of translating lyric poetry in any period include reconciling the demands of sound and sense, especially when the two conflict. For
William Herebert, these demands were especially urgent due to his dual pastoral obligations to appeal to the laity while conveying institutionally sanctioned doctrine. This problem finds formal expression in the French lyric
"Amours m'ount si enchaunté," which Herebert compiles, copies, and marks
for special attention with a rubric. This poem expresses the complex ways in
which the lyric genre's tactical practices can both promote and undermine
morality and how the more strategic practices of scholastic written texts can
support the former. These ideas find formal expression in the lyric's use of

equivocal and end rhymes. They further inform Herebert's own English translations of Latin hymns. In these translations, Herebert draws on the tactical practices of English lyrics in counterintuitive and inventive ways. Even as his aim in translating the hymns remains largely strategic—to communicate institutional doctrine—he uses tactical practices to achieve it. These apply to both his adaptation of scholastic textual forms such as academic prologues and rubrication, as well as to a variety of rhetorical and poetic devices. Throughout the manuscript, in his compilation, layout, and translation practices, Herebert takes care to accommodate both the doctrinal meaning and the emotional impact of song by putting the two into tactical relationships. Perhaps because of the high stakes of these texts to a member of the preaching orders, lyric emerges most clearly in Herebert's commonplace book as a genre defined by its tactical practices. The genre's performativity allows it to communicate effectively with a popular audience, while its written texts permit Herebert to stabilize its moral meanings by drawing on the scholastic apparatus of *auctorite* with his rubrics and translations.

The miscellanies examined above, British Library MS Harley 2253 and MS Additional 46919, have been chosen as case studies for their similarities as well as their differences. Each contains a relatively extensive lyric corpus, especially by comparison with other contemporary English manuscripts, and each was compiled by its primary scribe. Yet MS Harley 2253 was probably assembled for a wealthy secular household and contains a variety of profane and devotional texts apparently intended for entertainment and edification. MS Additional 46919 is pastoral in focus, befitting its fraternal compiler, who assembles and rubricates texts according to the needs of a preacher. While the material forms of these compilations differ, as do the forms of the lyrics within them, both draw on aspects of lyric tactics in their compilation and layout (and, in Herebert's case, translations) of these texts. The improvisatory and ad hoc capacities of the lyric genre influenced both of these scribe-compilers and offer modern readers a lens for understanding their presence and presentations in these two manuscripts. As we shall see, even as the English lyric changes significantly in its forms and influences, the kinds of tactical practices that these two manuscripts demonstrate continue to define the genre.

CHAPTER 3

Lyric Negotiations: Continental Forms
and *Troilus and Criseyde*

Up to this point, I have examined lyrics written and compiled prior to 1350, which, although often formally intricate, do not as a group follow fixed forms. As Christopher Cannon has observed, early Middle English literature generally is characterized by its formal variety rather than by its uniformity.[1] As we have seen in Chapter 1, the post-Romantic understanding of the lyric genre as a form of subjective expression also fails to unite these early lyrics. Instead, the genre of medieval English lyric is defined by its *practices*, which, in their ad hoc uses of conventional forms of written and performative textuality, are best described as tactical. As we have seen, lyric tactics determined aspects of manuscript compilation and layout as well as poetic forms and rhetoric. Features of medieval English lyric practice—broadly defined to include the collection, copying, and oral and sung performances of the poems—allowed two compilers to develop implicit lyric theories, centering respectively on voice, in BL MS Harley 2253, and on the relationship between meaning and affect (especially in relation to doctrinal authority), in the friar William Herebert's commonplace book. These miscellanies thus begin to demonstrate a poetics of lyric that, while nowhere explicitly or formally expressed, coheres around the concept of tactics, the improvisational use of existing forms and conventions.

The second part of this book turns to the later fourteenth century. In particular, it focuses on the inset lyrics in Geoffrey Chaucer's narrative poems and their relationships to contemporary forms and practices. The reason for this shift in emphasis is twofold. While there are, of course, many fascinating compilations of lyric that I have omitted from this study (the lyrics of the

Vernon Manuscript, the carols of British Library MS Sloane 2593, and the poems of John Audelay come to mind), this is not primarily a book about lyric manuscripts. My argument is that tactical practice defines the genre of lyric in medieval England. As such, it influences the insular lyric manuscripts that differ markedly from Continental "songbooks." But the implications of defining this genre through its practice extend beyond compilation. Just as post-Enlightenment definitions of lyric (e.g., as formally unified or as a subjective utterance) led modern poets to explore and develop these definitions within their poems, so too insular lyric tactics led medieval poets to develop the implications of the genre in their poetry. Because tactics are modes of relation, examining lyrics where they appear in relation to other literary forms illuminates further aspects of the medieval understanding of the genre. One of the most important of these relationships is between lyric and narrative poetry. Combining lyric and narrative was popular in the Middle Ages; the practice extends back at least as far as Boethius's *Consolation of Philosophy* and gains new popularity in later centuries with Dante's *Vita Nuova* and the *dits amoreux* of French poets such as Guillaume de Machaut.[2] While, as we have seen in the first half of this book, individual lyrics work through the implications of the ad hoc, improvisatory practices of lyric, these tactics become even clearer when the relationships between texts and their material contexts are explored. Thus, the shift in the second half of this book preserves the attention to lyrics in relation to other contexts, while directing its attention toward the literary and generic relations that bring the features of the lyric genre into clearer focus.

This way of understanding lyric implicates the genre in political and ethical questions that can expand our understanding of the poetics of the medieval insular lyric. To define a genre is to delimit an aesthetic category as well as to identify the modes of perception, analysis, and interpretation characteristic of that category. Such a definition is inherently political and ethical, creating and structuring relationships between an audience and an aesthetic object or experience that defines a subject's place and degrees of mobility within a community.[3] As I have argued elsewhere, early English genres are less prescriptive "laws" than adaptive "forms-of-life," shaping and shaped by experience and practice.[4] This brings me to the second reason for this book's shift in emphasis, from diverse, often anonymous, lyrics to those of a single poet. Why focus on Chaucer? Of the many poets writing in later medieval England, Chaucer is the one to whom lyrics seem most important, even in his narrative poetry.[5] He most likely began his career writing courtly lyrics, perhaps largely in French; he includes lyrics in most of his long poems, and he lists lyrics in two of his "bibliographies": "many an ympne [hymn] for [the God of Love's] halydayes / That highten balades, roundels, virelayes" in the prologue to the *Legend of Good Women*; "many a song and many a leccherous lay" in the Retraction to the *Canterbury Tales*.[6] While many of these, especially the lyric insertions in his narrative poems, demonstrate clear evidence of classical or Continental influences, Chaucer's adaptation of these influences is informed by tactical practices.[7] As we shall see, these practices enable Chaucer to explore the political and ethical implications of the lyric genre by at once aligning it with and differentiating it from other literary traditions. Although the two poetic works that make up the subjects of the next chapters, *Troilus and Criseyde* and the *Legend of Good Women*, clearly differ from the manuscript compilations of the book's first half, they also offer intriguing parallels. Like the two compilations, both of Chaucer's long poems include secular and moral elements. Yet just as MS Harley 2253 has a largely secular context and Herebert's book has a pastoral context, my readings of the two works will focus on secular and moral issues, respectively. Further, each of Chaucer's longer poems juxtaposes—we might even say "compiles"—lyrics with other literary forms.

This chapter focuses on *Troilus and Criseyde*, whose inset lyrics, numbering anywhere from ten to fifty-six, have attracted admiration for their style, their diversity of influences, and their centrality to the poem's literary ambitions and affective content.[8] While Continental models strongly influence this poem's lyrics, Chaucer's translations, adaptations, and metapoetics of these sources are tactical. My claim in this chapter is that such tactics connect Chaucer's lyricism to the earlier insular tradition. Put another way, for Chaucer, the established forms of French and Italian lyrics (and lyric insertion) constitute normative elements for reshaping and recombination. To some extent, of course, all medieval vernacular poetry—and perhaps all poetry, period—is engaged in a continual reworking of forms. Yet as we have seen in the first chapter, most Continental poetry is informed by a far more explicit set of formal constraints, defined in treatises on poetic form and manifested in the structure of poetic manuscripts like the troubadour *chansonniers*. For insular poets, these explicitly defined poetic and textual forms are mediated through a poetic culture that prizes the contingent, the improvisatory, and the recombinative. Thus, as for earlier English poets and anthologists, practice is at the center of Chaucer's understanding of the lyric genre and its cultural work. I do not argue for the direct influence of earlier English lyrics on Chaucer's poetry, since we can only speculate about whether Chaucer had any familiarity with these texts (indeed, one reader asserts Chaucer's "wholesale rejection of the indigenous vernacular lyric tradition" on formal grounds).[9] Rather, this chapter and the next demonstrate that a tactical approach to lyric sources and conventions remains the central feature of English lyric even as its forms and influences change.

Further, when read for tactics, *Troilus and Criseyde*'s lyric interpolations directly pose the longer work's most pressing political problem, that of the relationship between self and society, between individual and communal desires.[10] My reading proposes that we can understand this relationship in terms of a tension between negotiation and absolutism, bodied forth in the tactics of the poem's lyric interludes. That is, the ad hoc, improvisatory practices of certain kinds of lyric composition and performance in *Troilus and Criseyde* make it possible to imagine a political mode of negotiation, by contrast with other, largely Petrarchan, lyric practices that support and reify political absolutism. This becomes especially clear if we examine the practices surrounding *Troilus and Criseyde*'s lyric interludes—their diegetic performances and Chaucer's own practices of composition—in relation to their formal and stylistic features. This chapter begins with an episode in the poem that most clearly demonstrates the tactical practices of lyric composition, performance, and reception: the scene containing Antigone's song. This lyric creates tactical relationships among poetic forms, sources, and audiences, and its narrative frame implicates it in both the romance and the history that *Troilus and Criseyde* relates. As we shall see, these relationships suggest a poetics of negotiation (understood politically and aesthetically) that seeks to reconcile the political needs of self and society, of the lovers and of the polis. Taking this at once poetic and political reading of Antigone's song as paradigmatic of, rather than marginal to, Chaucer's lyricism in this poem, we can also understand the *cantici Troili* in a different light. These lyrics have been located within a Continental tradition that adduces authorship and authority to lyric composition.[11] However, read alongside the tactics of Antigone's song, the *cantici Troili* also demonstrate a debt to insular lyric practices. This hybrid view of Troilus's lyrics implies that the poetics of negotiation put forth in the forms and practices of Antigone's song also inform Troilus's solitary songs, suggesting that they critique totalizing models of power and authority.

In short, this reading of *Troilus and Criseyde* is interested in reevaluating Chaucer's debt to Continental lyricism in light of my prior discussion of insular lyric practices. Without diminishing the indisputable importance of

Continental forms and traditions to Chaucer's lyrics, I show how the tactical practices that define the insular lyric genre influence Chaucer's adaptation of these new forms. A second, but no less important, goal of this reading is to demonstrate that not only does Chaucer use these practices, but he also works through their at once poetic and political implications.

Lyric Import(s) and Antigone's Song

By the time Geoffrey Chaucer composed *Troilus and Criseyde* in the 1380s, the lyric landscape of England had shifted considerably. A new wave of fourteenth-century French lyrics and lyricists—Guillaume de Machaut, Oton de Granson, and Jean Froissart, among others—had arrived in England, inspiring many insular poets with their poetic styles and forms, including *formes fixes* like ballades, rondeaux, and virelais, as well as mixed lyric-narrative poems.[12] French *chansonniers*, along with other Continental types of lyric anthologies, contributed to the growing awareness of vernacular authorship in English literary culture and of the material forms through which it was produced.[13] Italian poetry, although less prominent in its influence on English poets, also informed Chaucer's later works. His travels in Italy in the 1370s seem to have brought him into contact with the works of Italian authors such as Dante, Boccaccio, and Petrarch.[14] These poets were prolific lyricists. Dante's standalone lyrics and intercalated songs were influenced by the *stil novo* of the thirteenth century, while Petrarch drew on classical and vernacular traditions in his *Canzoniere*. The lyricism of Boccaccio's *Il Filostrato* informed Chaucer's poetic style in *Troilus and Criseyde*, as we shall see. Further, the relationships among these "three crowns" of Italy, who translated, mediated, and commented on each other's poetry, influenced Chaucer's adaptations of their works.[15]

These Continental influences on Chaucer and other post-1350 English poets would seem to be a part of what is generally understood as a decisive transition in English lyric history. As English lyric forms and modes of expression, particularly of affectivity, drew on Continental influences, insular short poems more recognizably anticipated early modern lyric conventions.[16] The late fourteenth century is often identified as the period that completes the transition in English poetry from primarily oral to primarily written circulation (although oral and performed song maintained a vigorous cultural presence). These material and literary changes did result in notable formal and stylistic transformations of English lyrics. But they also merged with an existing lyric genre that, as we have seen, is marked by a tactical mode of practice. We can begin to understand Chaucer's lyric tactics by examining a set piece that has sometimes seemed out of place in *Troilus and Criseyde*: Antigone's song. With its communal practices of composition, performance, and reception, the song differs in important ways from the solitary perform-ances of the *cantici Troili*.

The relationship between Antigone's song and the other lyric interpola-tions is further complicated by its role in the poem's plot. W. H. Auden's assertion that "poetry makes nothing happen" and Jonathan Culler's claim that "if narrative is about what happens next, lyric is about what happens now" are both implicit in the solitary *cantici Troili*.[17] These moments suspend the action of the poem, foregrounding the poetic utterance of the emotional and philosophical content of the material.[18] But Antigone's song crosses the lyric-narrative border: it responds directly, point by point, to each doubt that Criseyde has expressed in her prior conversation with Pandarus, and it medi-ates her decision to accept Troilus as a lover that drives the plot forward, while at the same time exemplifying certain conventions of the courtly love poem.[19] With these negotiations, Antigone's song structurally and formally manifests the central political conflict in the poem, between individual desire and political exigencies. While many readings of *Troilus and Criseyde*'s lyri-cism take the *cantici Troili* as paradigmatic, this reading will begin by explor-ing the conflicting models of lyric put forward by the setting and text of Antigone's song and then using the stakes established in this scene to inter-pret the poem's other lyric interludes.

In short, I will argue that Antigone's song creates tactical relationships among the practices and forms of lyric: its performance, sources, and rhetoric. Every tactic also carries with it a political valence, from the interruption of written history with performed song to the reshaping of metaphors as politi-cally pointed proverbs. The politics of the tactics of Antigone's song can be described as "negotiation," a term I use both to refer to the political process of communal decision making, whereby plural voices contribute to an out-come, and to invoke Lee Patterson's use of this term as a methodology for medieval studies. Patterson proposes "negotiation" as a critical frame for understanding the historical past as constituted by its symbolic representa-tions and, most crucially, the centrality of the subject in "negotiating" these representations.[20] My use of the term seeks to foreground how literary forms and genres can exemplify and structure the degrees of freedom a subject has in her negotiations of political and ethical norms. As a genre defined by its practices, medieval lyric offers an especially cogent form for these negotiations. However, it is important to note that negotiation is not equivalent to tactics; rather, it is one political and formal mode made possible by lyric tactics.

Antigone's song is framed by invocations and allusions that connect historical change and political upheaval to lyric language. Chaucer invokes Cleo, the muse of history, in the proem to Book 2, just before the well-known passage on language change:

Ye knowe ek that in forme of speche is chaunge
Withinne a thousand yeer, and wordes tho
That hadden pris, now wonder nyce and straunge   *value; unusual*
Us thinketh hem, and yet thei spake hem so,
And spedde as wel in love as men now do;   *fared*
Ek for to wynnen love in sondry ages,
In sondry londes, sondry ben usages. (2.22–28)

Chaucer here reminds us of the fragility of language and custom in the face of larger historical forces.[21] Although Muscatine reads this passage as an assertion of the "insufficiency" of courtly language "to cope with the here and now," it seems to me that Chaucer is actually celebrating how this idiom's tactics can change with time and circumstance.[22] Winning love through speech is a tactical process: "For every wight which that to Rome went / Halt not o path, or alwey o manere"; "For to thi purpos this may liken the, / And the right nought; yet al is seid or schal" (2.36–37 and 2.45–46). Love's rhetoric is at once governed by broad cultural custom and yet highly sensitive to local contingencies.

The episode's Ovidian frame, too, suggests that song requires a different model of reception and interpretation in light of its historical context and Criseyde's subject position. The entire scene of Antigone's song is bookended by allusions to the tale of Philomela, Procne, and Tereus:

The swalowe Proigne, with a sorowful lay,
Whan morwen come, gan make hire waymentynge
Whi she forshapen was, and ever lay   *transformed*
Pandare abedde, half in a slomberynge,
Til she so neigh hym made hire cheterynge

How Tereus gan forth hire suster take,
That with the noyse of hire he gan awake. (2.64–70)

The allusion recurs at the end of the scene, when Criseyde hears the nightingale's "lay of love," which makes her heart "fressh and gay." James Simpson has argued that the poem's debt to Ovidian elegy enables "Troilus' and Pandarus' own turning away from the world of public action," even as political and historical concerns press in on the poem. Yet as he observes, Criseyde's relationship to this form is quite different, dependent on social and practical considerations.[23] Indeed, as medieval readers understood it, the tale of Tereus, Procne, and Philomela is explicitly political, linking desire with military and sexual violence.[24] In Ovid's telling, Tereus's marriage to Procne is a result of his intervention in the Athenian wars. Statius's *Thebaid*, a book that threads through *Troilus and Criseyde*, takes up the Ovidian tale as a touchstone for the ways in which women suffer—and protest—the ways the injustices of war are visited upon them.

Or, if you want deeds closer
To home, let Procnê—a *Thracian* wife—teach us resolve: she
Made her spouse a meal that paid him out for the marriage![25]

And also:

The women, too, in numerous speeches, made
Loud and frequent moan at Ogygian laws and Creon's
Inhumanity: plaintive, too, the nightingale's tortured
Song as under foreign eaves she sorrows, protesting
Her marriage betrayed, the cruel things Tereus did.[26]

As Catherine Sanok has demonstrated, the entire *Thebaid* emphasizes women's suffering in wartime.[27] In both of these allusions, Statius uses the Philomela story to show women's agency to respond to oppression, cruelty, and injustice in a time of war. When Chaucer frames the episode of Antigone's song with this Ovidian context, he positions song as a form of female agency during crises of history and desire.

When Pandarus arrives to convey Troilus's suit, Criseyde and her ladies are reading about the siege of Thebes, possibly from the *Thebaid*.[28] The forms of pleasure—dancing and singing—interrupt the totalized history of the book, as Pandarus urges, "Do wey [Put away] youre book, rys up, and lat us daunce" (2.111). Yet love's "pleye" cannot be decoupled from historical crisis. When Pandarus says, "Yet koude I telle a thyng to doon yow pleye" (2.121), meaning Troilus's love for her, Criseyde asks, "is than th'assege [the siege] aweye?" (2.123). Criseyde's hesitation to observe the rites of May during the siege resists the subordination of form to event, lyric to history. Her apparently innocent question reminds the reader that she is about to be personally besieged by Troilus's petition.

Where many of the poem's other lyric interludes are presented as privately composed and sung, community marks the composition, transmission, performance, and interpretation of Antigone's song. The song's performance setting is social and tactical, as Criseyde and her ladies enter the garden via wandering paths:

Adown the steyre anonright tho she wente
Into the gardyn with hire neces thre,
And up and down ther made many a wente—   *path*
Flexippe, she, Tharbe, and Antigone—
To pleyen that it joye was to see;
And other of hire wommen, a gret route,   *company*
Hire folwede in the gardyn al aboute. (2.813–19)

The song's audience is constituted as a community whose movements are tactical: Criseyde and her neces "made many a wente" through the garden paths "to pleyen," and her women go "al aboute" as they follow her. Multiple agents mediate its performance and interpretation: the song is attributed to "the goodlieste mayde / of gret estat in al the town of Troye" (2.880–81) and performed by Antigone for a responsive, interpreting listener, Criseyde. If we examine Chaucer's probable sources for this song, we can see that its composition also reflects the kind of plural relationships represented in the scene of its performance. Here is the song's opening stanza:

O Love, to whom I have and shal
Ben humble subgit, trewe in myn entente
As I best kan, to yow, lord, yeve ich al
For everemo myn hertes lust to rente;   *as tribute*
For nevere yet thi grace no wight sente

So blisful cause as me, my lif to lede

In alle joie and seurte out of drede. (2.827–33) *security*

George Kittredge finds its source in Machaut's *Paradis d'Amours*:

Et pour ce veuil loyaument

De cuer et joieusement

Amours servir

Tout mon temps.

[And therefore I want to serve love from my heart loyally and joyously for all my time.][29]

The echo, as we see, is very faint, demonstrating what Kittredge calls Chaucer's "adaptive mastery" of his source.[30] James Wimsatt proposes that the opening is influenced by some lines from Machaut's *balade* beginning, "Trop ne me puis de bonne Amour loer," from the *Louange des Dames*; in particular, he notes the following lines: "Et ren toudis à Amours la droiture / Que je li doi" (And I always give to love the right that I should).[31] Citing other Machauvian influences on Antigone's song, Wimsatt rightly notes, "Chaucer extracts from these [lyrics] their very essence in constructing his lyric."[32]

We might also note other sources for the opening stanza of Chaucer's song in the poetry of Machaut. For instance, Machaut's long poem *Le livre dou voir dit* (The Book of the True Poem, 1363–64) describes a courtship carried on between two lovers who have never met. The work, which includes many letters and poems between the lover and his lady, begins,

A la loange et a lonnour

De tresfine amour que ie honnour

Aim, oubey, et ser, et doubte

Quen lui ay mis mentente toute.

[In praise and honor / Of Love most refined, whom I honor, / Love, obey, serve, and fear, / Who has my complete devotion.][33]

Likewise, we might compare the following lines from Antigone's song—"In which myn herte growen is so faste, / And his in me, that it shal evere laste" (2.872–73)—to these lines from *Le livre dou voir dit*: "Que cuers scet si proprement / Entrelacier / Quon ne les puet deslacier / Legierement"

(Because [love] can so very properly / Link hearts together / They cannot be unlinked / With ease).[34] Perhaps the closest parallel between *Le livre dou voir dit* and Antigone's song occurs when she thanks love. Antigone's song reads,

Whom shulde I thanken but yow, god of Love,
Of al this blisse, in which to bathe I gynne?
And thanked be ye, lord, for that I love!
This is the righte lif that I am inne,
To flemen all manere vice and synne: *expel*
This dooth me so to vertu for t'entende,
That day by day I in my wille amende. (2.848–54)

The parallel passage in Machaut reads,

Premierement sans detrier
Weil tresbonne amour mercier
Quant si bien li est souvenu
De moy, questes yci venu
Pour moy doucement conforter. . . .
Yert de moy loiaument servie
Et si morray en son service
Sans villain penser et sans vice.

[First, without delay / I want to thank very good Love / For remembering me / So marvelously, in that you've come here / To provide me with sweet comfort. . . . (My lady) will be served loyally by me / Who will then die in her service / Without impure thoughts or vice.][35]

Like the sources suggested by Kittredge and Wimsatt, the excerpts from *Le livre dou voir dit* resonate only faintly with Chaucer's poem. This suggests that Chaucer was not, most likely, using any one of these poems as his source for Antigone's song but drawing on the idiom of contemporary French lyricism (and, in particular, lyrics and lyrical interludes in praise of love) for Antigone's song.

This survey is not intended primarily to argue for additional sources for Antigone's song. Rather, my point is that this poem exemplifies a tactical model of composition that creates a new song from disparate sources, by

adapting, borrowing, and modifying a variety of analogues from a more struc-
tured poetic lineage without translating a single source. The tactics of Antigone's song reflect a broader reality of the relationship between medieval
English and French lyrics. Ardis Butterfield has proposed that we think of
this relationship not in terms of source study, translation, or even intertextuality but as "citation," with lyrics citing their common idiom across languages. Refrains, in particular, are frequently cited across lyrics, acting as
both a "signal of difference" that marks the voice of the other and as a shared
"common currency."[36] As Butterfield rightly says of this kind of lyric language, "All of it is borrowed; none of it is original."[37] The intimacy between
English and French lyric language reflects the presence of French poets, their
poetry, and lyric performance practice in England. The language of French
and other Continental lyrics constitutes what Nancy Bradbury calls a "soft
source" for the poem as a whole. As Bradbury puts it, a soft source "need not
be a single written text. . . . [It] might be a pictorial image, cultural practice,
oral tradition, set of conventions, or real event, but the soft source as I con-
ceive of it leaves a distinct verbal imprint on the work in question to indicate
its special relevance."[38] The addition of *Le livre dou voir dit* to Chaucer's list
of potential sources suggests that Chaucer understood lyrics less as isolated
and totalized than as relational. Machaut's *Livre*, while not without narrative
elements, is permeated by lyric idioms that Chaucer selectively extracts and
adapts in Antigone's song. Chaucer's rendering of them in a discrete "song"
at once marks this language as lyrical and relates it to the larger field of
narrative poetics.

   If the above examples draw on the French courtly lyric idiom, the second
stanza also demonstrates another kind of influence, the epideictic tradition
of classical rhetoric.

Ye, blisful god, han me so wel byset
In love, iwys, that al that bereth lif
Ymagynen ne kouthe how to be bet;
For, lord, withouten jalousie or strif,
I love oon which is moost ententif
To serven wel, unweri or unfeyned,
That evere was, and leest with harm desteyned. (2.834–40)

The rhetoric of the praise poem originated in classical eulogy and migrated
in the Middle Ages both into Christian poetry in praise of God, martyrs, and

relics and also into secular lyrics in praise of nature or a beloved.[39] The stanza, indeed, alludes to the origins of its rhetoric by beginning with praise for the God of Love, which then becomes praise for the beloved. The passage uses the exemplarity topos—"moost ententif," "leest with harm desteyned"—to emphasize the superior character of the beloved.

But where these epideictic idioms imply permanence—of the lover's fidelity, of God's goodness—Antigone's song develops them with rhetorical forms of contingency and negotiation. In the third stanza, they appear in a series of metaphors.

As he that is the welle of worthynesse,
Of trouthe grownd, mirour of goodlihed,
Of wit Apollo, stoon of sikernesse,
Of vertu roote, of lust fynder and hed,   *originator*
Thorugh which is alle sorwe fro me ded—
Iwis, I love him best, so doth he me;
Now good thrift have he, wherso that he be! (2.841–47)   *prosperity*

In four lines, the beloved is rendered well, ground, mirror, Apollo, stone, root, "fynder," and head. These lines develop the exemplarity topos with a series of tropes, as we have seen in pre-Chaucerian lyrics, but with an important difference. Many lyrics extend a metaphor over a stanza or the entire poem or, as we have seen in "Annot and John," focus each stanza on a single lexis as the vehicle for its metaphors (lapidaries, herbals, etc.). By contrast, each line in this stanza of Antigone's song contains two heteroglossic metaphors, demanding interpretive agility on the part of the audience. As a rhetorical figure, metaphor is itself a tactic. Geoffrey of Vinsauf's elegantly organic definition makes this point:

> A comparison that is made in a hidden way is introduced with no sign to point
> it out. It is introduced not under its own aspect but with dissembled mien, as
> if there were no comparison there at all, but the taking on, one might say, of a
> new form marvelously engrafted, where the new element fits as securely into
> the context as if it were born of the theme. The new term is, indeed, taken
> from elsewhere, but it seems to be taken from there; it is from outside and does
> not appear outside; it makes an appearance within and is not within; so it
> fluctuates inside and out, here and there, far and near; it stands apart, and yet

is at hand. It is a kind of plant; if it is planted in the garden of the material the handling of the subject will be pleasanter.⁴⁰

If Geoffrey's description emphasizes the simultaneous disappearance of metaphor into material (via his own metaphor of "engrafting") and markedness of the trope, the quick succession of the metaphors of Antigone's song seems particularly to call attention to their own figuration. By introducing a string of unrelated images and concepts, Antigone's song encourages rapid cognitive "mapping" between unrelated conceptual domains that generates—or should generate—sensitivity to local meanings in its audience.⁴¹ The listener or reader who has thus far been treated to an extended apostrophe to the personified God of Love must follow more condensed, less conventional metaphors: the beloved as the "Apollo of wit" or the "stone of certainty." Cristina Cervone calls metaphor "conceptual," with an intended pun on gestation; that is, metaphor creates knowledge or new ways of understanding.⁴² Here, then, the tactics of metaphor (which, as Geoffrey points out, bring the outside world into the enclosed garden of the poem) encourage cognitive negotiations among its dual referents. Yet perhaps the technique goes too far: the stanza itself seems overwhelmed by its succession of tropes, failing to complete the anticipated simile ("As he that is") and instead breaking syntax: "Iwis, I love hym best." Inasmuch as these metaphors demonstrate formal negotiations, they also suggest their failure.

The breakdown of metaphor leads to a new formal tactic, the introduction of a string of proverbs near the end of the song. All of these are metaphoric, a widespread but by no means inevitable proverbial style. The *Auctores Octo*, a popular primer containing the didactic works of eight authors, includes both the *Distichs of Cato* (fourth century) and the *Liber Parabolum* of Alan of Lille (c. 1116–1202) among its selections.⁴³ The proverbs of the *Distichs* are declarative, relying on increasingly complex poetic stanzas for stylistic interest. By contrast, each of Alan's proverbs is a metaphoric couplet, the first line providing the vehicle and the second the tenor. The proverbs in Antigone's song follow a similar form.

Thei [those who disparage love] speken, but thei benten nevere his bowe!
What is the sonne wers, of kynde right,   *proper nature*
Though that a man, for fieblesse of his yen,   *eyes*
May nought endure on it to see for bright?
Or love the wers, though wrecches on it crien?

No wele is worth, that may no sorwe dryen.   *endure*
And forthi, who that hath an hed of verre,   *glass*
Fro cast of stones war hym in the werre! (2.861–68)   *beware*

The first line of the passage alludes to a proverb about Robin Hood that was known to medieval audiences; two manuscripts name Robin Hood in marginal glosses.[44] The source of the question beginning "What is the sonne wers" is a (now) little-known Latin proverb, "Non possunt oculi solem tolerare dolentes; / Vix manuum tactus languida membra gerunt" (Sorrowing eyes cannot tolerate the sun; / Weak limbs scarcely bear the hand's touch).[45] The echoes of "languida" with "fieblesse" and of "dolentes" with "wrecches," as well as the overall similarity of the metaphor, indicate the correlation. The Latin text has only one witness that I have been able to determine, a German manuscript from the late fourteenth century, where it appears in a list of proverbs.[46] However, an earlier English version appears in the *Ormulum* (c. 1200): "Yiff thatt tin eyhe iss all unnhal / Withthinnen o the sene, / Itt shuneththt, thatt tu wast te sellf, / The sunness brihhte leome."[47] The last two lines of the passage allude to the now familiar proverb, "Those who live in glass houses shouldn't throw stones." The proverb has no known English witness before Chaucer's time but is common in medieval Italian.[48] "An extreme form of convention," proverbs constitute a transhistorical textual tradition transmitted in both oral and written forms.[49] Chaucer's free adaptation of them suggests that he has internalized them as thoroughly as he has the idioms of the courtly lyric and praise poem.

Why does Chaucer shift into the proverbial mode at this moment in the poem? One explanation is surely C. S. Lewis's durable claim that Chaucer "medievalizes" his sources throughout *Troilus and Criseyde* by interpolating didactic material.[50] But I think that there is another reason for this shift that speaks to the poem's larger political concerns. By interrupting the elaboration of the stable feudal metaphors of courtly love with the rapid-fire metaphors of exemplarity ("welle of worthynesse," "stoon of sikernesse," etc.) and the metaphorical proverbs, the song performs negotiation by means of rhetorical and formal tactics. That is, the metaphors of exemplarity are rhetorical tactics that demand cognitive negotiation, and the introduction of proverbs is a formal tactic for negotiating between the individual desires of courtly expression and the communal values of the proverbs.

Further, these metaphorical proverbs revise two of the metaphors of exemplarity in the third stanza of the song: "Of wit Apollo, stoon of sikernesse." In this line, "Apollo" refers to the god's poetic mastery, while eliding the legend of the origins of his rhetorical gift, his pursuit and imprisonment of unwilling Daphne. But Apollo is also, of course, the god of the sun, whose danger is expressed in the proverb, "What is the sonne wers." As Jamie Fumo has demonstrated, Apollo's duality as prophet and traitor inform *Troilus and Criseyde*, which represents this god not only by way of the Ovidian affiliation with the poetic but also by way of his Virgilian nationalism.[51] As well, the "stoon" of the third stanza signifies the stability of the beloved's desire, but the proverb transforms an aspect of that quality, a stone's weight and hardness, into a threat: "Fro cast of stones war hym in the werre!" Indeed, had Criseyde interpreted the proverbs of Antigone's song tactically, with reference to her immediate situation, she would have noted that they warn the vulnerable *against* love. Those with weak eyes should *not* look upon the strong sun of love; someone with a glass head, or helmet, should avoid the stones of love's tribulations. The final proverb's allusion to war, indeed, reminds us of the source of Criseyde's vulnerability, the Trojan War that forms the backdrop to the longer poem. As James Simpson has observed, Criseyde cannot claim the masculine luxury of using desire to turn away from public life: "her emotional life is represented as a matter of circumstance, decision, and, therefore, of process."[52] The transformations of the metaphors of exemplarity that insert the possibility of flux into the praise-poem tradition in the proverb stanza remind us that Criseyde is vulnerable to the "stones of war." And the proverb stanza also recasts the relationship between love and sorrow. Whereas love "kills" sorrow in the third stanza—"Thorugh which is alle sorwe fro me ded"—the proverb stanza acknowledges the intimacy of love and sorrow: "No wele is worth, that may no sorwe dryen."

The song's formal tactics thus presage the political negotiations to which Criseyde will be subject later in the poem. As many readers have observed, her political subject position differs markedly from Troilus's; her agency is contingent on her historical circumstances and her relationships with other men in the poem.[53] Her father Calchas's abscondence to the Greeks left her vulnerable in warring Troy and perhaps more amenable to Troilus's suit. *Troilus and Criseyde*'s most famous negotiation, of course, is the decision to exchange Criseyde for Antenor in the Trojan Parliament, which some readers have likened to the Wonderful Parliament of 1386.[54] That parliament witnessed the magnates's bid to curtail monarchical power whose repercussions as directly affected courtiers and "king's men," including Chaucer himself, as they did Richard II. The Trojan negotiation—and its silencing of Criseyde's desires—likewise exposes the inequities of a representative governance not undergirded by universal suffrage. As Matthew Giancarlo has demonstrated, changes to English social and governmental structure in the fourteenth century gave rise to a parliament that attempted to provide a representative forum for the interests and voices of the commons. Yet in practice and in its documentary and literary representations, this new English parliamentarism struggled to reconcile "the twin ideals of multiplicity and unity, of *communitas* and *unitas*."[55] These ideals are especially confounded by the voicelessness of certain members of the community who lack the power to elect or otherwise influence their putative representatives.

The negotiations of the Trojan Parliament, then, stand in contrast to those of Antigone's song, which uses formal tactics to enact a more participatory negotiation. The poem's style and use of rhetoric demonstrate this. The opening stanza invokes the trope of subjection common to courtly love poetry. Although it seems to present a model of complete surrender to the personified Love's authority, the stanza in fact represents a nuanced negotiation between two agents. The speaker's willingness to be a "subgit" relies on her own "entente," and she provides her "hertes lust" as "rente" in return for Love's protection. The term "rente" signifies a tribute, payment, or salary, and here it represents the relationship between the speaker and Love as one of equals negotiating a mutually beneficial arrangement. The poem's speaker attempts to use service to love as insurance ("seurte") against historical rupture—and indeed, against "drede," the emotion that Criseyde has cited repeatedly as her reason for resisting Troilus's love. Criseyde's fear, said by Lewis to be her defining characteristic, is caused not primarily by the reason for women's fear in the courtly love tradition, loss of power over the beloved, but by the historical events of her time, the threat of capture, enslavement, and/or rape by enemy soldiers, to which Criseyde, as a widow who has lost her primary male protector when her father Calchas absconded, is especially vulnerable.[56] Just as Pandarus has interrupted the reading of the siege of Thebes, here lyric form interrupts an event-based form, narrative, but offers a formal space for putting desire in dialogue with its constraints and influences. Indeed, Antigone's song has sometimes been critiqued for being too close to the poem's narrative and thereby less lyrical than the poem's other lyric interpolations.

The song's use of proverbs offers particular insight into how lyric tactics suggest a form of participatory negotiation. Let us first recall Geoffrey of Vinsauf's description of the function of proverbs in poetry: "If a still more brilliant beginning is desired . . . make use of a proverb, ensuring that it may not sink to a purely specific relevance, but raise its head high to some general truth. See that, while prizing the charm of the unusual, it may not concentrate its attention on the particular subject, but refuse, as if in disdain, to remain within its bosom. Let it take a stand above the given subject, but look with direct glance towards it."[57] Geoffrey's description of the relationship between proverbs and the material of a story raises an issue of interpretation that continues to resonate throughout the poem. The proverb, according to Geoffrey (who is of course speaking primarily of narrative poetry), elevates the material from the particular to the universal, "stand[ing] above the given subject but look[ing] with direct glance towards it." This evocative image speaks to Chaucer's use of the now-obscure proverb that people with weak eyes shouldn't gaze on the sun. Read through the lens of Geoffrey's image, the version of this proverb in Antigone's song suggests that those without the perspective to understand love in its larger context—that of the historical moment of war-torn Troy in which his story is set—should not attempt to participate in love. Yet Geoffrey's hierarchical image obscures the fact that metaphorical proverbs "mediat[e] between two aspects of reality, two levels of classification."[58] And, as Karla Taylor observes, in *Troilus and Criseyde*, proverbs themselves constitute a kind of desire: "Proverbs are apt not to describe reality as it is, but only as we wish it to be."[59] Cognitive research has shown that "proverb comprehension rests upon mapping the similarities between two widely divergent domains of knowledge, one familiar and experiential, the other more remote and abstract."[60] This kind of mapping reminds us of the relationship between the abstractly conventional language of the lyric idiom and the contingent setting of the historical romance. The metaphorical proverbs in Antigone's song provide the key to how Criseyde is meant to understand the lyric. As several readers have observed, the poem portrays a feminized ideal of love, offering a " 'female' poetry of presence" by contrast with the "Petrarchan lyric of privation," as Claire Kinney puts it.[61] Yet the vehicles of the metaphorical proverbs remind us to locate such an ideal within the contingencies of a situation; in other words, to read tactically.

Geoffrey of Vinsauf's image of a proverb looking down from above also evokes the poem's palinode, in which Troilus's soul looks down on the earth: "And down from thennes faste he gan avyse [examine] / This litel spot of erthe that with the se / Embraced is, and fully gan despise / This wrecched world" (5.1814–17). Troilus's perspective, as many readers have noted, gives the poem a philosophical distance from the vagaries of earthly affairs that elevates the individual above history.[62] For Troilus, a tragic war hero who dies in battle, this teleology makes some sense. However, as Mary Carruthers has observed, a cold rationalism is not a satisfying moral outcome of the poem; rather, emotion, especially grief and suffering, amplifies a reader's judgment and acumen.[63] This is especially clear if we consider Criseyde's "ending." The scope of this chapter does not permit a full analysis of Criseyde's life after her infidelity, but we can find inklings of Criseyde's alienation from large, overarching structures of interpretation (precisely those intimated in the palinode, where Troilus escapes worldly cares) in her reading of Antigone's song.

As she grapples with the implications of the song to her decision about whether to love Troilus, Criseyde explores the emotional and communal foundations of lyricism.

"Now nece," quod Criseyde,
"Who made this song now with so good entente?"
Antygone answerde anoon and seyde,
"Madame, ywys, the goodlieste mayde
Of gret estat in al the town of Troye,
And let hire lif in moste honour and joye."   *leads*
"Forsothe, so it semeth by hire song,"
Quod tho Criseyde, and gan therwith to sike,
And seyde, "Lord, is ther swych blisse among
Thise loveres, as they konne faire endite?" (2.877–86)

Readers have discussed this song, and Criseyde's response to it, as both an affirmation of idealized love and as an intimation of the alienation and threat that a love affair with Troilus would pose for her.[64] The song describes a kind of desire that can find fulfillment only within the *hortus conclusus* of its space of performance and that purports to offer a vision of "blisse" at odds with the "double sorwes" that shape the poem's larger narrative. Yet it is precisely because of Criseyde's oblique position in the history and the narrative of this poem that the song's promise is unrealizable. Lee Patterson reads her as an alienated and passive subject in a masculine erotic history: Criseyde "knows and doesn't know that she desires," a double bind figured in the mediations of Antigone's song.[65] But as Aranye Fradenburg points out, Criseyde's vulnerability is due not to her exclusion from a masculine chivalric culture but is created by the very fabric of that culture. In her discussion of the twin engines of "entente" and enjoyment, or *jouissance*, that drive this poem, Fradenburg notes that the private intention or will is inscribed in an enjoyment that circulates through groups even as it relies on individual desire.[66] In other words, when Criseyde asks, "Who made this song now with so good entente," she seems to isolate love within individual experience. Yet when she reframes her question as, "Lord, is ther swych blisse among / Thise loveres, as they konne faire endite," she locates love's emotions and its lyricism in a communal experience.

In summary, Antigone's song puts forth a poetics of negotiation based on lyric tactics. Its poetics, performance, and reception all rely on contingent improvisations on established forms. French and classical poetic idioms, as well as the pedagogic form of the proverb, serve for Chaucer the role of institutionally established forms. His poetic tactics have political implications, as the episode's Ovidian frame suggests. The tale of Philomela was a medieval touch point for the interactions between erotic desire and the politics of war, and a warning against the violent potential of each. In *Troilus and Criseyde*, Chaucer demonstrates a poetics and politics of negotiation that aspires to a more peaceable and equitable expression of love and politics, by means of the tactical forms and agents of Antigone's song. These tactics are evident in the narrative of the song's performance, in its diffuse relationships to its disparate sources, and in its use of rhetorical figures and forms, particularly metaphor and proverbs. Antigone's song emphasizes the contingency and disjunction of these figures. The proem of Book 2 and the Ovidian frame of this lyric suggest that the adaptive tactics of this song can offer a form for female agency and desire within historical crisis. These ideas are practiced as formal, rhetorical, and interpersonal negotiations in Antigone's song, in which the use of the courtly poetic idiom of stable, faithful love encounters formal change, in its use of metaphor and metaphorical proverbs that set courtly ideals against Criseyde's wartime vulnerability. Interpretation based on scholastic models of literary authority breaks down and misleads Criseyde. Unlike Troilus, Criseyde cannot rely on the rhetorical and cultural structures of stability and transcendence; she cannot look down from above.

Cantici Troili; or, The Problem with Petrarch

The tactics of Antigone's song suggest a poetics of negotiation, forged from disparate sources and alert to local contingencies and the particularities of subject positions within a given community. This model of poetic and political praxis inflects other lyric interludes in *Troilus and Criseyde*: in particular,

the songs of Troilus. These songs differ in obvious formal ways from Antigone's; they more directly translate single lyric sources, and they are largely
performed in solitude, not in public. Yet as I will demonstrate, reading the
cantici Troili through the lens of the kinds of tactics practiced in Antigone's
song reveals how they critique, even as they draw on, their literary and political foundations. The first of Troilus's songs takes up the problem of the
intersection between self and ruler and between private desires and their
public expression in the form of the "complaint." Two of Troilus's most
poignant lyrics, in Book 5, yield darkly to a totalizing poetics of loss, rupture,
and the destruction of negotiation in favor of absolutism. Troilus's loss of
Criseyde is thus inseparable from the loss of the possibility of negotiation that
song can enable. As with my discussion of Antigone's song, representations of
lyric practice will figure in my analysis along with each song's sources and
rhetoric.

The songs of Troilus have formed a focal point for many readings of the
long poem's lyricism. For Charles Muscatine, Troilus's first song demonstrates Chaucer's presentation of this character as the epitome of a French
courtly love tradition.[67] Robert Payne, for instance, identifies a "structural
area" of the poem consisting of a "system of lyric and apostrophe" that
extends from the first to the last *cantici Troili* (i.e., 1.400–5.658).[68] Although
he includes Antigone's song among the ten lyric interludes of this "structural
area," Payne also identifies it as exceptional, since it is the only one that
influences the poem's plot. His ten lyrics "constitute a kind of distillation of
the emotional progress of the poem, held together by a thread of thematic
imagery in much the manner of a very condensed sonnet sequence."[69] Payne's
model for the poem's lyricism is thus deeply Petrarchan or, in Roland
Greene's term, "post-Petrarchan." Greene finds this lyric mode in the sonnet
sequences that proliferate in early modern England and continue to influence
modern poetry across cultures and languages. These sequences create an
"alternate world," which Greene calls its "fictional element," from the lyric's
qualities of sound and its emotional expressivity, which Greene calls its "ritual
element."[70] Other readings of the *cantici Troili*, especially the direct Petrarchan translation of Book 1, examine how they reflect Chaucer's relationship
to his literary influences. Thomas Stillinger reads the first and last *cantici
Troili* as Chaucer's claims to adduce the literary authority of the Continental
"lyrical book" to *Troilus and Criseyde*.[71] These Petrarchan lyrics within a
translation of Boccaccio's *Il Filostrato* suggest that Chaucer's relationship to
these medieval Italian poets, as well as to the "third crown," Dante, involves

multiple and attenuated interdependencies, which have been characterized as "a translation of his translations."[72] In short, *Troilus and Criseyde*'s lyricism is generally read, via the *cantici Troili*, as either drawing on or anticipating features of a European lyric tradition that bears identifiable formal, material, and literary historical continuities with modern lyricism.

But reading the first *canticus Troili* through the lens of the negotiations put forth in Antigone's song casts a different light on the relationship between this poem and the Petrarchan tradition. Petrarch's *Canzoniere* and his literary practices more generally involve dominance, mastery, and even violent dismemberment of the text and the body of the woman represented therein.[73] In David Wallace's concise summation of the founding humanist myth, "Masculine desire, of a specific social and educated level, finds itself locked out of social and erotic fulfillment and exiles itself from the city. Lost in thought (within a humanist landscape) a text comes to mind: one that sees the female body pursued by masculine desire. This text is captured, laid open or transcribed (with a dagger), and consumed. The knowledge of this text, gained in private, may then be exploited to influence behavior within the public domain. Control of the text, figured as a woman, facilitates control of woman in society."[74] Lyric performs this control as an act of descriptive dismemberment (frequently with a blazon), dividing the desired woman into body parts to be consumed in private delectation. As Nancy Vickers has shown, this kind of lyric originates in Petrarch's descriptions of Laura in the "scattered" poems of the *Rime Sparse*, which invert the Ovidian myth of Diana and Actaeon. When Actaeon illicitly gazes on Diana, she transforms him into a deer that her dogs tear apart. Petrarchan lyric, with its dismembered descriptions of Laura, switches the genders of the Ovidian myth, thereby rendering the woman a textual object to be consumed, glossed, and dissected by the masculine reader.[75]

Much of Petrarch's literary and political absolutism is related to his concept of the autonomous self, which is reflected in his proto-modern praise of solitude as an ideal environment for artists and thinkers. His "Letter to Posterity" describes a prolific sojourn in secluded Vaucluse, where he composes, among other works, *De Vita Solitaria*, his treatise in praise of solitude.[76] Likewise, all of Troilus's songs are sung in privacy or for a single listener. Yet the setting of the first *canticus Troili* interrogates as much as it enacts the authority accruing to this kind of lyricism. In the parallel scene in Boccaccio's *Il Filostrato*, Troilo "joyfully gave himself to singing, with high hopes and completely disposed to love Criseyde alone."[77] Chaucer's version inserts a much-studied passage that has inspired discussions of his own poetic authority:

And of his song naught only the sentence,
As writ min auctor called Lollius,
But pleinly, save oure tonges difference,
I dar wel seyn, in al, that Troilus
Seyde in his song, loo, every word right thus
As I shal seyn; and whoso list it here,
Loo, next this vers he may it finden here. (1.393–99)

Most readers accept that the name "Lollius" in this passage derives from a misreading of a Horatian text, whether Chaucer believed him to be a classical author or simply used the name as a cipher for authorizing his own multiply sourced fiction.[78] But other theories as to Lollius's identity have been put forth. The name may be Chaucer's wordplay on "lolling," or it may be a mistaken attribution to Petrarch's friend "Laelius," or Lellus Pietri Stephani de Tossetis, to whom he addressed many letters.[79]

The confusion surrounding the identity of Lollius contributes to the representation of lyric composition in this stanza, which emphasizes negotiation rather than authority. The negative invocation of the spurious source, "min auctor called Lollius," leads to a distinction between meaning and rhetoric. Lollius provided "only the sentence"—the moral/polemical meaning, or *sententia*—of Troilus's song, but Chaucer's narrator gives us "every word." The repetition of the verb "seyen," which in Middle English can mean to "recite" or even "sing," sandwiching a subordinate clause with "Troilus" as the subject with "I"-subject main clauses, syntactically reinforces the intimacy between the narrator and Troilus and excludes "min auctor" from this cozy exchange.[80] Yet, because it emphasizes rhetoric, any imagined transparency of translation is clouded by "oure tonges difference," a phrase that most obviously refers to translation (a theme Chaucer develops, as we have seen, at greater length in the proem to Book 2). But it also, on a literal level, reminds the reader of the distance between the source of the lyric and its translation, as lyric language negotiates linguistic and historical change.

The translation itself subtly modulates its Petrarchan source to introduce the possibility of negotiation into the original's binaries. As many readers have noted, Petrarch's "S'amor non è" is a poem of paradox, whose resolution requires a "turn inwards."[81] Chaucer's translation expands his source formally, converting the fourteen-line sonnet into three rhyme royal stanzas, for a total of twenty-one lines, and also expands it thematically, personifying love as an agent apart from the speaker and condensing the affective states of the original into a politically charged English.

If no love is, O God, what fele I so?
And if love is, what thing and which is he?
If love be good, from whennes cometh my woo?
If it be wikke, a wonder thinketh me,
When every torment and adversite
That cometh of him may to me savory thinke,
For ay thurst I, the more that ich it drinke. (1.400–406)

The problem of this lyric is at one level a problem of the ethics of desire. Is love good or bad, and why does the affective response to it—both pleasure and pain—divide the self? By comparison with its source, the first *canticus Troili* represents love more strongly as an agent separate from the voice that says "I." Love is twice personified as "he" in the first stanza of the translation. In the second stanza, the English version seeks an external source for the internal pain of love: "And if that at myn owen lust I brenne, / From whennes cometh my waillynge and my pleynte?" (1.407–8). Petrarch's original simply contrasts two affective states: "S'a mia voglia ardo, ond' è 'l pianto e lamento?" ("If I burn willingly, why weep and grieve?").[82]

Troilus, in his solitude, contemplates Criseyde in her entirety, seeing "al holly hire figure" in the "mirour of his mynde" (1.365–66). This lyric is less a private delectation and dismemberment of the female object of desire than a way of imaginatively working through other masculine, social, and political relationships. The intractable entity in this poem is not the desired woman but personified "love," gendered male: "every torment and adversite / That cometh of him may to me savory thinke."[83] In particular, the first *canticus Troili* takes up the problem of the intersection between the self and the ruler, between the private will and the public petition, and between "consent" and "complaint."

And if that at myn owen lust I brenne,
From whennes cometh my wailynge and my pleynte?
If harm agree me, whereto pleyne I thenne?

I noot, ne whi unwery that I feynte.

O quike deth, O swete harme so queynte,   *living; marvelous*

How may of the in me swich quantite,

But if that I consente that it be?

And if that I consente, I wrongfully

Compleyne, iwis. (1.407–15)

"Compleyne" and its forms ("pleynte" and "pleyne") are Chaucer's translations of two Italian affective terms, "lament/lamenter" and "doglio." The
English "complaint" signifies a complex of lyric forms, including elegiac
laments, Christian *planctus*, and the vernacular love laments of the later Middle Ages, as well as the legal form of petition that rose to prominence in the
late thirteenth century; diverse instances of the genre punctuate *Troilus and
Criseyde*.[84] As Wendy Scase has suggested, the introduction of the legal complaint, which gave peasants a mechanism by which to air their grievances,
offered vernacular poetry a new documentary and literary form.[85] Yet the
complaint as a poetic genre long predates the English legal form. As Lee
Patterson observes, the medieval literary complaint is so ubiquitous as to be
"virtually coextensive with poetry, indeed with writing itself. If language is a
form of action that mediates between the subject and the world, then complaint interrogates its relation to these two presences: can language objectify
the subject and/or have an effect upon the world?" Patterson's reading of the
first *canticus Troili* focuses the ways in which the mediating function of language reveals a complex, equivocal, and alienated self.[86]

But the song's dialectic between internal and external does not only bear
on selfhood; the question of this first song is "why do I publicly perform or
petition my private desire?" If much of Petrarch's literary politics justifies
repressive acts of tyranny, this poem uses the metaphor of governance common in courtly love lyrics to put forth a model of negotiation, both between
the lover and the God of Love and between love's private and public practices. This negotiation appears in Chaucer's text not only thematically but
formally. The *canticus Troili* is itself mediated by the poet-narrator's negotiation with his putative source, Lollius. A second lyrical interlude immediately
follows the Petrarchan translation, in which Troilus proposes specific terms
to the God of Love:

Wherefore, lord, if my service or I

May liken yow, so beth to me benigne;   *please*

For myn estat roial I here resigne
Into hire hond, and with ful humble chere
Bicom hir man, as to my lady dere. (1.430–34)

This passage alludes to an older poetic tradition, the address to the God
of Love, conventionally represented as an omnipotent ruler, that derives,
ultimately, from Ovid.[87] The conceit that Troilus is conducting a negotiation
with this ruler is underscored by the use of feudal and contractual language
("resigne"; "estat roial"; "bicom hire man"). Chaucer's juxtaposition of the
song and the Ovidian love petition situates the lyric within a network of
powerful forces that make private desire public. It also poses a question: how
can we reconcile the private authority of individual desire with the courtly
model that imagines that desire as a feudal contract? If individual desire, in
Petrarchan poetics, is conflated with literary *auctorite*, then lyric tactics offer
a practice distinct from authoritative translation in the distancing of the
song's "every word" from Lollius's "sentence."

Although the first *canticus Troili* is closer to a direct translation of a
single lyric than is Antigone's song, Chaucer's approach to translation here is
tactical. He adapts the closed form of the sonnet into the more permeable
and integrated rhyme royal of his narrative; he complicates the relationships
among source, author, translator, and singer; and he introduces the language
of English forms of political negotiation into the translation. All of these
features of the first *canticus Troili* anticipate the formal, literary, and political
tactics that we have seen in Antigone's song. Yet one important aspect of
these tactics is missing: the inclusion of the voices of all subjects of the negotiation. Criseyde is completely absent from Troilus's lyric. The negotiations
between Troilus and Love in many ways presage those of the Trojan Parliament, leaving Criseyde's private desires voiceless. Even as this first song
attempts a tactical reworking of Petrarchan lyricism, it cannot evade the troubling poetics and politics of the form.

Criseyde's absence from Troilus's lyricism is explicitly thematized in
Book 5. Troilus mourns Criseyde's departure using the *ubi sunt* (i.e., "Where
are they now?") topos most often found in didactic lyrics that denigrate
worldly pleasures, the so-called *contemptus mundi* tradition.

"Wher is myn owene lady, lief and deere?
Wher is hire white brest? Wher is it, where?
Wher ben hire armes and hire eyen cleere
That yesternyght this tyme with me were?" (5.218–21)

Best known to medieval audiences from a poem called *The Sayings of St. Bernard*, the *ubi sunt* topos appears in many longer poems, including *The Owl and the Nightingale*.[88] In didactic lyrics, it reminds its audience of the universality of death and is often used to urge repentance. A thirteenth-century lyric begins,

Where beth they biforen us weren?	
Houndes ladden and hawkes beren,	*led*
And hadden feld and wode;	
The riche levedies in here bour,	*their chambers*
That wereden gold in here tressour,	*head-dress*
With here brighte robe.[89]	

In *Troilus and Criseyde*, the *ubi sunt* topos suggests that Criseyde's transmutation into a lyric object is a kind of death. Troilus's lament employs the dismembering blazon of a Petrarchan love lyric for the first time in the poem, dividing Criseyde into "white brest," "armes," and "eyen cleere." In the quasi-death of her exile, Criseyde becomes a Petrarchan lyric object, to be dissected and examined. Troilus no longer sees her "al holly," as he did when she was inside the walls of Troy. The dissection of Criseyde heralds the abandonment of the hope to reconcile public and private desires through negotiation, instead turning to political and poetic absolutism. The *ubi sunt* lyric commonplace, which was typically used to induce contempt for worldly things and thereby turn penitents inward, here recasts interiority as despair.

The result of Troilus's mastery of Petrarchan lyricism is evident in the final, brief *canticus Troili*, which Troilus performs in solitude, "whan he was from every mannes syghte" (5.635). It is the only *canticus* that explicitly takes Criseyde as its object:

O sterre, of which I lost have al the light,	
With herte soor wel oughte I to biwaille	
That evere derk in torment, nyght by nyght,	
Toward my deth with wynd in steere I saille;	
For which the tenthe nyght, if that I faille	*lack*
The gydyng of thi bemes bright an houre,	
My ship and me Caribdis wol devoure. (5.638–44)	

As Thomas Stillinger demonstrates, this lyric has a strong correlation with Petrarch's sonnet 189 in the *Canzoniere*, in its imagery, metaphor, and what he calls its "double logic."[90] Troilus's use of a trope to describe Criseyde in this lyric is significant as well: in Criseyde's absence, Troilus begins to understand her as an object of hermeneutics, which he must explicate. In the two lyric utterances of Book 5, Criseyde is first dismembered, then doubled. When grieving Troilus asks himself, "Why twynned be we tweyne?" (5.679), he unknowingly hints at this rhetorical and erotic duplicity.

Troilus's physical and poetic distance from Criseyde is epitomized in the palinode, as his soul ascends above the earth and he looks down with disdain on its worldly pleasures and cares. Its closure is perhaps overdetermined in the anaphora of the stanza that concludes the poem's narrative:

Swich fyn hath, lo, this Troilus for love!
Swich fyn hath al his grete worthynesse!
Swich fyn hath his estat real above!
Swich fyn his lust, swich fyn hath his noblesse!
Swich fyn hath false wordes brotelnesse!
And thus bigan his lovynge of Criseyde,
As I have told, and in this wise he deyde. (5.1828–34)

If the "swich fyn"s did not adequately convey the sense of narrative ending, the final couplet leaves no doubt, summarizing the story's *materia*. But narrative closure inspires a final lyric tactic:

O yonge, fresshe folkes, he or she,
In which that love up groweth with your age,
Repeyreth hom from worldly vanyte,   *Return home*
And of youre herte up casteth the visage   *direct your attention*
To thilke God that after his ymage
Yow made, and thynketh al nys but a faire,
This world that passeth soone as floures faire. (5.1835–41)

In one sense, this is the moral of the *materia*, taking its natural place at the end of the story. But it is also marked by lyric rhetoric. It opens with an apostrophe, which John of Garland identifies as a foundational rhetorical figure for "rhymed poetry" and Robert Payne equates with lyric in this poem.[91] The final *rime riche*, "faire/faire," gestures toward an insular lyric commonplace, the world as a passing harvest, or "cherry" fair: "This life, I see, is but a cheyre fayre. / All thinges passene and so most I, algate."[92] The "floures faire" invoke not only transience but also poetry, by way of the commonplace of the "flower of rhetoric." Even as Troilus's lyricism collapses into Petrarchan binarism, insular lyric flowers briefly against the totalizing pressures of authority, narrative, and moral.

In summary, the lyrics in *Troilus and Criseyde* illustrate how a signal period of transition in the history of English lyric maintains continuity with the earlier insular tradition. Even as English lyrics are permeated by Continental forms and sources, the tactical practices of the insular tradition survive in its adaptation of these influences. In Antigone's song, these practices shape an aesthetic form with political consequences, as the song's adaptations of its sources and multivocal transmission suggest a model of inclusive negotiation of public and private desires. Tactics also inform the translations of the more unified forms and sources of the *cantici Troili*, which put Petrarchan poetics and politics into dialogue with this model of negotiation. Troilus's solitary lyric performances in *Troilus and Criseyde* explore the limitations of Petrarch's model of intellectual and artistic solitude and especially the political implications of its privileging of private desire. Yet these lyrics gradually abandon the possibility of negotiation for a more totalizing form and politics. The poem's ending suggests that the conversion is far from complete, however; tactics persist in opening every attempt at closure, as the mutability of the insular lyric finds new pathways through seemingly bounded forms.

CHAPTER 4

Form and Ethics in *Handlyng Synne*
and the *Legend of Good Women*

Troilus and Criseyde, though a romance, is fundamentally political. It is about how conflicting desires are negotiated in love and war. As we have seen, Chaucer's exploration of this problem is as much formal as thematic, with different models of lyric suggesting ways to negotiate (or abandon negotiations) between public and private desires. This chapter continues the project set forth in my reading of *Troilus and Criseyde*, that of understanding how tactical modes of relation inform the encounters between lyric and other literary forms and, further, what the broader implications are of such encounters. We turn here from politics to ethics as we examine the relationships between two medieval literary forms, lyric and exemplum, in Robert Mannyng of Brunne's *Handlyng Synne* (1303) and Chaucer's *Legend of Good Women* (1386–96).[1] Both works consist of collections of narrative exempla, generally well-known stories that conclude with a moral, and also draw on two other well-theorized forms of medieval exempla, as we shall see. Where Mannyng is concerned with Christian ethics, the *Legend*'s narrator, "Geoffrey," is charged by the God of Love with examining the ethics of erotic and emotional behavior, by documenting "good" women in a manner at once descriptive and prescriptive.[2]

In spite or perhaps because of the explicit theorization of medieval exemplary forms, both Mannyng and Chaucer use lyrics and lyricism tactically within these forms. Mannyng's tale of the "Dancers of Colbek" centers on its cursed carol, and Chaucer's exempla, and the much-admired prologue to the collection, are permeated with lyrics and lyricism, from set pieces such as the *balade* "Hyd Absolon" to lyricized translations of Ovid in the legends themselves. While the inclusion of lyric in narrative was a common practice in medieval poetry, as discussed in the previous chapter, the specific relationship between lyric and exemplum has implications for medieval modes of ethical thought and practice. In particular, both Mannyng and Chaucer use lyric conventions that are premodern (refrain and noesis) and proto-modern (temporal suspension, brevity, and rhetorical complexity) to challenge the accretive logic of an ethics based on exemplary forms.[3] Medieval exempla were central to the philosophical tradition of "casuistry," or reasoning from cases, which sought to amass a number of examples as a basis for ethical thought and action. By contrast with the progressive and telic practices of this kind of ethics, the tactics of interpolated lyrics in Mannyng's and Chaucer's poetry enable iterative and recursive ethical practices. As we shall see, the encounter between the literary forms of lyrics and exempla at once imagines and implements an ethics that is nonlinear, circumstantial, and improvisatory: in short, tactical.

While these readings will draw on three distinct exemplary forms, the most common of these, and the most overtly used by both Mannyng and Chaucer, is the exemplary narrative, or *paradigma*. Its narrative qualities, as some recent studies have discussed, are central to the complexity of this seemingly simple, didactic form, from its sequencing of events to the narrating "voice" that negotiates the authority and ethical guidance of the form's moral.[4] Exemplary narratives, by many accounts, are those in which the boundary between the audience and the narrator is most permeable. The very status of a narrative as exemplary invites its audience to internalize its ethical authority by aligning their experiences with events in the tale.[5] Yet the example's status as a model (positive or negative) of behavior is inseparable from the authority of its disseminator. That is, representing a narrative as exemplary locates its teller within what we, following Certeau, have called the "proper" of institutional space: a circumscribed space subject to centralized, well-defined power relations.[6] Nonetheless, in order to communicate its ethical content, the exemplum must reach toward those outside of that space. The form of the *paradigma*, a narrative with a moral, bodies forth the conflict between these two aims. As its narrative accrues specificity, contingency, and subjectivity, its moral attempts to totalize and abstract these particularities. To some extent, these two components of the exemplum are irreconcilable. Exempla as forms and exemplary ethics as practices thus encounter many of the same issues that we observed in our discussion of the fraternal use of lyrics in Chapter 2. Their aims are largely strategic, as they convey an ethics

that is institutionally sanctioned by ecclesiastic, academic, or social authorities. Yet they are unable to regulate the way they are applied outside of their
institutions, by the laity or the "lewed." Thus, the practices of case-based
reasoning put pressure on exemplary forms and tend toward a more tactical
form that would allow for improvisation and contingency.

It is in this gap that lyric enters. The presence of lyric within exemplum
suspends its drive toward closure, suggesting an alternate ethical praxis that
more closely follows Certeau's concept of the "opportunity": the subject's
manipulation of events in time to fit his circumstances.[7] Narrative exempla
whose complexity drives them toward iterative and recursive practices, in
particular, deploy lyric to expand their own formal constraints. Like exempla,
medieval lyrics may have narratives and/or morals, especially in their more
didactic instances, but many lyrics put these elements into cyclical, iterative,
or progressive forms. Further, lyrics' formal and material fluidity encourages
a practice that has the capacity to modify or even challenge the authority of
the exemplary moral. Although English lyric poetry is neither so well theorized nor so coherently witnessed as the exempla, both circulate in public and
popular channels whose practices shape and are shaped by their explicit or
implicit forms.[8] Lyric and exemplum are thus in some ways complementary
forms that, taken together, can refine and reform ethical practices.

My central claim in this chapter is that lyric tactics allow Mannyng and
Chaucer to imagine a hybrid ethical form and practice that reconciles the
exemplum's contingency and specificity with its moral aims. In particular,
the iterative and recursive tactics of medieval lyrics suggest an ethical practice
that is more contingent, plural, and flexible—and thus more representative
of actual ethical action—than the abstract closure of the defined exemplary
forms. In what follows, I first elaborate on these forms and their place in the
philosophical tradition of casuistic reasoning. By way of illustration, I discuss
the relationship between the carol's textual form and movement practices
and the "Dancers of Colbek" exemplum in Mannyng's *Handlyng Synne*. I
then turn to an extended discussion of the plural lyric and exemplary forms
in the *Legend of Good Women*, first in the prologue and then in the legends
themselves. As we shall see, Chaucer's poem both explicitly and implicitly
poses the question of how a medieval concept of "form"—which is at once
metaphysical and aesthetic—bears on ethical practice. Both Mannyng's and
Chaucer's juxtapositions of lyric and exemplum suggest tactical modes of
ethical practice that can respond to a subject's contingent circumstances. In
the *Legend of Good Women*, Chaucer goes further. He draws on multiple

features of lyric form in set pieces as well as interludes that are more contiguous with narrative, suggesting that the relationships between literary forms are as crucial to their ethical implications as the formal features of each. With this approach, Chaucer critiques exemplary ethics by means of lyric tactics, suspending the exemplum's drive toward closure and reimagining exemplary "showing."

"Why go we noght?": Exempla, Practical Ethics, and Lyric

Like didactic literature generally, exempla can seem "merely" instrumental (and therefore not aesthetic), heavy-handed, and inelegant. But examples and the exemplary mode pose a subtle formal problem that has informed their long history of use in literature and philosophy.[9] In this section, I first discuss the philosophical method of casuistry, or reasoning from cases, that relies on exempla and then locate exemplarity in its medieval context by describing the three main types of exemplary forms. To begin to understand the relationship between lyric tactics and these exemplary forms and practices, I examine the relationship between the carol and the *paradigma* in the "Dancers of Colbek" episode in *Handlyng Synne*. As we shall see, Mannyng's proposed reading practices for his collection exceed exemplary form and challenge totalizing and telic morality. He introduces a lyric form—that of the carol—to facilitate a more open, recursive, and iterative ethical practice. My main aim in this section is to demonstrate how this kind of ethical practice manifests in a hybrid form that combines lyric and exemplum, a tactic explored in Mannyng's collection and more fully realized in Chaucer's *Legend of Good Women*.

The exemplum's medieval forms reflect its centrality in the philosophical tradition of "practical" or "casuistic" reasoning. J. Allan Mitchell gives the following account of the process of case-based analysis: "The best approach to practical dilemmas, according to the casuist, is to model present solutions on successful past ones. And so the practitioner proceeds in an incremental fashion, by comparison and contrast, moving in and among known cases or groups of cases (paradigms, genera, taxonomies) to the outer limits of current understanding, looking for ways to accommodate new cases and circumstances by placing them under an existing genus, or modifying known genera, or a combination of strategies thereof."[10] Casuistic reasoning is linear and accretive. Rejecting top-down reasoning from abstract principles, the casuist "mov[es] crab-wise or laterally across known cases," building knowledge incrementally from particulars.[11] This kind of reasoning is often identified with medieval nominalism and reached its greatest popularity among the early modern Jesuits. But following a scathing critique by Pascal and the method of abstract reasoning from a priori principles championed by Kant and his followers, casuistic reasoning fell out of favor.[12] Recent proponents of practical ethics, especially as they pertain to medical and legal questions, have returned to case-based reasoning as a method of considering contingent and circumstantial factors in ethical thinking.[13] Thus, on one hand, casuistic reasoning seems to acknowledge the particularities that are key components in tactical practice. Yet, on the other, it tends to totalize those particularities in authorized cases.

A critique of case-based analysis thus invites a consideration of the relationships between centralized structures of power and their public subjects in the formation and propagation of examples that solidify into meaningful "cases." What constitutes an acceptable case, who defines it, and how does its reception and transmission affect its ethical work? As Lauren Berlant says, a case is fundamentally a "communicative action" that "organizes publics." As such, case making is deeply entrenched in discourses of power; a case "expresses a relation of expertise to a desire for shared knowledge."[14] Mitchell himself uses the term "strategies" (albeit not in a Certeauvian sense) to describe the accretive practices of building ethics from cases. These strategies are far-reaching, since in practice, casuistic reasoning is nearly universal: "Everybody depends upon it, even though few people say so explicitly."[15] Thus, it offers a potent yet dispersed dissemination of the power structures that authorize the case.[16]

The history and conventions of exemplary forms are bound up with those of legal and literary "cases."[17] Medieval treatises identify three distinct forms of exempla that do social and ethical work.[18] The first is the example from conduct, which clerics were exhorted to provide in their way of life. Twelfth-century handbooks of canonical life advised clergy to teach "by word and by example," making all of their speech, actions, and behaviors exemplary.[19] Treatises of canonical life use verbs meaning "to show," *ostendere* and *exhibere*, to refer to conduct. Thus behavior itself was a form or pattern (*forma*) for others to imitate.[20] Although this kind of active exemplum had no rhetorical counterpart, its model of exemplary conduct as a kind of showing or manifestation intersects in both Chaucer's and Mannyng's works, as we shall see, with other forms of textual exempla.

These textual exempla, sometimes called "showings" that allow their
audiences to "see" the moral outcome, emerged from two classical rhetorical
figures.[21] In the first, the *imago* or *eikon*, the name of a mythic or historical
figure is invoked to call to mind his most dominant quality. In its simplest
form, the *imago* is equivalent to a simile or any object of explicit comparison.[22] Medieval treatises also use the term to describe a historical or mythic
figure who exemplified a particular virtue or vice, the *imago virtutis/vitii*.[23] In
this kind of exemplum, the name of the person is a synecdoche for the most
salient feature of the character. For instance, later medieval penitential manuals identify biblical figures with their most prominent vices: Balaam and Delilah with extravagance, Jezebel with avarice, and so forth.[24] This form of
exemplarity also appears in vernacular literature. Virgil lists the souls con-
demned for lust in Circle Two of Dante's *Inferno*:

"Helen. You see? Because of her, a wretched
Waste of years went by. See! Great Achilles.
He fought with love until his final day.
Paris, you see, and Tristan there." And more
Than a thousand shadows he numbered, naming
Them all, whom Love had led to leave our life.[25]

Chaucer borrows and extends Dante's list for his description of the Temple
of Venus in the *Parliament of Fowls*:

Semyramis, Candace, and Hercules,
Biblis, Dido, Thisbe, and Piramus,
Tristram, Isaude, Paris, and Achilles,
Eleyne, Cleopatre, and Troylus,
Silla, and ek the moder of Romulus:
Alle these were peynted on that other syde,
And al here love, and in what plyt they dyde.[26]

In these two passages, "showing," or visual evidence, is central to exemplarity:
Dante repeats "*vedi*" ("you see"), and Chaucer's names refer to figures
painted on the walls of the temple. But these showings rely on a subsumed
narrative, whose particularity and contingencies collapse into a single attribute associated with that name, which takes on the force of an exemplary

"image." Indeed, Chaucer's exempla are doubly *imagines*: at once names stripped of narratives and actual paintings.

The third and best-known form of the example is the extended narrative called the *exemplum* or *paradigma*.[27] According to Isidore of Seville, "Paradigm (*paradigma*) is a model (*exemplum*) of someone's word or deed, or something that is appropriate to the thing that we describe either from its similar or from its dissimilar nature."[28] The *Rhetorica ad Herennium* demonstrates the figure in a sample speech on risk and glory: "It is this that, in my opinion, Decius well understood, who is said to have devoted himself to death, and, in order to save his legions, to have plunged into the midst of the enemy. He gave up his life, but did not throw it away; for at the cost of a very cheap good he redeemed a sure good, of a small good the greatest good. He gave his life, and received his country in exchange. He lost his life, and gained glory, which, transmitted with highest praise, shines more and more every day as time goes on."[29] The treatise later defines the figure and its effects as follows: "Exemplification [*Exemplum*] is the citing of something done or said [*alicuius facti aut dicti*] in the past, along with the definite naming of the doer or author. It is used with the same motives as Comparison. It renders a thought more brilliant when used for no other purpose than beauty; clearer, when throwing more light upon what was somewhat obscure; more plausible, when giving the thought greater verisimilitude; more vivid, when expressing everything so lucidly that the matter can, I may almost say, be touched by the hand."[30] In the later Middle Ages, this kind of narrative exemplum enjoyed a vigorous textual presence in two distinct strains, the pastoral (as in Jacques de Vitry's *Sermones Vulgares*) and the political (as in the pseudo-Aristotelian *Secretum Secretorum*).[31] These stories tended to be popular and appealing, but in their narrative specificity, they at times undercut the telic moral that they proclaim.[32] I might tell you a story about a farm boy who falsely tells his elders there is a wolf in the chicken coop so many times that when a real wolf comes, they fail to believe him. I can probably persuade you that the moral of the story is, preserve your credibility by always speaking the truth; or, it is dangerous to lie. But what if I continue the story? When the real wolf comes, no one believes the boy, so he kills it himself and brings the body to his detractors, who reward him for saving their chickens. Then the moral might become, always take seriously allegations of a threat (from the perspective of the farmers); or, it is never too late to redeem yourself for prior infractions (from the perspective of the boy). Depending on the details I use in the

story—how sympathetic the boy or the farmers seem, how valuable the chickens are, the boy's own backstory, and so forth—the moral lesson of the tale
may change. As this example shows, the details of narrative inform the moral,
but the very process of moralizing a narrative—that is, of making it
exemplary—elides these details and renders them abstract. The contingencies
of a story undergird its abstraction but are also erased by it. While narrative
and moral are co-constitutive of the exemplary form, they are at some level
irreconcilable.

To begin to understand how lyric tactics can address this irreconcilabil-
ity, let us consider the influence of one kind of lyric, a carol, on an exemplum
from Robert Mannyng of Brunne's *Handlyng Synne*. This early fourteenth-
century pastoral collection is a translation and adaption of the Anglo-French
Manuel de Pechiez. Mannyng's prologue describes a reading practice that
echoes the *Rhetorica ad Herennium*'s image of exemplum as something that
can be "touched by the hand." In his cleverly literal translation of the "*Manuel*" of his title, he enjoins his reader to "handle" sin in words rather than
deeds:

Handlyng yn speche ys as weyl
As handlyng yn dede euerydeyl.   *in every way*
On thys manere handyl thy dedys
And lestene & lerne wan any hem redys. (115–18)

Instead of the laterally progressive practices typical of casuistic reasoning,
Mannyng advocates an iterative and recursive use of his work:

Oueral ys begynnyng—oueral ys ende,
Hou that thou wylt turne hyt or wende.   *move through*
Many thynges ther yn mayst thou here;
Wyth ofte redyng mayst thou lere.   *learn*
Thou mayst nought wyth onys redyng   *one*
Knowe the sothe of euery thyng.
Handyl, hyt behouyth the, ofte sythys: *frequently*
To many maner synnys hyt wrythys. (123–30)   *addresses*

Mannyng's instructions use language more tactical than strategic to invite
readers to find their own contingent and ad hoc pathways through his work.
He describes a recursive ethical practice dictated by form ("Oueral ys

begynnyng—oueral ys ende") and demonstrated in the repetitions and restatements of this passage: for instance, "ofte redyng"/ "nought wyth onys redyng." Exemplary moralizing is ongoing, captured not merely in the final moral but in the particularities of narrative, which merits rereading. The reader's navigation of the treatise is as important as the stories themselves to ethical practice. Repeated "handlyng," via different entry points and pathways, is the best use of this book.

The carol offers one formal model for this practice; it is iterative and recursive and suspends contingency without reaching toward abstraction. To see how this works, we can consider Mannyng's version of the tale of the "Dancers of Colbek." On Christmas Eve, a group of twelve dancers arrive in Colbek and entice Eve, the daughter of the local priest, Robert, to join them in a carol-dance in the churchyard. When the dancers refuse Robert's plea to leave off their revels and come to Christmas mass, the priest curses them to continue caroling, their hands locked together, for exactly one year. Robert's son, Ayone, attempts to wrest Eve from the circle but only succeeds in pulling off her arm. Finally, at the end of the year, the dancers' bodies detach and they fall to the ground. All are unharmed except for Eve, who dies of her wound.

If we look closely at the tale's lyric, we see how its form enacts a temporal suspension that at once mirrors the cursed dance and speaks to the tale's ethics. Among the dancers are a man named Beune, a woman named Merswynde, and a poet named Gerlew. When they arrive at the churchyard, Gerlew composes a lyric for the dance:

Beune ordeyned here karollynge,	*arranged for*
Gerleu endyted what they shuld synge	*composed*
Thys ys the karol that they sunge	
As telleth the latyne tunge:	
Equitabat beuo per siluam frondosam	
Ducebat secum merswyndam formosam,	
Quid stamus, cur non imus.	
"By the leued wode rode beuolyne,	
Wyth hym he ledde feyr merswyne.	
Why stonde we, why go we noght?" (9047–56)	

Like the exemplum, the lyric also uses proper names to concretize its text, but rather than using past, authoritative figures, it names the present dancers Beune and Merswynde. This tactic repurposes elements of the narrative text in a lyric form. Beune and Merswynde's (imagined) actions appear in the carol not in the register of ethics but in that of aesthetic and erotic pleasure: Beune rides through the "leued wode" (*siluam frondosam*), leading "feyr" (*formosam*) Merswynde with him in a pastoral idyll. Suspended in this lyric image, the dancers' question becomes one of love-longing and desire: "Why stond we, why go we noght"—with the two lovers? But in another sense, the burden of the carol describes the physical action of the dance. In the round-dance form of the carol, the verses were generally sung by a leader while the dancers' steps navigated the circle their bodies delimited, traveling, for instance, three steps to the left during the verse. The burden, by contrast, was sung by all of the dancers as they performed steps in place.[33] In the exemplary context, the refrain seems ironic; the dancers cannot "stond" but must continually "go." But it can also be read as a commentary on the different relationships between words and actions in the lyric and exemplary forms. An exemplum is a verbal phenomenon that describes past actions and anticipates future ones; word and action are related linearly. Indeed, if "narrative is about what happens next," in Jonathan Culler's felicitous phrase, the exemplum is an especially driven kind of story, whose trajectory of events culminates in a moral. Whereas, if "lyric is about what happens now," the burden of the carol underscores the recursive and immanent quality of words and actions in the danced lyric, which, even when the dancers are in motion, goes nowhere.[34] But its very quality of suspension also makes the lyric an agent of the curse. We are told that "Thys ys the karol that grysly wroght," and the carolers "sunge that song that the wo wroght" (9057, 9160). The nearly interminable repetitions that the curse mandates exaggerate the way in which the lyric's present voice contrasts with the exemplum's reliance on a past, completed narrative. In its own right, this carol constitutes a kind of case *without* abstraction or moralization. If casuistic reasoning relies on accruing exempla laterally, gathering multiple tales that point to a higher level of abstraction, the carol's repetitive iterations enhance and amplify a delimited pattern or *forma*. The rhymes in the above excerpt, too, demonstrate the carol's integration with and challenge to narrative structure. Mannyng's treatise is composed of octosyllabic couplets, but the carol's incipit rhymes "aab" (with the refrain also rhyming internally), creating a three-line poetic unit. The sentence before and after the Latin verse mimics this structure, with end rhymes "karollynge/sunge/tunge" (a half-rhyme with a couplet) and "Beuolyne/

Merswyne/nought" (an "aab" echo of the Latin carol). While all of the English verses are part of a larger couplet structure, the syntactic divisions here underscore the influence of the carol form on the narrative.

The effects of the curse manifest the recursive and iterative qualities of the carol's form.

These men that yede so karolland	*went*
Al that yere hand yn hand	
They neure out of that stede yede,	*place*
No noun myghte hem thenne lede.	*from there*
There the cursyng fyrst bygan,	*Where*
Yn that place aboute they ran. (9142–47)	

Their hands locked together, the carolers trace a fixed circle delimited by their collective body. But it is not only their bodies that are locked in repetition; the lyric is also being repeated, as they "sunge that song that the wo wrought: / 'Why stonde we, why go we noght?'" (9160–61). Unlike the exemplum, this is a hidden text, recurring behind the exemplary narrative without showing its own conclusion. The exemplum gives only the incipit of the carol, the "beginning" that, as D. Vance Smith has discussed, is at once equivalent to the full text and gestures toward its signification of the extratextual, demonstrating how every text exists at the intersection of formal closure and indeterminate practices of reception and transmission.[35] As Mark Miller points out, attempts toward containment or closure of the cursed dancers fail. Robert repeatedly tries to bury Eve's arm after it has been ripped from the circle, but the arm appears above the grave each time. The emperor Henry, one of a number of spectators who come to witness the dance, tries to construct a shelter over the dancers that falls to the ground.[36]

Just as the carol and the events of the story resist containment, the narrative of the "Dancers of Colbek" exceeds exemplary form, with nested internal exempla and multiple final morals. In the middle of the story, Ayone admonishes Robert when he presents Eve's arm:

"Thy cursyng now sene hyt ys,	
Wyth veniaunce on thyn owne flesshe.	
Fellyche thou cursedest & ouer sone	*Wickedly*
Thou askedest veniaunce: thou hast thy bone." (9120–23)	*reward*

Ayone moralizes the priest's cursing, making it a negative exemplum against vengeance. Further, when the dancers recover from the curse, they identify Robert as an "ensample":

Thou art ensample and enchesun	*cause*
Of oure long confusyun.	*punishment*
Thou maker art of oure travayle	
That ys to manye ful gret mervayle. (9194–97)	

This use of "ensample" requires some unpacking: how is Robert the example of the dancers' confusion? The *Middle English Dictionary* tentatively defines this usage as equivalent to "enchesun": "?an argument, reason, cause."[37] It seems to me that "ensample," in this context, is more likely to mean something like the *imago*, an image of the endless dance. Like the dancers, Robert is both an agent and an image of the story's moral. The endless carol forces the dancers to obey him but also perpetuates the sinful behavior Robert wanted to stop.[38]

These intermediate exempla exist in an oblique relationship to the plural closing morals. The tale at first seems to conclude with a proverb: "Tharfore men seye & weyl ys trowed, / The nere the cherche, the ferthere fro god" (9246–47). Does this refer to the priest Robert, whose desire for vengeance belies his "nearness" to the church, or to the dancers, whose physical proximity to the church makes their dance sacrilegious? This maxim is followed by a warning against both cursing and churchyard revels:

A tale hyt ys of feyr shewyng,
Ensample & drede ayens cursing.
Thys tale y told to make yow aferd
Yn cherche to karolle or yn cherche yerd. (9252–55)

The exemplary "showings" within the tale are also plural, from Robert's display of Eve's arm in the church to the physical and visual example the dancers provide to their audience: "What man shuld thyr be yn thys lyue / That hyt ne wlde se & thyder dryue [hasten there]?" (9162–63). Mark Miller suggests that the tale demonstrates what he calls "phenomenological" exemplification, which creates examples not from the experiences of individual subjects but from a more collective set of repeated phenomena. As Miller points out, this approach demonstrates how sin is "holistic" rather than individual and accounts in part for the indeterminacy of the exemplary morals.[39]

In other words, the story's multiple internal "ensamples" and plural endings exceed univocal moralizing and the constraints of exemplary form. Lyric's tactics offer more improvisatory and contingent forms and practices for the kind of ethics suggested by Mannyng's plural morals. In "The Dancers of Colbek," the carol verse is inassimilable to any of these morals. Further, the repetition and suspension of its refrain offer an alternative to narrative exemplarity. The tale itself circles, carol-like, around its two morals, against vengeance and against sacrilegious revels. The more details the narrative accrues, the more its contingencies seem to overwhelm a univocal and totalizing moral.

In short, as Mannyng's recommended reading practices for his collection reach toward plural and recursive modes of ethical knowledge, the collection encounters the formal limits of the exemplary *paradigma*. In "The Dancers of Colbek," the carol offers a formal model for these practices based on iteration and recursion. The carol-lyric, though incomplete in the exemplary text, drives and even "makes" ("wroght") the narrative with its repetitive form. Both the poetics and movement practice of this lyric demonstrate a tactical response to exemplary morality.

Lyric in the Prologue to the *Legend*

Mannyng's project in *Handlyng Synne* was one of moral education, and the pressures he puts on one kind of exemplary form—the moralized narrative— result from his attempts to reconcile it with the recursive reading practices he advocates for ethical self-improvement ("oueral ys begynnyng—oueral ys ende"). In the *Legend of Good Women*, Chaucer also explores how lyric can reimagine the ethical practices implicit in exemplary form, but his interests are as much literary as didactic. The poem draws on all three modes of exemplarity discussed above (the example from conduct, the *imago* and the *paradigma*), and it is equally catholic in its lyricism. The poem's lyric interludes, from the standalone "Balade" in the prologue to lyricized excerpts from Ovid, use diverse formal features from medieval and emerging proto-modern poetics. But they share a common project of integrating lyric and exemplary forms for ethical ends. A lyrical ethics, Chaucer thus suggests, is one of suspension and openness, dwelling in details, emotions, and contingencies before or perhaps instead of driving toward a moral. Chaucer's use of multiple forms of exemplarity and lyricism demonstrates the richness of an ethics that emerges from putting these forms and practices into tactical relationships.

While the *Legend* has many detractors (with critics insisting that Chaucer intentionally writes "boring" or "bad" poetry to make a point about didactic literature), some readers have nonetheless defended the poem as a crucial stage in Chaucer's literary development, a transition between *Troilus and Criseyde* and *The Canterbury Tales*.[40] More recent readings of the *Legend* have focused on its ethical work, and in particular, the relationship between self and Other. To James Simpson, the Other in question is a figure of power, specifically the God of Love, who seeks to prescribe tyrannical reading practices that an ethical subject can recognize and resist. Aranye Fradenburg considers the self's relationship to a "proximate Other" as a structuring ethic of the *Legend*, which involves the dual and at times conflicting responses of erotic desire and a fantasy to redeem. Kathryn Lynch and Carolyn Collette locate the *Legend* within discursive contexts ranging from literary exemplarity to Aristotelian philosophy.[41] My own reading draws on these studies in order to unite the literary and ethical aims of the *Legend* by demonstrating how its lyric and exemplary forms suggest an ethical work generated from tactical modes of practice. Thus, in this section, I first discuss the Prologue's lyricism by way of its multiple sources and forms before turning in the following section to the lyricism of the first four legends. I conclude with a discussion of Chaucer's own explicit invocation of the medieval discourse of "form" in this poem, and its implications for the modes of ethical practice that lyric has introduced in the *Legend*.

The "F" Prologue, in particular, draws heavily on lyric and lyrical sources: French *marguerite* poems by Froissart, Deschamps, and Machaut; the courtly "flower and leaf" lyric debates; long poems such as Machaut's *Jugement dou roy de Navarre*, which judge lyric poets for their crimes against lovers; lyrical fragments of Boccaccio's *Il Filostrato*; and a number of French *balades*.[42] Its opening polemic in favor of reading ("Wel ought us thane honouren and beleve / These bokes, there we han noon other preve," F.27–28) turns into a lyrical reverie, as the narrator professes his distraction from his studies in the month of May, when he goes out into the meadows to look at the daisies. The naturalism of the initial description ("To seen this flour ayein the sonne sprede," F.48) quickly enters the ambit of lyric with a courtly idiom: "So glad am I, whan that I have presence / Of it, to doon it alle reverence, / As she that is of alle floures flour / Fulfilled of al vertu and honour" (F.51–54).[43] This opening invokes exemplarity and lyric metonymically, with books and flowers, and also speaks in their idioms, polemical in the discussion of books ("Than mote we"; "Wel ought us") and lyrical in praise of the daisy ("blissful sighte"; "alle floures flour").

A reflection on practices of poetic making that is followed by an inset lyric (F.66–96) sets up the poetics of the longer work. While the Prologue's best-known lyric is the standalone *balade*, this earlier, unmarked interlude demonstrates a lyric mode that will be integral to the narrator's exploration of courtly love. Longing to praise the daisy, the narrator petitions contemporary love poets:

Allas, that I ne had Englyssh, ryme or prose,	
Suffisant this flour to preyse aryght!	
But helpeth, ye that han konnyng and myght,	
Ye lovers that kan make of sentement;	*write poetry about*
In this cas oghte ye be diligent	
To forthren me somwhat in my labour,	
Whethir ye ben with the leef or with the flour.	
For wel I wot that ye han her-biforn	
Of makyng ropen, and lad awey the corn,	*reaped*
And I come after, glenyng here and there,	
And am ful glad yf I may fynde an ere	
Of any goodly word that ye han left.	
And thogh it happen me rehercen eft	
That ye han in your fresshe songes sayd,	
Forbereth me, and beth nat evele apayd. (F.66–80)	

This address to love poets ("ye lovers that kan make of sentement") seems particularly directed at Chaucer's Continental peers. As J. L. Lowes has shown, the preceding lines in praise of the daisy are a patchwork of borrowings from Machaut, Froissart, and Deschamps, and the subsequent passage—which takes the form of a praise lyric—translates Boccaccio's *Il Filostrato* 1.2.1–4.[44] The invocation also alludes to a particular lyric practice, the poetic debates between the adherents of the "flower" and the "leaf" that took place in French and English courts as part of the May-day celebrations.[45] Further, it adapts the petitionary rhetoric of love lyric to an appeal to poets, suggesting a metapoetics of lyric that will be more explicitly realized in the following lines. In other words, this passage integrates lyric forms and their practices, an approach to lyricism that, as we shall see, has implications for its use later in the poem.

By his own admission, Chaucer's lyricism is belated: "I come after." Yet the two terms he uses to describe his poetic making, "glenyng" and "rehercen," merit examination. While the comparison between the poet's stale "glenyngs" and the "fresshe songs" of the French lyricists demonstrates the humility topos, the two terms also present lyric making as a recovery and revitalization of what might otherwise rot in the field once these poets have "lad awey the corn."[46] Without this poet's gleaning, good "ears" might go to waste; his rehearsing brings existing lyrics into new modes of circulation—that is, into practice. In this passage, Chaucer's georgic metaphor aligns even derivative poetry with social value.[47] Gleaning and rehearsing are tactics of preservation; the poet, here, is the tactician who recombines established forms into new lyrics.

The praise lyric that follows the invocation demonstrates this poetics.

She is the clernesse and the verray lyght
That in this derke world me wynt and ledeth.
The hert in-with my sorwfull brest yow dredeth
And loveth so sore that ye ben verrayly
The maistresse of my wit, and nothing I.
My word, my werk ys knyt so in youre bond
That, as an harpe obeieth to the hond
And maketh it soune after his fyngerynge,
Ryght so mowe ye oute of myn herte bringe
Swich vois, ryght as yow lyst, to laughe or pleyne.
Be ye my gide and lady sovereyne!
As to myn erthly god to yow I calle,
Bothe in this werk and in my sorwes alle. (F.84–96)

The more one reads it, the more complex this apparently straightforward lyric becomes. On its surface, it is a praise poem to the lady-daisy, a "gleaning" from the lyric makers whose help the poet has just invoked. This inset lyric amalgamates the opening lines of Boccaccio's *Il Filostrato* (which Chaucer omitted from *Troilus and Criseyde*) with language inspired by the long poems of Machaut and Deschamps.[48] In Chaucer's version, we notice the change in point of view, from third to second person, in line 86. The "She" of line 84 distinguishes the epideictic lyric from the invocation. Yet the rapid return to the second person invites a parallel reading of the inset lyric, in which it addresses the poets as much as the lady. Read in this way, the lyric expresses the speaker's sense of thralldom to his literary antecedents: "My word, my werk ys knyt so in youre bond."

The striking metaphor of the speaker as the "harp" that sings at the behest of the "hand" of his lady merits examination. Some readers have suggested that this metaphor derives from Guillaume de Machaut's *Dit de la harpe*, given the extensive Machauvian influence on the Prologue as a whole.[49] Machaut's poem allegorically compares his lady to a harp, enumerating her twenty-five virtues that correspond to the harp's twenty-five strings. As a modern editor of the poem notes, there is little direct correlation between the language of Machaut's poem and that of Chaucer's metaphor in the prologue.[50] In Chaucer's metaphor, the poet (or the poet's heart's voice) is the harp, and the lady is the hand; by contrast, Machaut's lady is the harp. Nonetheless, Machaut's allegory is not completely consistent, and features of it suggest that the harp is also to be understood as a metonym for lyric poetry. In the poem's opening section, Machaut defends the harp as the most noble of instruments, describing its affiliations with Orpheus, Apollo, and David. Its sound, too, is of the highest quality:

[I]e puis legierement prouuer,
Qu'on ne porroit pas instrument trouuer
De si plaisant ne de si cointe touche,
Quant blanche main de belle et bonne y touche,
Ne qu'en douceur a elle se compere. (25–29)

[I can easily show that you can find no other instrument of such a pleasant or elegant sound, when the white hand of a beautiful and good lady touches it, and that nothing compares to it in sweetness.][51]

Thus, before the extended allegory begins, Machaut's poem associates harp playing both with prominent mythic lyricists and with a lady. These allusions suggest that the harp signifies multiply, as the heart of the poet (a suggestion Chaucer makes explicit) and as an artist's musical or poetic work. In the poem's conclusion, Machaut claims he has hidden an anagram of his own name as well as that of his lady, but modern readers have been unable to discern her identity. Sylvia Huot has suggested that the solution to this crux is to understand the beloved as "none other than the conflation of lyricism and writerly craft that makes up his poetic oeuvre." But this association is inherently unstable; as Bruce Holsinger demonstrates, the very fragmentation of the poet by means of these figures and riddles "points to the perilously Orphic nature of medieval authorship."[52] In other words, this poem multiply figures the harp: as an exemplary lady, as the poet's heart, and as poetry itself. While we have no conclusive evidence that this poem is a source for Chaucer's inset lyric, we have seen in our discussion of Antigone's song that Chaucer's adaptation of Machaut's poetry is frequently tactical. The figure of the harp in Chaucer's Prologue, then, may express the speaker's affective response to the "rehersyng" of earlier lyrics, which brings forth in his own poetry "swich vois, ryght as yow lyst, to laughe or pleyne." But if the harp must obey the hand, it nonetheless produces the lyric voice, speaking while the hand is dumb. The image conveys the symbiosis of convention and voice, of text and practice. In the final couplet, poetic work ("this werk") and love-longing ("my sorwes alle") are at once subject to existing forms and invitations for improvisation and adaptation.[53]

Thus, the inset lyric at once practices tactical poetic making, in its contingent "gleaning," and sets up parallels between desire, poetic making, and the ethics of self-Other relations. The ostensibly constrained "voice" of the harp speaks from poetic conventions that it combines tactically. Further, the fact that this is, on its surface, a praise poem, gives it a certain formal kinship with the exempla to follow; for, although exempla are not by their nature epideictic, the poet "Geoffrey" is explicitly charged to write legends in praise of faithful women. This praise poem's plural readings thereby offer an alternative to exemplary totalizing. The lyric asks us to hold multiple meanings simultaneously: the addressee as lady, daisy, other poets, and harp-plucking hand; the speaking poet as lover, vassal, and harp. The lady's superior qualities are, of course, part of the convention of praise poetry, but note that this woman is, especially, a guide to the lover.[54] In this, she takes on the exemplary function, but in the doubling of the courtly love object and the Continental poets, Chaucer suggests that lyric's tactical practices can replace exemplary moralizing. Perhaps most important, Chaucer here transforms the language of his longer poetic sources into a lyric set piece. His gleanings yield both a guiding lyric and lyric object.

In short, Chaucer's invocation of the courtly love poets presents "glenyng" as a lyric tactic that at once evokes the accretive and lateral practices of casuistic reasoning (amassing sources and selecting among them) yet also offers an alternative ethical and interpretive practice in which the self multiplies by way of its relationships to multiple others (the lady, the poets) and thereby considers an array of ethical options. Such a practice is further developed in the Prologue's standalone *balade*, "Hyd Absolon." Positioned as an occasional poem celebrating the arrival of the God of Love and his court, Chaucer's *balade* in praise of Alceste is an adaptation of three French versions by Thomas Paien, Guillaume de Machaut, and Jean Froissart.[55] All three French poems have a similar structure; they begin with allusions to figures of classical myth and conclude with the refrain, "Je voy assez, puis que je voy ma dame" ("I see enough, when I see my lady"). Chaucer's translation at once amplifies and challenges the latent exemplarity of his French sources. Consider the first stanza of each French *balade*. Paien's begins,

Ne quier veoir la biauté d'Absolon
Ne d'Ulixès le sens et la faconde,
Ne esprouver la force de Sanson,
Ne regarder que Dalila le tonde,
Ne cure n'ay par nul tour
Des yeux Argus ne de joie gringnour,
Car pour plaisance et sanz aÿde d'ame
Je voy assez, puis que je voy ma dame.[56]

[I don't seek to see the beauty of Absolon, nor the wit or eloquence of Ulysses, nor to test the strength of Samson, nor to watch Delilah tonsure him. I care not at all for the eyes of Argus or any greater joy, since for pleasure and without the help of any soul, I see enough when I see my lady.]

Machaut's creation, the second in a "double *balade*" that includes Paien's version, begins thus:

Quant Theseus, Herculès et Jason
Cercherent tout, et terre et mer parfonde,
Pour acroistre leur pris et leur renom
Et pour veoir bien tout l'estat dou monde,
Moult furent dignes d'onnour.
Mais quant je voy de biauté l'umble flour,
Assevis sui de tout, si que, par m'ame,
Je voy assez, puis que je voy ma dame.[57]

[When Theseus, Hercules, and Jason searched everywhere, both the deep sea and the land, to increase their glory and fame, and to see the whole state of the world, they were very worthy of honor. But when I see the modest flower of beauty, I am completely satisfied, so that, by my soul, I see enough when I see my lady.]

And Froissart's *balade* begins,

Ne quier veoir Medee ne Jason,
Ne trop avant lire ens ou mapemonde
Ne le musique Orpheüs ne le son,
Ne Hercules, qui cerqua tout le monde,
Ne Lucresse, qui tant fu bonne et monde,
Ne Penelope ossi, car, par Saint Jame,
Je voi assés, puisque je voi ma dame.[58]

[I do not seek to see Medea nor Jason, nor to read too deeply into the map of the world, nor do I seek the sound and music of Orpheus, nor Hercules, who circled the whole world, nor Lucrece, who was so good and virtuous, nor Penelope either, because, by Saint James, I see enough when I see my lady.]

All three of these *balades* take as their theme the sufficiency implied in the refrain's "assez" (enough). The sight of the lady is enough to satisfy all of their longings for experience, honor, glory, and worldliness. The French poems use classical allusions as points of comparison that gesture toward the capaciousness of human experience by representing its extremes: the epic quests of Theseus, Jason, and Hercules; the extraordinary qualities of Absolon, Ulysses, and Samson; the unearthly music of Orpheus. To some extent, these allusions are exemplary *imagines*, yet they do not function as models for the speaker or audience. Rather, the three French *balades* use these mythic figures to emphasize the *speaker's* willingness to forswear other forms of sublime experience in favor of the sight of his lady. Only incidentally do they imply that the lady in question is therefore exemplary.

   Chaucer's version transforms these allusions into exempla of beauty and virtue—in other words, the qualities he will go on to praise in the legends themselves—while simultaneously challenging the logic of exemplarity. Here is the F Prologue's *balade* in full:

Hyd, Absolon, thy gilte tresses clere;
Ester, ley thou thy meknesse al adown;

Hyd, Jonathas, al thy frendly manere;
Penalopee and Marcia Catoun,
Make of youre wifhod no comparysoun;
Hyde ye youre beautes, Ysoude and Eleyne:
My lady cometh, that al this may disteyne.

Thy faire body, lat yt nat appere,
Lavyne; and thou, Lucresse of Rome toun,
And Polixene, that boghten love so dere,
And Cleopatre, with al thy passyoun,
Hyde ye your trouthe of love and your renoun;
And thou, Tisbe, that hast for love swich peyne:
My lady cometh, that al this may disteyne.

Herro, Dido, Laudomia, alle yfere,
And Phillis, hangyng for thy Demophoun,
And Canace, espied by thy chere,
Ysiphile, betrayed with Jasoun,
Maketh of your trouthe neythir boost ne soun;
Nor Ypermystre or Adriane, ye tweyne:
My lady cometh, that al this may dysteyne. (F.249–69)

Chaucer's list of names invokes the exemplary *imago*, with biblical and classical characters standing for their most notable qualities. Many of these characters will be subjects of narrative exempla (*paradigma*) in the legends
themselves. The use of the exemplary image in the *balade* suggests the tension
between the exemplary attribute and the contingencies of narrative, as well
as the partiality of any kind of exemplary "showing." Instead, the anaphora
on "hyd" challenges the premise that exempla can make visible and manifest
the salient ethics of old stories and mythic characters. Yet the naming of
exemplary women is itself a kind of showing, as is the *occupatio* by which the
lyric names their traits to be concealed: "Hyd Absolon, thy gilte tresses clere";
"Thy faire body, lat yt nat appere, / Lavyne"; "Phillis, hangyng for thy
Demophon."

Further, the *balade*'s refrain reminds us of the circular logic of exemplarity, in which the more exemplary a figure, the more she exceeds exemplarity
itself: "My lady cometh, that al this may disteyne." The French analogues say
"Je voy assez, puis que je voy ma dame" ("I see enough, when I see my lady"):

seeing the lady is sufficient to replace all manner of extraordinary experience. But Chaucer's refrain omits the repetition of "see," instead using the unusual verb "disteyne." According to the *Middle English Dictionary*, Chaucer's use of the verb is one of the first in English, meaning "*fig.* to dim or obscure."[59] Since this use has no known English precedent, it is possible that Chaucer was thinking more directly of the French *desteindre*, which means to put out or extinguish a source of light such as a candle; in other words, to eliminate the very possibility of seeing.[60] The French meaning even more literally suggests what Aranye Fradenburg calls Alceste's "power to drain the heat and light, the life and visibility, from her rivals" that demonstrates her exemplary exemplarity.[61] Alceste is the Prologue's example from conduct, the "kalender . . . / To any woman that wol lover bee," as the God of Love says (F.542–43).[62]

In short, Chaucer's *balade* foregrounds the exemplarism latent in the French sources in order to challenge the ethical logic of exemplary form. Exempla can obscure as much as they can illuminate. What Ernst Robert Curtius calls the "outdoing" topos thus seems to be another context for the *balade*.[63] In this idiom, the poet elevates a person or event by disparaging antecedents. Frequently used to praise poets, the commonplace was probably known to Chaucer from Statius, Lucan, or Dante. In Latin, it is often signaled by *cedat* or *taceat*: "let . . . yield" or "let . . . be silent." Using the outdoing topos with verbs of seeing emphasizes a particularly medieval form of exemplarity based on showing. It also opens up a temporal gap between Alceste's lyric presence and the exemplary figures of the past. This is especially true in the F Prologue's version of the *balade*, which does not use Alceste's classical name but calls her only "my lady." The making present of the past is, as we have seen, a constitutive feature of both lyric and exemplum, in the tactics of "gleaning," the recursiveness of refrain, and in the historical claims of exemplary narrative. "Hyd Absolon" brings together these common formal features in a practice that introduces recursiveness and repetition into the lateral acquisitiveness of conventional exemplarity.

Alceste's plurality, in lyric and exemplum, is important to Chaucer's formal project. As the daisy and the object of the lover's desire, she is a figure for multiple lyric idioms: the "flower" of the flower and leaf lyric debates, the "marguerite" of the *dits de la marguerite*, the lady of courtly love poetry. As the subject of the outdoing topos, as well as of the ultimate legend in the God of Love's plan for the work, she participates in all three exemplary forms: the example from conduct, the *imago*, and the *paradigma*.[64] This is not to reduce Alceste to a mere cipher; rather, it is this character's ability to signify multiply (as historical figure, as flower, and as lyric) that allows her to body forth the effects of lyric tactics on exemplary ethics.[65] As we have seen, in Chaucer's conception, the lyric object is implicated in lyric making, the "hand" that brings forth the voice of the "harp."

Both the *balade* and the praise poem, then, demonstrate lyric forms that are determined by tactical practices: gleaning and recombining poetic commonplaces, conjoining typically discrete forms, and reimagining centralized power relations into eccentric "wandering lines" (Certeau's *lignes d'erre*). The prologue's lyrics further present their tactics as directly engaging with exemplary form and ethics. Repurposing the "goodly words" left by prior poets into a praise-lyric, using the repetitions of the *balade* form, lyric, like exemplum, makes present what was in the past. Chaucer's literary treatment of Alceste in the *balade* demonstrates lyric's ability to suspend the exemplary drive toward closure and "showing." Less "grisly" than the carol in the "Dancers of Colbek" episode, lyric in the Prologue of the *Legend* is equally recursive. If casuistic reasoning resists the top-down imperatives of ethics derived from abstract principles, lyric's tactics introduce recursion and iteration into exemplarity's totalizing tendencies.

Lyric and Form(s) in the Legends

While the Prologue has often been praised as the most lyrical section of the long poem, lyric maintains a minor but pervasive presence throughout the legends themselves and continues the formal and ethical project set forth in the Prologue. Robert Frank's reading of the *Legend* claims that while Chaucer excises lyric from this poem's narrative, lyric nonetheless informs Chaucer's exemplarity in the affective quality of the tales' morals.[66] In this section, I show how lyric interludes in the first four legends—Cleopatra, Thisbe, Dido, and Hypsipyle and Medea—reform exemplary authority. Sheila Delany has said that "the Prologue and legends are related as theory and practice"; in fact, the lyric presence in both the prologue and legends shows how a lyric theory emerges out of practice.[67]

The first two legends in the collection appear to absorb lyric into the exemplary narrative. Both "Cleopatra" and "Thisbe" conclude with a penultimate speech by the heroine, followed by a moral that provides formal closure. These interludes draw on a range of lyric features, from the specifically medieval lyric language of noesis, or unity-in-diversity, to features more commonly associated with modern conceptions of the lyric genre, such as figuration and temporal suspension. What distinguishes them all is their place in the narratives, conjoint with or even supplanting the closing moral of a typical exemplum. Each lyrical soliloquy tactically navigates the apparent closure of exemplary morality in order to pose its own ethical issue, that of the relationship between the self and what Aranye Fradenburg has called the "proximate Other," the at once strange and familiar figure that inspires erotic and redemptive drives in the beholding subject.[68] For instance, in Cleopatra's speech, addressed to Antony's corpse, she affirms the "covenant" she made when she swore her love to him:

And in myself this covenaunt made I tho
That ryght swich as ye felten, wel or wo,
As fer forth as it in my power lay,
Unreprovable unto my wyfhod ay,
The same wolde I fele, lyf or deth—(688–92)

Cleopatra's speech unites the lovers in "feeling"; their affective experiences, although separated by their individual physical forms, will be united as far as her agency ("power") allows. Although, in Frank's view, this lament is not a courtly love "complaint," it draws on a medieval lyric idiom.[69] Cleopatra's vision of radical intersubjectivity engages what Peter Dronke identifies as the "unity-in-diversity" of the noetic vision of love between earthly and divine beings that characterizes many medieval love lyrics.[70] But it also recognizes the disparity of experience and emotion between the self and Fradenburg's "proximate Other." The lyric is thus also about the aspirations of the exemplum, the ways in which it hopes to reconcile these differences by relating the narrative's characters to the audience. Cleopatra's speech integrates lyrical noesis with an ethical practice that accounts for difference.

In the next legend, "Thisbe," Pyramus commits suicide when he believes Thisbe dead; finding his body, she utters a lyric soliloquy before killing herself. Like Cleopatra, Thisbe asserts her suicide as a means for achieving unity-in-diversity with her lover:

And thogh that nothing, save the deth only,
Mighte thee fro me departe trewely,
Thow shalt no more departe now fro me
Than fro the deth, for I wol go with thee. (896–99)

But unlike Cleopatra, Thisbe self-exemplifies: "But God forbede but a woman can / Ben as trewe in lovynge as a man! / And for my part, I shal anon it kythe [show]" (910–12). As some readers have noted, this legend creates a problem for the God of Love's exemplary mandate, to praise women by vilifying men, since both Pyramus and Thisbe are equally martyrs for love.[71] The conclusion to Thisbe's soliloquy uses a lyric convention to address this problem. Lyric language of unity-in-diversity becomes the basis for Thisbe's self-moralization. In her soliloquy, the lyric voice assumes the authoritative voice of exemplarity within its own form. The conclusion of the tale, the narrator's statement of the exemplary moral ("Here may ye se, what lovere so he be / A woman dar and can as wel as he," 922–23), reads as a belated echo of this powerful lyric voice.

The first two legends integrate the moral or *sententia* with a lyric voice, whose noetic navigation between self and Other provides the audience less with a maxim than with a pattern or *forma* of experience. The next two legends, "Dido" and "Hypsipyle and Medea," adapt segments of Ovid's *Heroides* into lyrical interludes that suspend narrative and ethical closure. These legends do not place their explicit morals at the end of the text. In Dido, the polemical voice interjects after the private "marriage" of Dido and Aeneas and before his desertion:

O sely wemen, ful of innocence,
Ful of pite, of trouthe and conscience,
What maketh yow to men to truste so?
Have ye swych routhe upon hyre feyned wo,
And han swich olde ensaumples yow beforn? (1254–58)

In what is likely the most familiar of the legends to Chaucer's audience, the moral can precede the narrative of betrayal because that narrative is already a common currency. But this is also a moral about the failure of exemplarity; women will trust unworthy men despite the "olde ensaumples."[72] Although the moral is already part of the audience's storehouse of exemplary knowledge, they disregard it.

Where narrative fails, can lyric be more effective? In this and the next legend, Chaucer adapts excerpts from Ovid's *Heroides* into set pieces with proto-modern lyric features, such as brevity, apostrophe, and rhetorical density.[73] Consider the conclusion of "Dido":

She wrot a lettre anon that thus began:
"Ryght so," quod she, "as that the white swan
Ayens his deth begynnyth for to synge,
Right so to yow make I my compleynynge.
Not that I trowe to geten yow ageyn,
For wel I wot that it is al in veyn,
Syn that the goddes been contraire to me.
But syn my name is lost thorugh yow," quod she,
"I may wel lese on yow a word or letter,
Al be it that I shal ben nevere the better;
For thilke wynd that blew youre ship awey,
The same wynd hath blowe awey youre fey."
But who wol al this letter have in mynde,
Rede Ovyde, and in hym he shal it fynde. (1354–67)

Although its source, Ovid's *Heroides* 7, is a letter containing both lyric and narrative elements, this passage excerpts and rearranges its parts in order to separate them.[74] Ovid's poem begins with the lyrical metaphors translated in the passage above before turning to a more narrative account of seduction and betrayal. By concluding his tale with this rich figurative language, Chaucer foregrounds the lyricism of the *Heroides* and puts the lyric form in the position of the exemplary moral. Indeed, Chaucer's conclusion directs the reader, essentially, to yet another telling of the tale, the version in the *Heroides*. The apparently conclusive lyric, then, points to the recursiveness of practical reasoning, which must retread the same ground over and over. The lyric voice is lost speech ("I may wel lese on yow a word or letter") to Aeneas but may perhaps be retained by the audience. Given that explicit moralizing in the middle of the tale bemoans the failure of exemplarity to change behavior, positioning this lyric at the end of the tale suggests that perhaps lyric provides a more apposite form for ethical reasoning than the *paradigma*.

The next legend, "Hypsipyle and Medea," continues to experiment with the arrangement of its formal elements. The twenty-eight-line introduction to the tale begins, "Thow rote of false lovers, Duc Jasoun" and concludes, "On Jason this ensaumple is wel ysene / By Isiphile and Medea the queene" (1368, 1394–95). Jason is the exemplum in this story, and moralizing him before narrating his deeds suggests the failure of exemplarity to affect behavior.[75] Indeed, the description of Jason in the "Medea" section portrays him as a collection of appearances and similarities, an exemplary *similitudo*: "Now was Jason a semely man withalle, / And lyk a lord, and hadde a gret renoun, / And of his lok as real as a leoun" (1603–5). Medea's concluding letter, again occupying the formal place of the moral, puts these exemplary features in lyric form:

"Whi lykede me thy yelwe her to se
More than the boundes of myn honeste?
Why lykede me thy youthe and thy fayrnesse,
And of thy tonge, the infynyt graciousnesse?
O, haddest thow in thy conquest ded ybe
Ful mikel untrouthe hadde ther deyd with the!"
Wel can Ovyde hire letter in vers endyte,
Which were as now to long for me to wryte. (1672–79)

Chaucer uses lyric compactness to powerful effect here. The "Whi lykede me" anaphora unites Jason's outward appeal with Medea's suffering in a way that narrative seriality cannot. The first four lines of Medea's lament take their inspiration from two lines of *Heroides* 12: "Why did I too greatly delight in those golden locks of yours, in your comely ways, and in the false graces of your tongue?"[76] In Chaucer's version, Medea regrets that Jason's physicality, which was introduced in terms of the exemplary *similitudo*, dulled her ethical acumen. The polyptoton of the final couplet ("ded"/"deyd") reminds the audience of the bloody coda of this tale that Chaucer omits: Medea's ruthless killing of King Pelias; of Jason's third wife, Creusa; and of their own children. These two lines derive from Medea's lament, in the *Heroides*, that Jason was not killed by the Theban warriors that sprang up when he sowed dragons' teeth.[77] Chaucer's adaptation of the Ovidian source transforms Medea's exemplarity, making her, if only briefly, into an object of sympathy (as a betrayed woman) rather than a figure of murderous female iniquity. Although some readers have read this omission as evidence of this legend's comic or ironic intention, I think Chaucer had a more serious formal purpose.[78] Medea's utterance here demonstrates how lyric can replace the showings of the exemplum (recalling "Hyd Absolon") and suspend us in contingency without turning a blind eye to outcomes. Our own seduction, as readers, by the vivid imagery and plangency of this lyric makes us receptive to Medea's sorrow. The polyptoton "ded/deyd" and the concluding reference to the full story in Ovid gesture toward an ending—and moral—that the audience knows well even as the rhetoric and form of this passage suspend its readers in a lyric moment.

*   *   *

By way of conclusion, I will briefly discuss two passages in the *Legend of Good Women* that suggest Chaucer's interest in addressing medieval concepts of form, which is at once metaphysical and literary, with tactical practices. These passages use metaphysical language to pose the problem of the protean nature of exemplary narrative and its moral. Taken together, they suggest that in collecting and aggregating exempla in the *Legend*, Chaucer is meditating on literary form. The first occurs in "Hypsipyle and Medea" as a simile for Jason's fickleness:

As mater apetiteth forme alwey
And from forme into forme it passen may
Or as a welle that were botomles
Ryght so can false Jason have no pes. (1582–85)

The second is the opening to the "Legend of Philomela," which begins with the epigraph *Deus dator formarum*, followed by a translation and amplification:

Thou yevere of the formes, that hast wrought
This fayre world and bar it in thy thought
Eternaly er thow thy werk began,
Why madest thow, unto the slaunder of man,
Or, al be that it was nat thy doing,
As for that fyn, to make swich a thyng,
Whi sufferest thow that Tereus was bore,
That is in love so fals and so forswore,
That fro this world up to the firste hevene
Corrumpeth whan that folk his name nevene? (2228–37)

Although these two invocations of form appear to allude to conflicting metaphysical theories, Chaucer's adaptation of his sources in both instances unites them in a critique that announces his own formal project in the poem. The first passage, "As mater apetiteth forme alwey . . . ," expresses the Aristotelian theory of hylomorphism, in which matter could only exist with a shaping form.[79] Describing his concept, Aristotle likens matter to female lust: "the form cannot desire itself, because it is not in need of anything. . . . It is the matter which does the desiring. You might liken it to a woman longing for a man."[80] However, Chaucer's language derives from Guido della Colonne's *Historia Destructionis Troiae*. Guido uses the Aristotelian concept and the verb *appetere* to describe Medea's typically feminine lust. "For we know that the heart of woman always seeks [*appetere*] a husband, just as matter always seeks [*appetit*] form. Oh, would that matter, passing once into form, could be said to be content with the form it has received. But just as it is known that matter proceeds from form to form, so the dissolute desire of women proceeds from man to man, so that it may be believed without limit, since it is of an unfathomable depth."[81]

The sources of the epigraph, "*Deus dator formarum*," and of Chaucer's amplification, "Thou yevere of the formes . . . ," are uncertain. However, it is clear that both refer to a neo-Platonic conception of the relationship between form and matter, in which God's ideal forms become imperfectly material. These ideas were widely disseminated among medieval philosophers and poets: Augustine, Boethius, Jean de Meun, Avicenna, and a number of scholastic commentators allude to a "giver of forms."[82] While the direct referents of both passages are metaphysical, medieval thinkers also understood the concept of "form" in a rhetorical and literary sense. Boethius, for instance, uses Aristotelian language in Book 4 of *De Topicis Differentiis* to demonstrate how *materia* is coextensive with its rhetorical form. "The matter of this discipline [of rhetoric] is every subject proposed for a speech. But, for the most part, it is a political question. The species of rhetoric come into this [matter, namely, the political question] and take [the] matter to themselves as if they were forms of a certain sort; . . . so that the political question [i.e., the matter], which heretofore was without form as far as the species go, accepts bounds and becomes subject to one or another of the species of rhetoric."[83] In other words, the "matter," which Boethius calls "the political question," cannot be found independent of its rhetorical form in one of the three species of rhetoric: judicial, deliberative, or epideictic.[84] By the thirteenth century, as Alastair Minnis has observed, "The human *auctor*, writer of the literal sense, produced the *forma* of his text."[85] He shaped his "matter," or content, by two means: the *forma tractandi*, or the style of the work, and *forma tractatus*, its structure. The form of a work is explicitly linked to its function and effects. Thus, the style of a treatise on what medieval thinkers called "human science"—philosophy or the natural sciences—should be analytical and unadorned in order to appeal to the intellect. By contrast, scripture and theological writings ("divine science") should appeal to the "disposition" or affective part of the human mind and use a full range of rhetorical figures. Because of form's duality, the *forma tractatus*, or structure of a work, was understood to be the physical shape best suited to its style. This kind of structure was most often discussed in terms of the work's divisions into books and chapters. Organizing knowledge was the prerogative and obligation of the author.

In short, the medieval sense of "form" was always multiple: metaphysical and literary, abstract and material, social and textual. Many of the above descriptions of form seem to reach toward a notion of tactical practice that would accommodate the improvisatory and inconclusive ("endless," to Guido) relationships between form and matter. The *Legend of Good Women*'s passages on form suggest one such tactic in their adaptations of their sources. The poem's version of Guido's Aristotelian simile in "Medea"—"Mater apetiteth form alwey"—reverses the typical gendering of matter and form. Matter, conventionally feminized for its mutability, corresponds to Jason in the simile, while the women he betrays are the forms. This change fulfills the God of Love's exemplary mandate to praise faithful women and disparage faithless men, and it also comments on how literary form and matter are mutually constitutive. Along with the legend of Cleopatra, "Medea" is the story that is perhaps the most altered by its conversion into an exemplum. Like Chaucer's audience, most of us know Medea's tale as a tragedy of female vengeance and Jason's as that of heroic conquest. Changing the form of these stories to an exemplum with lyric insets demonstrates just how protean *materia* can be. Although many readers have accounted for Chaucer's alteration of this tale by saying it is intentionally "bad" or comic, in rebellion against his charge, such readings overlook an opportunity to take seriously the poetics expressed in the translation of Guido.[86] It is, in fact, the tale's passing from form to form—from exemplum to lyric—that allows the *Legend* to suggest a tactics of ethical practice by means of a tactics of form.

Chaucer's elaboration of the epigraph to "Philomela" suggests that Tereus's negative exemplarity—represented here in the dual form of the *imago*, or his name, and his exemplum or narrative—corrupts the idealized forms of the "firste hevene." If neo-Platonic formalism relies on an increasingly weakened imitation of the divine forms, Tereus's crimes perturb a hierarchy that should proceed in a logical and subordinated relationship. Chaucer's change of form, in his translation, also critiques exemplarity. He turns a maxim, *Deus dator formarum*, into a critique by using a lyric rhetoric of apostrophe: "Thow yevere of the formes."[87] Indeed, apostrophe governs the structure of the tale's opening sentence: "Why madest thow . . . Whi suffrest thow . . . ?" Here, in miniature, is the lyric conversion of exemplary morality, the transformation of polemical closure (*Deus dator formarum*) into plural, unanswerable questions. The apostrophized questions are at once a tactic of adaptation and a tactic of reading, asking for a suspension of conclusiveness. The passage thus serves as both a formal and metaphysical critique. It disputes the top-down Platonic doctrine of forms by remaking its source along Aristotelian lines, and it transforms prescriptive exemplarity into lyric recursiveness and indeterminacy.

As the *Legend* suggests, matter's appetite for form, if promiscuous, can also be generative. The women's stories need not be bound by the God of Love's mandate or indeed by the form of the exemplum that fuses narrative and moral. Introducing lyric and its tactics into the exemplary form is at once radical and natural, a literary hylomorphism that acknowledges the interdependence of form and practice. The *Legend of Good Women* explores the formal and ethical potentials of a lyric genre that is shaped as much by its formal features as by its practice: in particular, its tactics for transforming a positivist exemplarity into a suspensive and iterative ethical practice. While its formal qualities comprise both earlier medieval and later proto-modern lyric conventions, their prominence in relation to the exemplum implies that form has practical motivations and effects. In Chaucer's *Legend*, lyric tactics suspend both the didactic trajectory of the exemplum and the lateral movement of its logic, inviting new pathways through the old forms and new forms for the old matter.

Conclusion

One founding myth of modern lyric is Ovid's tale of Orpheus and Eurydice, in which poetry emerges from irreparable loss. When Eurydice dies of snake-bite on their wedding day, the harper Orpheus pursues her to the underworld. The beauty of Orpheus's song persuades Hades to defy what seems to be a universal law, the finality of death, and to surrender Eurydice. But Orpheus disobeys Hades's one proscription as he leads her out of the underworld: with a single backward glance of love and fear, Orpheus loses Eurydice forever. According to one reading of this legend, lyric is born of Orpheus's subsequent lifelong laments for his frailty. In this model, the genre is tinged with, if not identical to, elegy, a literary "work of mourning" that offers consolation even as it confirms loss.[1]

The work of mourning sometimes seems to extend to the recovery, editing, and publication of early English lyrics, whose anthologists often adopt an elegiac tone. Richard Tottel's 1557 collection, *Songs and Sonnettes, written by the ryght honorable Lorde Henry Howard late Earle of Surrey, and other* (commonly called "Tottel's *Miscellany*"), is a landmark in lyric history. This first anthology of Tudor Petrarchan verse largely consists of works by Surrey and by Thomas Wyatt, as well as other named and anonymous poets. Tottel's address to his readers is perhaps disingenuously defensive: "It resteth now (gentle reder) that thou thinke it not evil don, to publishe, to the honor of the english tong, and for profit of the studious of Englishe eloquence, those workes which the ungentle horders up of such tresure have heretofore envied the."[2] Tottel's collection saves these lyrics from the exclusive delectation of the "ungentle horders" by putting them into print. Older lyrics, like medieval literature generally, are further threatened by the fragility and sometimes outright abuse of their material forms. In the preface to the fourth edition (1794) of his *Reliques of Ancient Poetry*, Thomas Percy describes the editorial challenges of working with his sources: "[T]he Editor has endeavored to be as faithful as the imperfect state of his materials would admit. For, these old popular rhimes being many of them copied only from illiterate transcripts, or the imperfect recitation of itinerant ballad-singers, have, as might be expected, been handed down to us with less care than any other writings in the world. And the old copies, whether MS. or printed, were often so defective or corrupted, that a scrupulous adherence to their wretched readings would only have exhibited unintelligible nonsense."[3] The story of origins of Percy's folio manuscript is indeed one of near loss; according to an oft-repeated tale, he claimed to have rescued it from the house of Humphrey Pitt, whose maids "were using it to light the fire."[4] Elegiac antiquarianism is by no means limited to earlier compilers of medieval poetry; R. M. Wilson's 1952 collection of what he calls the "lost literature" of medieval England, which includes marginal or fragmented lyrics, demonstrates how modern readers of premodern literature, too, are haunted by an Orphic prospect of loss.

But the Middle Ages had another legend of Orpheus, marked by Eurydice's return from the underworld, which replaces the losses of the Ovidian version with accretion, recuperation, and transformation.[5] The anonymous Middle English verse romance *Sir Orfeo*, a version of this tradition, was probably composed early in the fourteenth century. Its protagonist is a figure of poetic and social stature, a harper and English "king" of Winchester. His queen, "Herodis," dreams that she will be abducted by the king of fairies. Upon waking, Herodis is mad with fear: she tears her skin and clothes and finally falls into a faint. Orfeo's first words in the poem are a lyrical response to her death-like state:

O lef liif, what is te	
That ever yete hast ben so stille	
And now gredest wonder schille?	*cries; shrilly*
Thi bodi, that was so white y-core,	*beautifully*
With thine nailes is al to-tore.	
Allas! thi rode, that was so red,	*complexion*
Is al wan, as thou were ded. (102–8)[6]	

As Bruce Holsinger has observed, many medieval versions of the Ovidian Orphic legend emphasize the fragmentation of *Orpheus*'s body after his loss of Eurydice. Such readings center on the homoerotic coda to Ovid's legend, in which Orpheus rejects the love of women in favor of sex with young boys and men.[7] It is significant, then, to note that Sir Orfeo's first lament describes the destruction of Herodis's body and, further, that he employs specific lyric conventions—the *ubi sunt* topos, an inverted blazon—in this speech.[8] The *ubi sunt* topos appears again in a subsequent lyric interlude, after Orfeo, having lost Herodis to the fairies, abandons his kingdom and flees to the wilderness.

He that hadde y-werd the fowe and griis,	*speckled and gray fur*
And on bed the purper biis,	*linens*
Now on hard hethe he lith,	
With leves and gresse he him writh.	*covers himself*
He that hadde had castels and tours,	
River, forest, frith with flours,	*meadows*
Now, thei it comenci to snew and frese,	
This king mot make his bed in mese.	*moss*
He that had y-had knightes of priis	*nobility*
Bifor him kneland, and levedis,	
Now seth he nothing that him liketh,	
Bot wilde wormes bi him striketh.	*snakes; go about*
He that had y-had plenté	
Of mete and drink, of ich deynté,	
Now may he al day digge and wrote	*dig*
Er he finde his fille of rote. (241–56)	

The *ubi sunt* topoi suggest death, but this poem is marked by a number of partial and incomplete deaths rather than the doubled but conclusive loss of Eurydice that characterizes Ovid's version. Sir Orfeo famously encounters an uncanny scene in the fairy kingdom:

Than gan he bihold about al	
And seighe liggeand within the wal	
Of folk that were thider y-brought,	
And thought dede, and nare nought.	*seemed*
Sum stode withouten hade,	
And sum non armes nade,	
And sum thurth the bodi hadde wounde,	
And sum lay wode, y-bounde,	*crazed*
And sum armed on hors sete,	
And sum astrangled as thai ete;	

And sum were in water adreynt,   *drowned*

And sum with fire al forschreynt. (387–98)   *shriveled*

As Elliot Kendall notes, these mangled human forms, which would be dead in the natural world but survive in the land of fairy, mark the inassimilable in the poem. They challenge the purported restorations (of life and of status) of the poem's ending.[9] But given the close connection between lyric and death marked by the *ubi sunt* passages, we might also think about what these uncanny figures mean for the poem's lyricism. Indeed, a modern reader might see parallels between these human forms and those of medieval lyrics, which frequently survive "without heads" or wounded "through the body." Even as Orfeo divests himself of the trappings of power and social identity, he retains his identity as a musician. In his ten years of his exile in the woods, he finds solace playing his harp, the only possession from his previous life, for birds and beasts. In the kingdom of the fairies, he introduces himself repeatedly as a "minstrel" and, as in the Ovidian version, charms the fairy king with his music. He maintains this identity once he returns with Herodis to Winchester, where "he tok his herbarwe [lodging] . . . / As a minstrel of pover liif" (484, 486). Minstrelsy and harping in particular provide continuity across imagined and false deaths: in the guise of an itinerant musician, Orfeo tells his loyal steward that he found his harp next to the dead body of a man in the woods, whom the steward presumes was his lord. And, once Orfeo is reinstated, poetic and musical agency passes to others: he and Herodis process into town accompanied by minstrels, and after his death, Breton harpers compose the lay of *Sir Orfeo*.

Lyrics and lyricism, in this poem as in medieval culture generally, have an oblique relationship to harping, minstrelsy, and the genre of the Breton lay. Like lyrics, lays seem to have been originally set to music but survive largely as unnotated texts. As Seth Lerer has observed, Sir Orfeo's powers lie as much in his rhetorical as in his musical talents, uniting in the poem's central figure the verbal and musical arts that converge in lyric and lay.[10] *Sir Orfeo*'s lyric interludes both punctuate and imitate the poem's dominant genre. They figure as tactics of a musico-poetic landscape through which the poem navigates questions of loss, often very differently than its Ovidian source. The emphasis in the Middle English poem is less on loss than on transformation, as each of the poem's simulacra of death comes to signify not obsolescence but change. As Peter Dronke puts it, versions of this tale in which Eurydice returns offer "the intimation that the here and the beyond are not irrevocably opposed to each other, that they form one world, that one who is endowed with a more-than-human power of vision (expressed in the figure of prophetic, quasi-divine song), or endowed with a more-than-human power of love, can know this greater whole, can pass from here to the beyond and back again."[11]

We might extend Dronke's interpretation of the redemptive ending—that it links the worlds of the living and dead—to reflect on the historicism and transhistoricism of lyric. Like human bodies, older lyrics are made of materials—text and music—that are subject to decay and loss. Heather Dubrow has thoughtfully articulated both the pitfalls and potential of trying to define this genre across traditional literary-historical boundaries. As she observes, while discussing a genre necessarily assumes transhistorical and constant characteristics for a body of texts, crossing period boundaries in a single study threatens to overlook the historical specificities of individual poems.[12] But just as Dronke suggests that "the here and the beyond are not irrevocably opposed to each other, that they form one world," the past and the present, too, can speak to each other through the persistence of lyric poems and lyric theory across periodizing boundaries. While much of this discourse has emphasized the vulnerability of older lyrics—Tottel's "ungentle horders," Percy's "reliques," Wilson's "lost literature"—the medieval Orphic myth suggests an alternate story of lyric origins, in which its losses—of the beloved, of the imagined "originary" or complete poem—are tactics of transformation, positive signs of a network of practice and protean agglomeration rather than entropic decay. Understood in this way, the "fragments" and "relics" of medieval lyric that survive into our day are also lyric tactics, instances of the genre's navigation of its available modes, in writing, in performance (for instance, in modern recordings of these lyrics), and in the modern editing and criticism of medieval lyrics that accrete meanings to these persistent forms. In a thoughtful essay on anachronism, Margareta de Grazia makes the case for reconsidering our revulsion toward this term and concept. Antipathy toward anachronism, in her view, emerges less from a desire to respect historical "difference" than from a disciplinary anxiety, which requires that the past be irrecoverably lost, dead, and buried. "Would the past vanish if, like Eurydice, it were viewed head on?" asks de Grazia. Strict historical periodization, while valuable, leaves in the shadows other ways of understanding the past, through literary rather than empirical methods.[13]

The anachronisms of the medieval *Sir Orfeo* align with this book's premise, that medieval insular lyrics can be integrated with a larger lyric tradition if they are understood through their practices rather than their forms and, further, that such a model promotes a more diverse literary-historical narrative of genre. *Sir Orfeo*'s lyric insets represent death through its commonplaces but forestall complete loss. Instead, each of the poem's false deaths is accretive, recuperative, and restorative. Forms change—Orfeo loses his title, Herodis is abducted from her home—yet lyric practice navigates these changes and turns loss into transformation. *Sir Orfeo*'s lyrics constitute a tactic of elegy, invoking loss while evading it. What matters is less the substitution of symbol for presence than the *transformation* of a persistent lyric presence into a constellation of practices. Thus, to conclude this book, I discuss two lyrics that anticipate certain material and formal features conventionally associated with modern lyricism, yet draw on medieval lyric tactics as they do so. I wish to suggest, with these readings, that the plural practices of the medieval lyric genre may inform the development of modern lyric and should be included in a more expansive understanding of the history of English lyric.

My two poems, the anonymous "Adam lay ibounden" and Sir Thomas Wyatt's "Whoso list to hunt," might appear to form a diptych of medieval and modern lyric conventions. Yet when analyzed through the practices they represent and their material witnesses, we see that in fact each involves a dialectic of medieval lyric practices and modern lyric forms. "Adam lay ibounden" survives in one of the first exclusively lyric anthologies of England, the fifteenth-century British Library MS Sloane 2593. Here is the poem in full:

Adam lay ibounden
Bounden in a bond;
Foure thousand winter
Thowt he not too long.
And all was for an appil,
An appil that he took,
As clerkes finden wreten
In here book.

Ne hadde the appil take ben,
The appil taken ben,
Ne hadde never our lady
A ben hevene quen.

Blissed be the time
That appil take was!
Therfore we moun singen
"Deo gracias!"[14]   *Thanks be to God*

This poem's simple language and repetition, as well as its invocation of two
medieval commonplaces—the *felix culpa*, or "happy sin," and the *vinculum
amoris*, or "chain of love"—might seem to exemplify the kind of medieval
lyric poem that early modern lyricists did not so much reject as completely
ignore, in favor of the secularism, classical style, and psychological complexity
of Petrarchan lyric.[15] Yet its practices exemplify both the lyric tactics that
have been the subject of this book as well as anticipating the cohesion of the
modern lyric genre. MS Sloane 2593 collects mostly carols (without musical
notation), frequently recorded with their refrains at the head of the text as a
kind of incipit. It is one of the earliest English "songbooks," the genre-
making books that had been produced for centuries on the Continent that
collect these poems according to form and author, delimiting a discrete category, if not yet quite a genre, of lyric poetry. As Daniel Wakelin points out
in his study of this manuscript, carols had well-defined written forms that
determined their performance. "The carol is not only sound: it is inherently
a form of writing, too."[16] "Adam lay ibounden" at once inscribes itself in
and differentiates itself from clerical written practice, as authorized salvation
history ("As clerkes finden wreten / In here book") is formally supplemented
by song in the parallel place in the next stanza: "Therfore we moun singen /
'Deo gracias!'" The Latin song is both internal and external to the lyric,
which inscribes and describes its performance.

The poem's rhetoric suggests how textual practices change with time and
thematizes temporality as literary accretion. Although not apparently a carol,
its use of repetition evokes the structure of the carol's burden (as discussed
in Chapter 4). The conduplication of "bounden," "appil," and "taken ben"
amplifies the significance of these elements of the poem and the salvation
history on which it is based. Its expansive temporality is signaled in its third
and fourth lines: "Foure thousand winter / Thowt he [Adam] not too long"
to wait for salvation. This etiological history, with original sin causing the
need for redemption, takes the material form of the book: "As clerkes finden
wreten / In here book." The second stanza's subjunctives pose an alternate
history, linked to the first with the repeated "appil." Because the apple was
taken and Mary became the queen of heaven, we can express our thanks by

using song's affective mode: "Therfore we moun singen / 'Deo gracias!'"
These parallel couplets resonate with the distinction between lyric's affective
performance and its doctrinal meaning that we have seen in William Herebert's Commonplace Book. The second stanza's etiology concludes with
song, a tactic of salvation as well as of lyric temporality. "Adam lay ibounden"
asserts a concurrent and interdependent lyric practice of performance and
writing, and conduplication is a rhetorical form of this dual practice, as the
repetition of words inscribes the past onto the present. But it also participates
in the genre-making force of the lyric anthology, surviving alongside and in
formal dialogue with a group of English carols.

Thomas Wyatt's "Whoso list to hunt" differs strikingly from "Adam lay
ibounden," secular and classical in style where the earlier poem is devotional
and plain. A translation of Petrarch's poem 190 from the *Canzoniere*, it adapts
the classical trope of the loved woman as the hunted deer that has its origins
in myth, especially the story of Diana and Actaeon. Here is Wyatt's sonnet:

Whoso list to hunt, I know where is an hind,
But as for me, helas, I may no more.
The vain travail hath wearied me so sore,
I am of them that farthest cometh behind.
Yet may I by no means my wearied mind
Draw from the deer, but as she fleeth afore
Fainting I follow. I leave off therefore
Sithens in a net I seek to hold the wind.   *Since*
Who list her hunt, I put him out of doubt,
As well as I may spend his time in vain.
And graven with diamonds in letters plain
There is written her fair neck round about:
"*Noli me tangere* for Caesar's I am,
And wild for to hold though I seem tame."[17]

A more literal English translation of Petrarch's poem 190 demonstrates
Wyatt's poetic license:

A doe of purest white upon green grass
Wearing two horns of gold appeared to me
Between two streams beneath a laurel's shade
At sunrise in that season not yet ripe.

The sight of her was so sweetly austere
That I left all my work to follow her,
Just like a miser who in search of treasure
With pleasure makes his effort bitterless.
"No one touch me," around her lovely neck
Was written out in diamonds, and in topaz:
"It pleased my Caesar to create me free."
The sun by now had climbed the sky midway,
My eyes were tired but not full from looking
When I fell in the water and she vanished.[18]

Again, the temporality of each poem is significant. Petrarch's original is written in a simple narrative past tense, describing the poem's events sequentially and concluding with a kind of death: the speaker's near drowning, the doe's disappearance. The tone of Wyatt's speaker is world-weary: although he has played the game of love and professes to have abandoned it, his loss remains inconclusive: "Yet may I by no means my wearied mind / Draw from the deer, but as she fleeth afore / Fainting I follow." Addressing the poem to "whoso list to hunt," he anticipates how others will repeat his labors. This adaptation more strongly evokes the partial and transformative losses of the English "Sir Orfeo" than the conclusiveness of Ovid's legend and Petrarch's sonnet.

Wyatt's lyric labors, too, are tactical. His translation alters the conclusive telos of the Petrarchan sonnet, suggesting multiple (if unsuccessful) attempts to entrap the deer. It also poses the lyric poem as a multigeneric and multilingual form. Wyatt's "helas" is, of course, a variant of the English "alas." But more specifically, it is what the *Oxford English Dictionary* describes as a "parallel French expression" that gained popularity in early modern English. While the more common "alas/allas" spelling is witnessed as early as the thirteenth century, "helas" invokes the French etymology, "ha, las."[19] Wyatt elsewhere transforms Petrarch's Italian with the biblical Latin phrase "*Noli me tangere*" (John 20:17). His rendering of the inscription is, in fact, doubly mediated, since it derives most directly from the editorial commentary in a popular anthology of Petrarch's poetry that circulated in Tudor England.[20] Even as Wyatt's sonnet takes up themes of exhaustion and imprisonment, it exemplifies a vital and expansive lyricism that integrates multiple sources and languages. In "Adam lay ibounden," the Latin phrase "*Deo gracias*" is liturgical and performative; in Wyatt's poem, "*Noli me tangere*" is emphatically written ("graven"). Where the medieval poem begins in bondage that is released in Latin lyric utterance, the early modern sonnet concludes with writing as a fetter. Yet, as readers of this sonnet have observed, for Wyatt, poetry is far from a closed practice. His adaptations of Petrarch, while perhaps expressing his own futile and dangerous love for Anne Boleyn, participate in an early modern practice of "imitation" that is layered and allusive, wherein a single poem might invoke multiple sources.[21] This practice influenced not only poets but also readers, inviting them into a "participatory poetics" of mediation and interpretation.[22]

The prolepsis of "Whoso list to hunt," as it anticipates others' vain pursuits of the deer, reflects the poem's own material history as well. The poem's earliest witness is British Library Egerton MS 2711, simply called the "Egerton" manuscript by Wyatt scholars. Largely compiled during the poet's lifetime, this manuscript contains fair and working copies of many of Wyatt's poems in his hand and three others, one of which copied "Whoso list to hunt" on folio 7v.[23] The sonnet does not appear in the early canon-making lyric anthology, Tottel's *Miscellany*, although it is possible that Tottel used the Egerton manuscript to select poems for his collection.[24] Instead, the poem undergoes a process of early modern editing *within* the Egerton manuscript. Although Wyatt appears to have corrected or modified several of the poems in this manuscript that were not written in his own hand, signified by his informal signature, "Tho" or "Tho.," in the margin, this poem lacks the signature or any signs of Wyatt's editing.[25] Nicholas Grimald edited this poem, writing an "a" over "helas" among other emendations, and copied beside it the first stanza of Wyatt's "The restful place (To his bed)." Another editor wrote "Wyat" in the poem's margin and labeled it a "sonnet."[26] These editing practices appear to have their own coherence whose interest in canon making and standardization recalls, even as it differs from, conventions of printers like Tottel. Their accretions demonstrate that Wyatt's poem, in manuscript, is not being "hoarded" away but rather conceived as a text of record in the canon of Wyatt's poetry. And while it was not printed in Wyatt's lifetime or even in Tottel's *Miscellany*, "Whoso list to hunt" has entered the print canon of early modern Petrarchan sonnets in our own era, appearing continuously in the Norton *Anthologies of English Literature* from the second edition (1968) onward. Just as Wyatt's poem suggests that others will come after him to continue (if unsuccessfully) his work of chasing the deer, so too does the editorial history of this poem demonstrate how multiple and cross-temporal agents have transformed it. The poem itself draws on diverse written forms and sources, imagining them tactically as plural practices and witnesses. For Wyatt and for this poem, the written text is less definitive than generative, less a closed authorial product than an open space of interpretive and adaptive practice.[27]

Both "Adam lay ibounden" and "Whoso list to hunt" demonstrate how the past makes an indelible mark on the present, shaping practices of expression and representation. Their material forms bear witness to the tactics of lyric writing and performance, even as they occupy very different places in modern lyric canons and criticism. Like *Sir Orfeo*, each poem is constituted by loss, yet these losses leave behind not irreplaceable absence but rather proliferating representations, practices, tactics, and poems. Medieval lyric tactics, too, persist as poetry takes on a more recognizably modern form, suggesting that the practices that define the genre in later medieval England might profitably inform studies of later poetry. Like Sir Orfeo, perhaps we can find in these small deaths the transformations and persistence of a vital tradition.

NOTES

AND   Rothwell, William, gen. ed. *The Anglo-Norman Dictionary Online.*
Aberystwyth University and Swansea University, 2001.
http://www.anglo-norman.net/.

DIMEV   Mooney, Linne R., Daniel W. Mosser, and Elizabeth Solopova, eds.
Digital Index of Middle English Verse. http://dimev.net.

MED   McSparran, Frances, gen. ed. *Middle English Dictionary.* Ann Arbor:
University of Michigan, 2001. http://quod.lib.umich.edu/m/med/.

OED   *Oxford English Dictionary.* Oxford: Oxford University Press, 2016.
http://www.oed.com.

INTRODUCTION

1. Skeat suggests that the date of this version of the lyric is after 1100 and probably close to 1200 but that the lines may represent "an earlier tradition." See Stubbs, *Historical Memorials*, 50. The chronicle probably dates to the last quarter of the twelfth century; its translator suggests a date between 1170 and 1177. See Fairweather, trans., *Liber Eliensis*, xxii–xxiii.

2. Fairweather, trans., *Liber Eliensis*, 181–82. Here and in what follows, I silently emend the Middle English letter forms "þ," "ð,"and "ʒ." I have omitted Fairweather's modern English translation of the lyric and substituted the corrected Middle English proposed by Skeat in Stubbs, *Historical Memorials*, 51. "[S]ung publicly in choirs" translates "*in choris puplice cantantur*" (Blake, ed., *Liber Eliensis*, 154). R. L. Greene suggests, following Francis Gummere, that the song forms the burden of a carol dance, interpreting "*in choris*" as "in dance." See Greene, *Early English Carols*, xlix; Gummere, *Beginnings of Poetry*, 275.

3. On the liturgy as a foundation for vernacular literary invention, see Holsinger, "Parable of Caedmon's Hymn" and "Liturgy."

4. As the chronicle's modern editor notes, this aspect of the story is probably a fiction; the river Ouse does not pass close enough to the site of the monastery for a rower to hear its offices. Fairweather, ed. and trans., *Liber Eliensis*, 182 n. 385.

5. Zieman, *Singing the New Song*.

6. Holsinger, *Music, Body, and Desire*.

7. The Latin is "Hoc rex agitans, non quievit cum venerabili collegio pie ac dulciter concinere": Blake, ed., *Liber Eliensis*, 154. "Agitans" could also refer to the king's emotional response to the song.

8. Kay, *Parrots and Nightingales*, 131.

9. Wimsatt and Beardsley, *Verbal Icon*, x.

10. A key text in historical poetics that focuses on lyric poetry is Jackson, *Dickinson's Misery*. The term "New Formalism" was introduced in Dubrow, *Happier Eden*, 268–70. The best recent discussion of the history and current state of this critical movement appears in Levine, *Forms*, 1–23; see also Levinson, "What Is New Formalism?"

11. The essays are Butterfield, "Why Medieval Lyric?" "Afterwords," and "Construction of Textual Form"; Zeeman, "Imaginative Theory"; Brantley, *Reading in the Wilderness*, 121–66. More recent books than Woolf's, such as Gray, *Themes and Images*, and Boklund-Lagopoulou, *I Have a Yong Suster*, have not had the same widespread influence on the field.

12. The literature on medieval performativity is vast and growing. Key works on the relationship between literature and performance include the classic Chambers, *Mediaeval Stage*, as well as more recently Coleman, *Public Reading and the Reading Public*; Symes, *A Common Stage*; Holsinger, "Analytical Survey."

13. See Butterfield, *Familiar Enemy*; Baswell et al., "Competing Archives, Competing Histories."

14. Baswell et al., "Competing Archives, Competing Histories," quot. 673.

15. Butterfield, "Why Medieval Lyric?" esp. 326–27. For recent work on Continental lyric, see Galvez, *Songbook*.

16. Zumthor, *Toward a Medieval Poetics*.

17. Green, *Crisis of Truth*, 41–77.

18. Sutherland, Quo Warranto *Proceedings*, esp. 33–70; Clanchy, *From Memory to Written Record*, esp. 21–28.

19. See, e.g., Ong, *Orality and Literacy*; Stock, *Implications of Literacy*.

20. Stock, *Implications of Literacy*, 3.

21. For the concept of lyric "networks," I am indebted to Butterfield, "Construction of Textual Form."

22. For Godric's lyrics, see Dobson and Harrison, *Medieval English Songs*, 103–9. The tale of the priest is recorded in Gerald of Wales, *Jewel of the Church*, 92.

23. For texts of the Rawlinson D.913 poems, see Robbins, *Secular Lyrics*, 11–13, as well as Dronke, "Rawlinson Lyrics"; for discussion, see Wilson, *Lost Literature*, 177–87. The "Simenel hornes" fragment appears in Cambridge, Trinity College MS O.2.5: see the record in James, *Western Manuscripts*, 3.91, and on this manuscript, see Hunt, "*Deliciae*

Clericorum." A "simenel horn" is a loaf of fine bread made with pointed ends (*MED* "simenel" (a)); the meaning of this verse is obscure.

24. Boffey, "Middle English Lyrics," 17–18.

25. Boffey, "Middle English Lyrics," 1.

26. For a detailed discussion of these contexts, see Boffey, "Middle English Lyrics," 6–15, 16–17.

27. Wenzel, *Preachers, Poets*, 3–20.

28. Huot, *From Song to Book*; Gaunt, "Orality and Writing"; Nichols, "'Art' and 'Nature.'"

29. Huot, *From Song to Book*, 46–80.

30. Galvez, *Songbook*, 4.

31. Butterfield, *Familiar Enemy*, xxi, and see also 66–101; Baswell et al., "Competing Archives, Competing Histories"; essays in Wogan-Browne et al., eds., *Language and Culture*; Hsy, *Trading Tongues*. Anglicized French in this period is called "Anglo-Norman," "Anglo-French," or the "French of England." For a discussion of the history and implications of these terms, see Wogan-Browne, "General Introduction"; Rothwell, "Introduction." I use "Anglo-French" throughout to designate French language texts written in England.

32. See Brown, *English Lyrics of the XIIIth Century*, 14; *DIMEV*, 3272.5.

33. Text and translation from Fein et al., *Complete Harley 2253*, 2.234–37.

34. Symes, *A Common Stage*; Brantley, *Reading in the Wilderness*.

35. Taylor, "Myth of the Minstrel Manuscript," 60–65.

36. "hanc rotam cantare possunt quatuor socii": Dobson and Harrison, eds., *Medieval English Songs*, 300; see also Boffey, "Middle English Lyrics," 6; Taylor, *Textual Situations*, 76–136, discusses this manuscript.

37. English lyrics accompanied by music in manuscripts are collected in Dobson and Harrison, eds., *Medieval English Songs*. See also Hughes and Wooldridge, eds., *Early English Harmony*.

38. Butterfield, *Poetry and Music*, 103–21; Kay, *Parrots and Nightingales*, 131–33.

39. Hughes and Wooldridge, eds., *Early English Harmony*, 2.66–68. French folk tradition contains several versions of songs about "Bele Alis," one of which was taken as the text of a medieval sermon; see Greene, *Early English Carols*, cxlv–cxlvii; Butterfield, "Construction of Textual Form," 49–50.

40. Dobson and Harrison, eds., *Medieval English Songs*, 122–36, 242–43.

41. Greene, *Early English Carols*, xxxviii–xlii; see also Chaganti, "Dance in a Haunted Space."

42. Wenzel, *Preachers, Poets*; Waters, *Angels and Earthly Creatures*. See also my discussion in Chapters 1 and 2.

43. Förster, "Kleinere Mittelenglische Texte," 152, and see discussion in Wenzel, *Preachers, Poets*, 213–14; on "Bele Aelis," see Butterfield, "Construction of Textual Form," 49–50.

44. Summerfield, "Political Songs"; Matthews, *Writing to the King*, 52–80.

45. The foundational study of *auctorite*, Alastair Minnis's *Medieval Theory of Author-ship*, links it to the scholastic production and apparatus of written texts. Minnis shows how scholastic practices created a material form and a vocabulary of textual *auctorite*, at once "authority" and "authorship," that was appropriated and transformed by English vernacular poets. In particular, prologues found in scholastic manuscripts of the works of the *auctores*—Scripture, classical philosophy, and the works of the Church fathers—constitute a corpus of medieval literary theory, taking up a work's style, structure, inten-tion, order, material, utility, and so forth (*forma tractandi, forma tractatus, intentio auctoris, ordo, materia, utilitas*). Minnis's seminal monograph demonstrates how Ricardian authors, especially Chaucer and Gower, drew on and developed this lexicon to create a model of vernacular literary authorship. In subsequent decades, a vast critical literature of medieval *auctorite* has appeared, exploring topics ranging from translation to exempla. For a discus-sion of the prefaces and these terms, see Minnis, *Medieval Theory*, 9–39; Minnis and Scott, eds., *Medieval Literary Theory*, 1–11.

46. See Stillinger, *Song of Troilus*, and my critique of his argument in Chapter 3; also Watson, *Richard Rolle*; Woolf, *English Religious Lyric*, 5.

47. Zumthor, *Toward a Medieval Poetics*; Butterfield, *Poetry and Music*, 103–21.

48. Recent work that uses the lyric to challenge these textual models includes Zee-man, "Imaginative Theory," and Butterfield, "Construction of Textual Form"; but see Steiner, *Documentary Culture*, on the ways in which the "Charters of Christ" lyrics draw on legal documents for their form. Of these kinds of lyrics, however, most survive from the fifteenth century.

49. Wogan-Browne et al., eds., *Idea of the Vernacular*; see esp. the essay by the edi-tors, "The Notion of Vernacular Theory," 314–30.

50. Steiner, "Authority," 142.

51. Wogan-Browne et al., eds., *Idea of the Vernacular*, 316.

52. Certeau, *Practice of Everyday Life*, xviii–xx.

53. Certeau, *Practice of Everyday Life*, 45–49, quot. 47.

54. Buchanan, "Introduction: Other People," 97.

55. Certeau, *Practice of Everyday Life*, xix.

56. Le Goff, *Medieval Civilization*, 134.

57. See, e.g., Wallace, "Problematics" and "Europe: A Literary History"; the essays in the special issue of *postmedieval* on "Medieval Mobilities" (ed. Fincke et al.); Nelson, "Premodern Media."

58. Butterfield, "Construction of Textual Form," "Afterwords," and "Why Medieval Lyric?"

59. Zeeman, "Imaginative Theory."

60. Curtius, *European Literature*, 79–105.

61. Warren, "Introduction: Relating Philology," 286. For older readings of topoi, see, e.g., Woolf, *English Religious Lyric*; Gray, *Themes and Images*.

62. Luria and Hoffman, *Middle English Lyrics*, 7.

63. See Moser, "'And I Mon Waxe Wod'" for a survey of possible readings and contexts, summarized in this paragraph.

64. See Butterfield, "Construction of Textual Form," 54–55, for a discussion of these sources.

65. Chickering, " 'Foweles in the Frith,' " argues for liturgical music; Moser, " 'And I Mon Waxe Wod,' " 328, argues for musical ambiguity. Holsinger, "Vernacular Legality," 178 n. 60 and n. 61, provides a summary of the appropriation of liturgical music for secular songs.

66. Aristotle, *Physics*, 4.3 (trans. Waterfield).

67. Aristotle, *Physics*, 4.4. *Physics* 4.1–5 contains the complete discussion of place.

68. Aristotle, *Physics*, 4.4.

69. For more on the interdependence between place and motion in Aristotle's theory, see Morison, *On Location*, esp. 54–55.

70. Curtius, *European Literature*, 82–83.

71. Oxford Bodleian MS Douce 139, f. 179v; Dean and Boulton, *Anglo-Norman Literature*, no. 115.

72. For a detailed discussion of the history of the lyric genre, see Culler, *Theory of the Lyric*, 39–90.

73. See, e.g., Sidney, "Defence of Poesy," 11; Puttenham, *Art of English Poesy*, 115; Webbe, "From a Discourse of English Poetry."

74. Isidore of Seville, *Etymologies*, 180 (trans. Barney).

75. Isidore of Seville, *Etymologies*, 98 (trans. Barney).

76. Conrad of Hirsau, "Dialogue on the Authors," 44 (emphasis in original).

77. Some of these relationships, particularly as they pertain to the courtly love lyric, are discussed in Dronke, *Medieval Latin*: see esp. 1.112–25 on the Harley lyrics. But Dronke largely treats the courtly tradition from the twelfth century onward; for a more representative sample of the Latin lyrics to which Isidore and Conrad are referring, see Raby, *Oxford Book of Medieval Latin Verse* and *History of Secular Latin Poetry*.

78. Boffey, "Forms of Standardization," 67 (emphasis in original).

79. Duncan, "Introduction," xxiii–xxiv.

80. John of Garland, *Parisiana Poetria*, 159–223.

81. Dante Alighieri, *De Vulgari Eloquentia*, 71.

82. Kay, *Parrots and Nightingales*; Vidal, *Razos de Trobar*; Deschamps, *L'Art de Dictier*.

83. See Geoffrey of Vinsauf, *Poetria Nova*; Matthew of Vendôme, *Ars Versificatoria*. Martin Camargo's edition and translation of the *Tria Sunt* is in preparation; see excerpts in Copeland and Sluiter, eds., *Medieval Grammar and Rhetoric*, 670–81, as well as Camargo and Woods, "Writing Instruction."

84. Brown, *English Lyrics of the XIIIth Century, Religious Lyrics of the XIVth Century*, and *Religious Lyrics of the XVth Century*; Robbins, *Secular Lyrics*. The Brown and Robbins collections remain the most comprehensive critical editions for studying the corpus. More recent anthologies, such as Luria's Norton Critical edition, are more up-to-date but less inclusive. A new forthcoming Norton Critical edition, edited by Ardis Butterfield, promises to provide a much-needed comprehensive anthology.

85. Medieval lyric scholarship through 1997 is well catalogued in the annotated bibliography compiled by Greentree, *Middle English Lyric*. For a helpful more recent survey, see Duncan, *Companion*.

86. Woolf, *English Religious Lyric*. For works influenced by Woolf, see Gray, *Themes and Images*; Brantley, *Reading in the Wilderness*, esp. 123.

87. Wenzel, *Preachers, Poets*; Scattergood, "Authority and Resistance"; see also Boffey, *Manuscripts*.

88. Dillon, "Unwriting Medieval Song," 607.

89. Brantley, *Reading in the Wilderness*, quot. 1.

90. Cervone, *Poetics of the Incarnation*; McNamer, *Affective Meditation*, quot. 85. For psychoanalytic readings of English and French lyrics, see Zeeman, "The Gender of Song"; Kay, "Desire and Subjectivity."

91. Greene, *Early English Carols*; Zeeman, "Imaginative Theory."

92. An important exception is the work of Ardis Butterfield, esp. "Why Medieval Lyric?"

93. Transhistorical reassessments of the lyric form that omit consideration of the English medieval lyric include Hošek and Parker, eds., *Lyric Poetry*, which contains an essay on troubadour lyric but not on English medieval lyric, and the *PMLA* cluster "Theories and Methodologies: The New Lyric Studies" (ed. Jackson), which similarly overlooks the medieval English lyric. Jackson and Prins, eds., *Lyric Theory Reader*, does include essays on medieval lyric, perhaps indicating a new openness to premodern lyric studies. Culler, *Theory of the Lyric*, 64–68, includes Continental and English medieval lyrics in his historical survey; however, his discussion of English medieval lyrics is not comprehensive.

94. Hegel, *Aesthetics*, 2.959–1257. See also the discussion of Hegel's lyric theory in Culler, *Theory of the Lyric*, 92–105.

95. Joyce, *Portrait of the Artist*, 188.

96. See, e.g., Sidney, "Defence of Poesy"; Genette, *Architext*, esp. 8–14.

97. Mill, *Essays on Poetry*, 12 (emphasis in original); Frye, *Anatomy of Criticism*, 249.

98. Abrams, "Structure and Style," 527.

99. Richards, *Principles of Literary Criticism*, 71–72.

100. Richards, *Principles of Literary Criticism*, 102.

101. Eliot, *Three Voices of Poetry*, quot. 27 and 31; see also 6–7, 21–22.

102. Brooks, *Well Wrought Urn*, 74–75.

103. Wimsatt and Beardsley, *Verbal Icon*, 5 (emphasis in original).

104. Vendler, *Soul Says*.

105. Culler, *Theory of the Lyric*, 33–38.

106. Culler, *Theory of the Lyric*, 89.

107. See, e.g., Parker, "Introduction"; Culler, "Changes in the Study," 41–42; Jeffreys, "Ideologies of Lyric"; Kaufman, "Lyric Commodity Critique."

108. Adorno, "Lyric Poetry and Society."

109. Bernstein, "Academy in Peril," 246.

110. Andrews and Bernstein, "Repossessing the Word," ix.

111. Silliman, "Disappearance of the Word," quot. 122.

112. Perloff, "Can(n)on to the Right of Us."

113. Bakhtin, "Discourse in the Novel"; Jameson, *The Political Unconscious*.

114. See n. 9 above. For a discussion that directly addresses medieval literary studies, see Lerer, "Endurance of Formalism."

115. Terada, "After the Critique," quot. 199.

116. See Cameron, *Lyric Time*; Frye, "Approaching the Lyric"; Vendler, *Soul Says*; Culler, *Theory of Lyric*, esp. 86–90.

117. Troubadour lyrics are sometimes discussed in these accounts, but the insular tradition, if mentioned, is considered largely an adjunct of Continental lyricism. See n. 93 above.

118. Classic epoch-making work on fourteenth-century literature includes Salter, *Fourteenth-Century English Poetry*, and Burrow, *Ricardian Poetry*. See the argument for uniting pre- and post-1350 literature in Matthews, *Writing to the King*, ix–x. On early Middle English, see Hahn, "Early Middle English." Fifteenth-century studies have a vast bibliography. As a starting point, see Boffey and Edwards, eds., *Companion*.

119. Dryden, "Preface to Fables," 527; Minnis, *Medieval Theory of Authorship*.

CHAPTER 1

1. Nichols, "Introduction," quot. 4.

2. See esp. Zumthor, *Toward a Medieval Poetics*; Butterfield, *Poetry and Music*, 13–71; Brantley, *Reading in the Wilderness*, 121–66; Chaganti, *Medieval Poetics of the Reliquary*.

3. Woolf, *English Religious Lyric*, 4. While Woolf explicitly excludes secular lyrics, and in particular the Harley lyrics, in her study, as we shall see, the model of lyric voice put forward in this chapter has implications to the devotional lyrics that Woolf's study addresses as well.

4. See esp. the essays in Fein, ed., *Studies in the Harley Manuscript*, which offer incisive analyses of the range of the manuscript's lyric and nonlyric texts.

5. See Woolf, *English Religious Lyric*, 4–7; Allen, "Grammar, Poetic Form"; McNamer, *Affective Meditation*; Brantley, *Reading in the Wilderness*; Spearing, *Textual Subjectivity*, all discussed in greater detail below.

6. Fein, ed., *Complete Harley 2253*, 2.278.

7. McNamer, *Affective Meditation*, 1.

8. Patterson, "Writing Amorous Wrongs," 56. On the relationship between legal documentary forms and poetic forms, see also Scase, *Literature and Complaint*; Simpson, *Reform and Cultural Revolution*, 128–31; Steiner, *Documentary Culture*, 47–90.

9. Peraino, *Giving Voice to Love*. I would even speculate that Scribe B may have written this envoy. There is some evidence that he practices what has been called "scribal improvisation" elsewhere in the manuscript, modifying prefatory material to fit his layout: Nelson, "Performance of Power"; Chavannes-Mazel, "Expanding Rubrics." On scribal

improvisation, see Machan, "Editing, Orality," 229–45; Machan, *Textual Criticism*, 136–76.

10. Peraino, *Giving Voice to Love*, 32.

11. Spitzer, "Note on the Poetic and Empirical 'I,'" esp. 414–15.

12. Aquinas, *Commentary*, 242 (trans. Pasnau).

13. Aquinas, *Commentary*, 247 (trans. Pasnau).

14. Copeland and Sluiter, eds., *Medieval Grammar and Rhetoric*, 87.

15. Copeland and Sluiter, eds., *Medieval Grammar and Rhetoric*, 172–73.

16. For an extensive summary of grammatical theories of voice, see Leach, *Sung Birds*, 24–43, 297–300.

17. Wise, *Dionysus Writes*; Enders, *Rhetoric and Origins*.

18. Pound, *ABC of Reading*.

19. See Hunt, *Teaching and Learning Latin*, 1.120–43, for examples and discussion.

20. Hunt, *Teaching and Learning Latin*, 1.137, translation mine.

21. Hunt, *Teaching and Learning Latin*, 1.138, translation mine. I have translated this stanza colloquially. A more literal translation is "Let '*augustus*, -ti, -to' have [the meaning] of Caesar or the month; '*Augustus*, -tus, -ui' wants to say divination. If it becomes mobile [i.e., able to attach to another word], '*augustus*' should mean noble. 'Augeo' gives the first, 'gustus' and 'auis' give the second." The final line describes the etymologies of *augustus* (*auis* + *gustus*), as John understands them.

22. Quintilian, *Institutio Oratoria*, 1.19 (trans. Butler).

23. Quintilian, *Institutio Oratoria*, 1.185–87 (trans. Butler).

24. Quintilian, *Institutio Oratoria*, 1.325 (trans. Butler).

25. Ward, *Ciceronian Rhetoric*, 147–55, 270–305; Camargo, "Latin Composition Textbooks"; Enders, *Rhetoric and Origins*, 19–68.

26. *Rhetorica ad Herennium*, 197 (trans. Caplan).

27. *Rhetorica ad Herennium*, 199 (trans. Caplan).

28. Isidore of Seville, *Etymologies*, 96 (trans. Barney et al.).

29. John of Salisbury, *Metalogicon*, 10–11 (trans. McGarry).

30. Ward, *Ciceronian Rhetoric*, 275.

31. Kennedy, trans. *Progymnasmata*, 115.

32. Kennedy, trans. *Progymnasmata*, 116.

33. Woods, "Rhetoric, Gender and the Literary Arts," 113–14.

34. Specht, "'Ethopoeia' or Impersonation," 2–5; Woods, "Weeping for Dido," 287–89.

35. Isidore of Seville, *Etymologies*, 74 (trans. Barney et al.).

36. *Rhetorica ad Herennium*, 399 (trans. Caplan).

37. Priscian, "Fundamentals," 64 (trans. Miller).

38. Geoffrey of Vinsauf, *Poetria Nova*, 63 (trans. Nims).

39. Geoffrey of Vinsauf, *Poetria Nova*, 34 (trans. Nims).

40. Matthew of Vendôme, *Ars Versificatoria*, 1.41–116 (trans. Parr). A critical edition and translation of *Tria Sunt* by Martin Camargo is in preparation for the Dumbarton

Oaks Medieval Library. An excerpt from the work's concluding summary states that its twelfth chapter "is about the attributes of persons and actions, by means of which one provides the characteristic details that are suited to a particular subject matter"; it appears in Camargo and Woods, "Writing Instruction," 120. See also Camargo, "Latin Composition Textbooks," 277–80, and "*Tria Sunt.*"

41. Augustine of Hippo, *Confessions*, 1.17; Hutson, "*Ethopoeia*," 140–42.

42. Lanham, "Writing Instruction"; Woods, "Weeping for Dido," esp. 288.

43. Chaucer, *Troilus and Criseyde*, 5.1054–85; Chaucer, *House of Fame*, 300–60; see Specht, "'Ethopoeia' or Impersonation," 8–11, for a discussion of these examples. All Chaucer citations refer to the *Riverside Chaucer*.

44. Specht, "'Ethopoeia' or Impersonation," 2.

45. Hegel, *Aesthetics*, 2.1038.

46. Derrida, *Voice and Phenomenon*, esp. 60–74.

47. Lawton, "Voice and Public Interiorities," quot. 306.

48. Spitzer, "Note on the Poetic and the Empirical 'I,'" 415.

49. Woolf, *English Religious Lyric*, 5; Allen, "Grammar, Poetic Form," quot. 217.

50. Spearing, *Textual Subjectivity*, esp. 1–36 and 174–210, quot. 189 and 196.

51. Zink, *Invention of Literary Subjectivity*, 37–60.

52. Kay, *Subjectivity and Troubadour Lyric*, 4–5.

53. Morris, *Discovery of the Individual*; Bynum, *Jesus as Mother*, 82–109; Aers, "A Whisper in the Ear"; Zink, *Invention of Literary Subjectivity*, esp. 1–19.

54. For a seminal discussion of medieval literary publics, see Middleton, "Idea of Public Poetry."

55. McNamer, *Affective Meditation*; Brantley, *Reading in the Wilderness*, esp. 121–66.

56. Certeau, *Practice of Everyday Life*, 131–53, esp. 134–35.

57. Certeau, *Practice of Everyday Life*, 152 (emphasis in original).

58. This description summarizes Fein, ed., *Complete Harley 2253*, 2.1–12, 2.483–86.

59. Chambers, "Some Aspects," 274–75; Brook, *Harley Lyrics*, 1–26; Birkholz, "Harley Lyrics," 179; Pearsall, *Old English and Middle English Poetry*, 125–29; Scattergood, "Love Lyric Before Chaucer," esp. 42–43.

60. Fein, "A Saint 'Geynest Under Gore.'"

61. On the term "manuscript matrix," see Nichols, "Introduction."

62. On the Harley scribe as compiler of this manuscript, see Fein, ed., *Complete Harley 2253*, 2.8–12; Fisher, *Scribal Authorship*, 100–3. For a dissenting view, see Birkholz, "Harley Lyrics."

63. See Brown, *English Lyrics of the XIIIth Century*, 161–63, 235–37; Green, "The Two 'Litel Wot Hit Any Mon' Lyrics"; as well as my discussion below.

64. For the view of the manuscript as a miscellany, see Brown, *English Lyrics of the XIIIth Century*, xxxvi; Pearsall, *Old and Middle English Poetry*, 120–32, and "Medieval Anthologies." Occupying a self-described "middle course," see Stemmler, "Miscellany or Anthology?" For discussions of the anthologistic character of Harley 2253, see Revard, "Gilote et Johan" and "Oppositional Thematics"; Lerer, "Middle English Literature"; Fein, "Compilation and Purpose"; Fisher, *Scribal Authorship*, 100–145.

65. Revard, "Gilote et Johan" and "Oppositional Thematics"; Durling, "British Library MS Harley 2253."

66. Revard, "Scribe and Provenance," 91–100 and pl. 1–27, contains reproductions and descriptions of the legal documents.

67. Ker, ed., *Facsimile*, xx–xxiii.

68. Birkholz, "Harley Lyrics," 185.

69. Turville-Petre, *England the Nation*, 198–217.

70. Matonis, "Investigation of Celtic Influences" and "Harley Lyrics."

71. Birkholz, "Harley Lyrics," 186–91.

72. Fein, ed., *Complete Harley 2253*, 2.236–39 (text and translation).

73. Rothenberg, *Flower of Paradise*.

74. Fein, ed., *Complete Harley 2253*, 2.238–39 (text and translation).

75. Spitzer, "Note on the Poetic and Empirical 'I'"; Allen, "Grammar, Poetic Form," quot. 212.

76. Fein, ed., *Complete Harley 2253*, 2.112–13 (text and translation).

77. Fein, ed., *Complete Harley 2253*, 2.116–17 (text and translation).

78. See, e.g., Frere and Brown, eds., *Hereford Breviary*, 348. This phrase also appears in the *Memento Mori*.

79. Fein, ed., *Complete Harley 2253*, 2.276.

80. Fein, ed., *Complete Harley 2253*, 2.276.

81. Fein, ed., *Complete Harley 2253*, 2.276.

82. Durling, "British Library MS Harley 2253."

83. Fein, ed., *Complete Harley 2253*, 2.120.

84. Fein, ed., *Complete Harley 2253*, 2.122.

85. Coleman, *Public Reading and the Reading Public*, 35–36, points out that the medieval English word "read" has a range of significations, from private reading to public performance.

86. Fein, ed., *Complete Harley 2253*, 3.240, 3.242.

87. Fein, ed., *Complete Harley 2253*, 3.240, 3.242.

88. An exception is Kuczynski, "An 'Electric Stream,'" 145–49.

89. Stemmler, "Miscellany or Anthology?" 114–15, 121.

90. In particular, items 99–101, 105–8, 109a–111, 113, and 115. All item numbers are from Fein, ed., *Complete Harley 2253*.

91. Fein, ed., *Complete Harley 2253*, 3.266–67 (text and translation).

92. Fein, ed., *Complete Harley 2253*, 3.270–71 (text and translation).

93. Fein, ed., *Complete Harley 2253*, 3.276–77 (text and translation).

CHAPTER 2

1. Newman, *Medieval Crossover*, esp. 1–53.

2. On the friars as lyricists, see Wenzel, *Preachers, Poets*.

3. On the pastoral effects of the Fourth Lateran Council, see Wenzel, *Latin Sermon Collections*, 229–34; Reeves, "Teaching the Creed," 41–72.

4. Waters, *Angels and Earthly Creatures*.

5. Reimer, "Introduction," *Works of William Herebert*, 1–5. See also Little, *Grey Friars in Oxford*, 167–68; Jotischky, "Herbert, William (d. 1333/1337?)." Reimer convincingly argues against some of the assertions in this article, notably the claim that Herebert was in Paris in the 1290s.

6. For a full list of the manuscript's contents, see the entry for Add'l. MS 46919 in British Library, *Catalogue of Additions to the Manuscripts: 1946–51, Pt. 1*.

7. Studies of the hymns include Pezzini, "Versions of Latin Hymns"; Ready, "Marian Lyrics"; Robbins, "Friar Herebert and the Carol."

8. I take the text of the rubric and poem from the edition in Rothwell, ed., *Le Tretiz*, 99–102. Rothwell agrees with Herebert's attribution of the poem to Bibbesworth; in what follows, I explain why this attribution seems spurious. Translations of this poem and rubric are mine.

9. Dean and Boulton, *Anglo-Norman Literature*, no. 799. For a discussion and text of Bibbesworth's "Tretiz," see Rothwell, ed., *Le Tretiz*.

10. Hunt, "Wordplay Before the 'Rhétoriqueurs'?"

11. Rothwell, ed., *Le Tretiz*, 99. Translation mine. Because the poem relies so heavily on puns and wordplay, a single translation cannot do justice to all of its possible meanings; many valid translations are possible. Here, I have attempted to provide the clearest and most literal meaning of the poem. In general, I translate "chaunt/er" as song/sing, "deschaunt/er" as descant/sing badly/disenchant/contradict, and "enchaunt/er" as sing/charm/enchant.

12. For a discussion of the wordplay in "Amours m'ount si enchaunté," as well as the analogues of Gautier de Coinci and other poets, see Hunt, "Wordplay Before the 'Rhétoriqueurs'?" For the text of Gautier's poem, see Gautier de Coinci, *Miracles de Nostre Dame*. Studies of Gautier include Switten, "Borrowing, Citation, and Authorship"; Hunt, *Miraculous Rhymes*; Butterfield, *Poetry and Music*, 103–21.

13. Gautier de Coinci, *Miracles de Nostre Dame*, 1.24.

14. Rothwell, ed., *Le Tretiz*, 99, translation mine. I have emended Rothwell's "trer-ray," a direct transcription from the manuscript, to "terray," following Hunt, "Wordplay Before the 'Rhétoriqueurs'?" 286. If Rothwell's reading, "trerray" (to draw/derive), stands, these lines would translate as "My song will draw from Maryot because I wish to sing of Mary"; Rothwell, ed., *Le Tretiz*, 99 n. 19, explains that "Maryot" could mean "an image of the Virgin." However, I find this reading less plausible because of Gautier's contrast between "Maryot" and "Mary," discussed below.

15. Rothwell, ed., *Le Tretiz*, 99–100, translation mine. I have interpreted "faufee" as a misspelling of "maufee," a devil or evil spirit (following Hunt, "Wordplay Before the 'Rhétoriqueurs'?" 286). In his notes on the text, Rothwell suggests that "faufee" could be a variant of "fauvel," a metaphor for falseness or hypocrisy.

16. The word "manga," literally "ate," can also mean "swallowed, accepted with credulity." See Rothwell, ed., *Le Tretiz*, 99 n. 24.

17. Gautier de Coinci, *Miracles de Nostre Dame*, 3.277.

18. Gauiter de Coinci, *Miracles de Nostre Dame*, 3.279 and 3.290, e.g.

19. See Hunt, "Wordplay Before the 'Rhétoriquers'?" 288–89, for some of these texts; also Switten, "Borrowing, Citation, and Authorship."

20. For the grammar, see Rothwell, ed., *Le Tretiz*, and discussion in Orme, *Medieval Schools*, 74–75; Crane, "Anglo-Norman Cultures," 48–49.

21. Waters, *Angels and Earthly Creatures*, esp. 2–7.

22. Wooldridge, *Oxford History of Music*, 1.289.

23. Leach, *Sung Birds*, 186–87; Page, *Owl and the Nightingale*, 134–54; Wooldridge, *Oxford History of Music*, 1.290 n. 1.

24. Page, *Owl and the Nightingale*, 145–47.

25. Luria and Hoffman, *Middle English Lyrics*, 84–85.

26. Page, *Owl and the Nightingale*, 149; Leach, *Sung Birds*, 108–60.

27. Leach, *Sung Birds*, 175–237.

28. Rothwell, ed., *Le Tretiz*, 101, translation mine. I have emended "chaunçouns rymé" from Rothwell's transcription to "chaunçoun rymé."

29. John of Garland, *Parisiana Poetria*, 159–61 (trans. Lawler).

30. Rothwell, ed., *Le Tretiz*, 102, translation mine.

31. Wooldridge, *Oxford History of Music*, 1.295.

32. Quoted in Smalley, *English Friars and Antiquity*, 43. From MS Bâle, Univ. Libr. B.V.6, f. 46v (unexamined by me).

33. John of Grimestone, *Descriptive Index*, 3.

34. Fein, ed., *Moral Love Songs*, 34–35.

35. Owst, *Literature and Pulpit*, 41–47; see examples in Wenzel, *Verses in Sermons*, 51, 153; Wenzel, *Preachers, Poets*, 88.

36. The sermon is printed in Förster, "Kleinere Mittelenglische Texte," 152–54, and discussed in Wilson, *Lost Literature*, 174–75; Greene, *Early English Carols*, cxlvii; Boklund-Lagopolou, *I Have a Yong Suster*, 23.

37. Förster, "Kleinere Mittelenglische Texte," 152.

38. Förster, "Kleinere Mittelenglische Texte," 152.

39. The biblical citation appears in Latin in the witness: "Legimus in evangelio Matthaei recordi quod de omni verbo otioso, quod locuti fuerint homines, reddent rationem de eo in die iudicii" (We read written in the gospel of Matthew that of all idle words that men speak, they will give a reason for them on judgment day). Förster, "Kleinere Mittelenglische Texte," 152, translation mine.

40. Förster, "Kleinere Mittelenglische Texte," 152.

41. Durand, *Rationale*, 4.26; Powicke and Cheney, eds., *Councils & Synods*, 2:900–1; see discussion in Wenzel, *Latin Sermon Collections*, 232–37.

42. Charland, ed., *Artes Praedicandi*, 373, translation mine.

43. Minnis, "Quadruplex Sensus, Multiplex Modus," 232.

44. Murphy, ed., *Three Medieval Rhetorical Arts*, 131.

45. Murphy, ed., *Three Medieval Rhetorical Arts*, 143; Latin text from Charland, *Artes Praedicandi*, 258. I have made one emendation to Murphy's translation, rendering "accipieretur" in the first sentence as "should undertake," rather than Murphy's "does not use."

46. Wenzel, *Preachers, Poets*, 61–100; Rouse and Rouse, *Preachers, Florilegia, and Sermons*, esp. 3–42; Rouse and Rouse, "Statim Invenire."

47. Fein, ed., *Complete Harley 2253*, 2.276.

48. Mayhew, ed., *Promptorium Parvulorum*, 513–14; see also *MED*, "walken," esp. 2a, 2b, 9; "gon" (v.), esp. 1a.

49. For a summary of the affectivity of liturgical song, see Zeeman, "Theory of Passionate Song," 240–50.

50. Zieman, *Singing the New Song*; Hunt, *Teaching and Learning Latin*, 1.38–39.

51. Isidore of Seville, *Etymologies* 147 (trans. Barney). See also Zeeman, "Theory of Passionate Song," 241.

52. Bede, *Ecclesiastical History*, 415–17.

53. Kieran, "Reading Cædmon's 'Hymn,'" 162; O'Keeffe, "Orality and the Developing Text."

54. Holsinger, "Parable of Caedmon's Hymn."

55. "Si sit laus et dei laus et non cantetur, non est ymnus." Quoted in Hunt, *Teaching and Learning Latin*, 1.40. Translation from Pezzini, "Versions of Latin Hymns," 299.

56. Flanigan, Ashley, and Sheingorn, "Liturgy as Social Performance," 701.

57. Page, *Owl and the Nightingale*, 152.

58. Jeffrey and Levy, *Anglo-Norman Lyric*, 233, translation mine.

59. Wright and Halliwell-Phillipps, eds., *Reliquiae Antiquae*, 2.168. The only known witness to this song, BL MS Royal 16.E.8, has now been lost. Wright and Halliwell-Phillipps date this poem to the early thirteenth century; *ANL* (no. 147) dates it to the second half of the thirteenth century.

60. See Minnis, *Medieval Theory of Authorship*, 9–39, and Minnis et al., eds., *Medieval Literary Theory*, 12–36, for examples and discussion of the *accessus ad auctores*.

61. BL MS Additional 46919, f. 15b.

62. BL MS Additional 46919, f. 38, f. 87, f. 154.

63. Reimer, ed., *Works of Herebert*, 19, translation mine.

64. For an in-depth discussion of this tradition, see Copeland, *Rhetoric, Hermeneutics*, 33–35, 42–55.

65. Cicero, *De Inventione*, 365 (trans. Hubbell).

66. Horace, *Satires*, 460–61 (trans. Fairclough).

67. Jerome, *Liber De Optimo*, 13, translation mine.

68. Copeland, *Rhetoric, Hermeneutics*, 51.

69. See also the list of liturgical occasions for Herebert's hymns in Pezzini, "'Velut Gemma Carbunculus,'" 13–14.

70. Reimer, ed., *Works of Herebert*, 111–13; Julian, *Dictionary of Hymnology*, 1.4–5, 2.1220. Specifically, the latter hymn was sung on the Saturday before Passion Sunday (the fifth Sunday of Lent) until Maundy Thursday.

71. Reimer, ed., *Works of Herebert*, 113–16; Julian, *Dictionary of Hymnology*, 1.426.

72. Reimer, ed., *Works of Herebert*, 118–21; Julian, *Dictionary of Hymnology*, 1.99. I omit discussion of the intervening translation, *Libera me, Domine*.

73. Reimer, ed., *Works of Herebert*, 121–25. For the liturgical uses of these hymns, see Julian, *Dictionary of Hymnology*, 2.1206–8, 1.52, 1.257, and 1.228, respectively.

74. Robbins, "Friar Herebert and the Carol." See also Gneuss, "Latin Hymns in Medieval England," 416; Wenzel, *Preachers, Poets*, 24–25.

75. Daniel, ed., *Thesaurus Hymnologicus*, 1.204, translation mine.

76. Although the lack of attribution for this poem in the manuscript led Gneuss to suggest that this is not Herebert's translation, I agree with Reimer's assertion that this is an oversight; Reimer, ed., *Works of Herebert*, 120 n. 1. Regardless, the identity of the translator matters less to my reading than the fact that Herebert included the poem in his compilation.

77. Reimer, ed., *Works of Herebert*, 120.

78. See Pezzini, "Versions of Latin Hymns," for a more extensive discussion of how Herebert's translation practice fulfills specific preaching functions.

79. Daniel, ed., *Thesaurus Hymnologicus*, 1.147.

80. Reimer, ed., *Works of Herebert*, 111.

81. On these lines, see also Pezzini, "Versions of Latin Hymns," 300.

82. Pezzini, "Versions of Latin Hymns," 301–3.

83. Daniel, ed., *Thesaurus Hymnologicus*, 1.160; Reimer, ed., *Works of Herebert*, 112; these are also the references for the next two stanzas cited.

84. Daniel, ed., *Thesaurus Hymnologicus*, 1.78–79; Reimer, ed., *Works of Herebert*, 125.

85. Daniel, ed., *Thesaurus Hymnologicus*, 1.215.

86. *MED* "greden" 1a.

87. Reimer, ed., *Works of Herebert*, 113.

88. Daniel, ed., *Thesaurus Hymnologicus*, 1.215; Reimer, ed., *Works of Herebert*, 114.

89. Daniel, ed., *Thesaurus Hymnologicus*, 1.216; Reimer, ed., *Works of Herebert*, 114.

90. Reimer, ed., *Works of Herebert*, 135.

91. Reimer, ed., *Works of Herebert*, 135; BL MS Additional 46919, f. 211r.

92. Reimer, ed., *Works of Herebert*, 136.

93. Reimer, ed., *Works of Herebert*, 132.

94. Reimer, ed., *Works of Herebert*, 133; BL MS Additional 46919, f. 210r.

95. Reimer, ed., *Works of Herebert*, 133.

CHAPTER 3

1. Cannon, *Grounds of English Literature*, 10–15.

2. Butterfield, "Interpolated Lyric," offers an extensive study of this tradition; Johnson, *Practicing Literary Theory*, is an important recent study of verse and narrative mixed forms.

3. Rancière, *Politics of Aesthetics*, esp. 7–14.

4. Nelson and Gayk, "Introduction."

5. On this point, see Holsinger, "Lyrics and Short Poems."

6. On Chaucer's possible early French lyrics, see Wimsatt, *Chaucer and the Poems of "Ch."* Quotations from Chaucer, *Legend of Good Women*, F.422–23, and Chaucer, *Canterbury Tales*, X.1087.

7. Discussions of these influences include Butterfield, "Interpolated Lyric," esp. 134–231; Stillinger, *Song of Troilus*; Windeatt, *Troilus and Criseyde*; Wimsatt, *Chaucer and His French Contemporaries*; Ginsberg, *Chaucer's Italian Tradition*, 1–28, 105–47.

8. For the low estimate, see Payne, *Key of Remembrance*, 185; for the high estimate, see Wimsatt, "French Lyric Element," 31. For a concise yet comprehensive discussion of the role of lyrics in the poem, see Windeatt, *Troilus and Criseyde*, 163–69. On the literary authority of *Troilus and Criseyde*, see Wetherbee, *Chaucer and the Poets*; Stillinger, *Song of Troilus*; Kinney, " 'Who Made This Song?' " On their Boethian and French influences, see Butterfield, "Interpolated Lyric," 170–231. On their affectivity, see Payne, *Key of Remembrance*, 184–87; Muscatine, *Chaucer and the French Tradition*, 158; Borthwick, "Antigone's Song as 'Mirour.' "

9. Holsinger, "Lyrics and Short Poems," 189.

10. This reading has some kinship with James Simpson's discussion of the relationship between Ovidian elegy and the historical/political situation of the poem. Simpson, *Reform and Cultural Revolution*, 138–48. For the most comprehensive discussion of the political parallels between Troy and England in the 1380s, see Patterson, *Chaucer and the Subject of History*, 155–64.

11. See esp. Stillinger, *Song of Troilus*.

12. On the French tradition of lyric "interpolation" or "insertion," see Butterfield, "Interpolated Lyric," 87–133; Boulton, *The Song in the Story*; Butterfield, *Poetry and Music*, 217–90.

13. Huot, *From Song to Book*; Galvez, *Songbook*; Stillinger, *Song of Troilus*.

14. Pearsall, *Life of Geoffrey Chaucer*, 102–9.

15. On the relational influences of Dante, Boccaccio, and Petrarch on Chaucer and *Troilus and Criseyde*'s lyricism, see Ginsberg, *Chaucer's Italian Tradition*, esp. 105–89. On Dante's *Vita Nuova* as a model of lyric authority, see Stillinger, *Song of Troilus*, 44–72. On Chaucer's translation of Petrarch's poem 132 as the first *canticus Troili*, see Rossiter, *Chaucer and Petrarch*, 109–31, and the discussion below.

16. On the affectivity of medieval lyric, see McNamer, *Affective Meditation*, and Zeeman, "Gender of Song" and "Theory of Passionate Song." On medieval and early modern Petrarchism, see Boitani, "Petrarch and the '*barbari Britanni*' "; Dubrow, *Echoes of Desire*; Greene, *Post-Petrarchism*; Rossiter, *Chaucer and Petrarch*; Wallace, *Chaucerian Polity*, 261–98.

17. Auden, *Collected Poems*, 197; Culler, "Why Lyric?" 202. Culler is reformulating Alice Fulton's statement, "Fiction is about what happens next. Poetry is about what happens now," from Fulton's *Feeling as a Foreign Language*, 7.

18. Payne, *Key of Remembrance*, 184–87; Vance, *Mervelous Signals*, 271–72.

19. Borthwick, "Antigone's Song as 'Mirour.'"

20. While Patterson is of course known as the preeminent advocate for "New Historicism" in medieval studies, his conception of this methodology became increasingly concerned with literary form throughout his career. A classic statement of Patterson's New Historicism in relation to medieval studies appears in *Negotiating the Past*, 3–74. More recently, Patterson, *Temporal Circumstances*, 1–18, articulates what Patterson himself calls a "negotiation" (6) between historicism and formalism.

21. The passage adapts Horace, "Ars Poetica," lines 70–71; on possible intermediate sources that may have influenced Chaucer, see Barney's notes to this passage in *The Riverside Chaucer*. Two readings that focus on how the stanza conveys the tenuousness of language and custom are Payne, *Key of Remembrance*, 70–71, and Muscatine, *Chaucer and the French Tradition*, 138.

22. Muscatine, *Chaucer and the French Tradition*, 138.

23. Simpson, *Reform and Cultural Revolution*, quot. 138; see 128–48.

24. For readings of how the Ovidian allusions engage issues of the representation of trauma, see Fradenburg, *Sacrifice Your Love*, 224–26, and Ingham, "Chaucer's Haunted Aesthetics," 235–38.

25. Statius, *Thebaid*, 5.120–22 (trans. Joyce) (emphasis in original).

26. Statius, *Thebaid*, 12.476–80 (trans. Joyce).

27. Sanok, "Criseyde, Cassandre, and the Thebaid."

28. See Barney, "Explanatory Notes to *Troilus and Criseyde*," in Benson, ed., *Riverside Chaucer*, 1031, and notes to 2.84, 2.100–8.

29. Machaut, *Poésies Lyriques*, 346.

30. Kittredge, "Antigone's Song of Love," 158.

31. Wimsatt, "French Lyric Element," 18–32, and "Guillaume de Machaut and Chaucer's *Troilus and Criseyde*," 287–91. The text of Machaut's lyrics may be found in Machaut, *Poésies Lyriques*, as follows: *Mireoir amoureux*, 2.362–70; "Trop ne me puis de bonne Amour loer," 1.202–3; "Je ne croy pas c'onques à creature," 1.159; and "Moult sui de bonne heure née," 2.630.

32. Wimsatt, "Guillaume de Machaut and Chaucer's *Troilus and Criseyde*," 291.

33. Machaut, *Livre dou voir dit*, 1–4; all translations of this work by Palmer.

34. Machaut, *Livre dou voir dit*, 1025–28.

35. Machaut, *Livre dou voir dit*, 226–30, 247–49. I have emended Palmer's translation of the French *vice* as "impropriety" to its English cognate "vice" in order to highlight the similarity between Machaut and Chaucer.

36. Butterfield, *Poetry and Music*, 243–70, quot. 243.

37. Butterfield, *Familiar Enemy*, 264; see also 241–44.

38. Bradbury, "Proverb Tradition," 238.

39. Curtius, *European Literature*, 154–59; Burrow, *Poetry of Praise*, 6–28.

40. Geoffrey of Vinsauf, *Poetria Nova*, 25 (trans. Nims).

41. For a discussion of the cognitive science of how the brain performs metaphor mapping, see Lakoff, "Neural Theory of Metaphor."

42. Cervone, *Poetics of the Incarnation*, 14–15.

43. Pepin, ed., *English Translation of Auctores Octo*, 5–24, 149–75.

44. Whiting, *Chaucer's Use of Proverbs*, 68.

45. Walther, ed., *Proverbia*, 3.352 (no. 18242).

46. According to Walther, this is München, Bayerische Staatsbibliothek clm 24514, f. 152v (unseen by me).

47. Holt and White, eds., *Ormulum*, 9393–96. See Whiting, *Proverbs, Sentences*, E226.

48. von Düringsfeld and von Reinsberg-Düringsfeld, *Sprichwörter*, 1.600.

49. Taylor, "Proverbs and the Authentication of Convention," 278.

50. Lewis, "What Chaucer Really Did," 56–75.

51. Fumo, *Legacy of Apollo*, 124–62.

52. Simpson, *Reform and Cultural Revolution*, 138–48, quot. 147.

53. Dinshaw, *Chaucer's Sexual Poetics*; Simpson, *Reform and Cultural Revolution*; Patterson, *Chaucer and the Subject of History*.

54. McCall and Rudisill, "Parliament of 1386"; Patterson, *Chaucer and the Subject of History*, 155–64.

55. Giancarlo, *Parliament and Literature*, quot. 88.

56. Lewis, *Allegory of Love*, 185.

57. Geoffrey of Vinsauf, *Poetria Nova*, 20 (trans. Nims).

58. Barley, "Structural Approach," 737.

59. Taylor, "Proverbs and the Authentication of Convention," 285.

60. Bradbury, "Transforming Experience into Tradition," 266.

61. Kinney, " 'Who Made This Song?' " 279; see also Borthwick, "Antigone's Song as 'Mirour.' "

62. See esp. Muscatine, *Chaucer and the French Tradition*, 132; Patterson, *Chaucer and the Subject of History*, 84–86.

63. Carruthers, "On Affliction and Reading."

64. For the first view, see Borthwick, "Antigone's Song as 'Mirour,' " and Kinney, " 'Who Made This Song?' "; for the second, see Patterson, *Chaucer and the Subject of History*, 146; Fradenburg, *Sacrifice Your Love*, 219–20.

65. Patterson, *Chaucer and the Subject of History*, 146.

66. Fradenburg, *Sacrifice Your Love*, 199–238.

67. Muscatine, *Chaucer and the French Tradition*, 134.

68. Payne, *Key of Remembrance*, 184.

69. Payne, *Key of Remembrance*, 186.

70. Greene, *Post-Petrarchism*, 5, 10.

71. Stillinger, *Song of Troilus*, 165–206.

72. Ginsberg, *Chaucer's Italian Tradition*, 8, and see 1–28, 148–89; see also Rossiter, *Chaucer and Petrarch*, esp. 1–33, 109–31.

73. Vickers, "Diana Described"; Wallace, *Chaucerian Polity*, 261–98.

74. Wallace, *Chaucerian Polity*, 277.

75. Vickers, "Diana Described."

76. Petrarch, *Letters of Old Age*, 2.672–80, and *Life of Solitude*.

77. Barney, ed., *Troilus and Criseyde*, 28.

78. Kittredge, "Chaucer's Lollius"; Pratt, "Note on Chaucer's Lollius"; Millett, "Chaucer, Lollius."

79. Bright, "Chaucer and Lollius"; Hornstein, "Petrarch's Laelius."

80. *MED* "seien (v. (1))," 5.

81. See, e.g., Muscatine, *Chaucer and the French Tradition*, 134; Rossiter, *Chaucer and Petrarch*, 110–11, quot. 111.

82. Petrarch, *Canzoniere*, 216–17 (trans. Musa).

83. Simpson, *Reform and Cultural Revolution*, 121–90.

84. On the complaint form in Chaucer's poem, see Windeatt, *Troilus and Criseyde*, 166–67. For a history of lyric complaint, see Davenport, *Chaucer*, 4–8; on the legal complaint and its effect on English literature, see Scase, *Literature and Complaint*.

85. Scase, *Literature and Complaint*, esp. 33–41.

86. Patterson, "Writing Amorous Wrongs," quot. 56.

87. Simpson, *Reform and Cultural Revolution*, 130.

88. Woolf, *English Religious Lyric*, 94–96, 107–10.

89. Luria and Hoffman, *Middle English Lyrics*, 12.

90. Stillinger, *Song of Troilus*, 175–78.

91. John of Garland, *Parisiana Poetria*, 175; Payne, *Key of Remembrance*, 184–87.

92. Luria and Hoffman, *Middle English Lyrics*, 229.

CHAPTER 4

1. See Shaner and Edwards, "The Prologue," in Benson, ed., *Riverside Chaucer*, 1060, for a discussion of the dating of the *Legend of Good Women*.

2. For a recent discussion of the *Legend* as an ethical text, see Collette, *Rethinking Chaucer's* Legend, 77–115.

3. On refrain, see Chaganti, "Choreographing Mouvance," and John Hollander, "Breaking into Song"; on noesis, see Dronke, *Medieval Latin*, 75. On all three of the proto-modern qualities of lyric, see Frye, "Approaching the Lyric." On modern lyric's rhetorical density, see Dubrow, *Challenges of Orpheus*, 26–31; on its temporal suspension, see Cameron, *Lyric Time*, and Culler, "Why Lyric?"

4. See, esp., some important recent studies on medieval exemplarity: Scanlon, *Narrative, Authority and Power*; Miller, "Displaced Souls"; Mitchell, *Ethics and Exemplary Narrative*; Allen, *False Fables*. On Chaucer's literary models for stories of exemplary women, see Collette, *Rethinking Chaucer's* Legend, 33–75.

5. Mitchell, *Ethics and Exemplary Narrative*; Scanlon, *Narrative, Authority, and Power*.

6. Certeau, *Practice of Everyday Life*, xviii–xx.

7. Certeau, *Practice of Everyday Life*, 37.

8. On the institutional contexts of exempla, see Kemmler, *"Exempla" in Context*; Scanlon, *Narrative, Authority, and Power*; Mitchell, *Ethics and Exemplary Narrative*; Allen, *False Fables*.

9. For a concise history of the use of examples in "practical" or "case-based" philosophical reasoning, see Mitchell, *Ethics and Exemplary Narrative*, 22–35, and my discussion below.

10. Mitchell, *Ethics and Exemplary Narrative*, 24.

11. Mitchell, *Ethics and Exemplary Narrative*, 27.

12. For a comprehensive discussion of this history, see Jonsen and Toulmin, *Abuse of Casuistry*, esp. 89–175 on medieval and early modern casuistry and 231–49 on Pascal's critique. On the Jesuit uses of casuistry for both moral and political ends, see Sampson, "Laxity and Liberty." On Kant's critique, see Kittsteiner, "Kant and Casuistry."

13. See the discussions in Jonsen and Toulmin, *Abuse of Casuistry*, 304–32, and Mitchell, *Ethics and Exemplary Narrative*, 24–25.

14. Berlant, "On the Case," 664–65.

15. Jonsen and Toulmin, *Abuse of Casuistry*, 15.

16. See discussion in Scanlon, *Narrative, Authority, and Power*, esp. 27–36.

17. van Dijk, *John Gower*, 15–32; Mitchell, *Ethics and Exemplary Narrative*, 26–28.

18. Kemmler, *"Exempla" in Context*, 66, lists four kinds of exempla that he finds in Mannyng's *Handlyng Synne*, of which 1, 3, and 4 correspond to the three kinds I discuss here. Kemmler's second usage, "to give an example—not necessarily a 'narrative,'" is rhetorically distinct in Mannyng but alludes to one of the other three kinds and does not constitute a separate form.

19. Bynum, Docere Verbo et Exemplo, 9–98.

20. Bynum, Docere Verbo et Exemplo, 79–81.

21. See, e.g., Mannyng, *Handlyng Synne*, 329, 9252; Chaucer, *Legend of Good Women*, 922, 2560. All subsequent citations of these texts will be noted parenthetically.

22. *Rhetorica ad Herennium*, 384–86 (trans. Caplan); Isidore of Seville, *Etymologies*, 64 (trans. Barney).

23. Curtius, *European Literature*, 59–61 (trans. Trask); Kemmler, *"Exempla" in Context*, 62–63, 66.

24. Kemmler, *"Exempla" in Context*, 62–63.

25. Dante Alighieri, *The Divine Comedy*, Inferno 5.64–69 (trans. Kirkpatrick).

26. Chaucer, *Parliament of Fowls*, 288–94.

27. *Rhetorica ad Herennium*, 382–84; Isidore of Seville, *Etymologies*, 64; see discussion in Curtius, *European Literature*, 59; Kemmler, *"Exempla" in Context*, 63–66.

28. Isidore of Seville, *Etymologies*, 64.

29. *Rhetorica ad Herennium*, 373 (trans. Caplan).

30. *Rhetorica ad Herennium*, 383–85.

31. See the discussion of these two exemplary modes in Scanlon, *Narrative, Authority, and Power*, 55–134, who calls them the "public" exemplum and the "sermon" exemplum. I have changed his terms to reflect a broader usage of, in particular, moral exempla in the *pastoralia*.

32. Scanlon, *Narrative, Authority, and Power*, esp. 1–26.

33. Chaganti, "Choreographing Mouvaunce," 82–83. See also the discussions of this dance form in Greene, *Early English Carols*, xliv–xlvi; Dronke, *Medieval Lyric*, 189–90. It is also possible that the movement occurred during the burden while the dancers stayed in place during the verses.

34. Culler, "Why Lyric?" 202.

35. Smith, *Book of the Incipit*, esp. 1–17.

36. Miller, "Displaced Souls," 611.

37. *MED* "ensaumple," 3d. The *MED*'s other citation under this definition, also from Mannyng, is better understood as a narrative exemplum.

38. On this point, see Miller, "Displaced Souls," 619–21.

39. Miller, "Displaced Souls," 614, 622.

40. See, e.g., Frank, *Chaucer and the* Legend; Kiser, *Telling Classical Tales*, 95–131; Patterson, *Chaucer and the Subject of History*, 231–43. Some readings frame these literary issues within the context of the sexual economies and ideologies of the legends. See Dinshaw, *Chaucer's Sexual Poetics*, 65–87; Delany, *Naked Text*, 187–228.

41. Simpson, "Ethics and Interpretation"; Fradenburg, *Sacrifice Your Love*, 176–98; Lynch, *Chaucer's Philosophical Visions*, 111–39; Collette, *Rethinking Chaucer's Legend*, 33–115.

42. As is well known, the *Legend* has two prologues, "F" and "G." "F" is widely agreed to be the earlier of the two, composed between 1386 and 1388, and "G," which omits references to Queen Anne found in "F," is supposed to be composed after her death in 1394. For a discussion of the dating of the two prologues, see Shaner and Edwards, "Prologue," 1060, in Benson, ed., *Riverside Chaucer*. In this discussion, I focus primarily on the "F" prologue, with its more pervasive lyricism, commenting on the "G" revisions when they are relevant to my argument. On the relationship between French and Italian sources and Chaucer's prologue, see Lowes, "Prologue to the *Legend*"; Pearsall, ed., *Floure and the Leafe*, 22–29; Wimsatt, *Chaucer and His French Contemporaries*, 161–68, 181–87, 263–66. But see also Lossing, "Prologue to the *Legend*," 15–35, which argues against Lowes's claim for Deschamps's *Lai de Franchise* as a source and more generally makes the case for the difficulty of establishing sources in a culture of widespread imitation.

43. On these idioms in medieval lyric, see Dronke, *Medieval Latin*; Butterfield, "Afterwords."

44. Lowes, "Prologue to the *Legend*," 611–20.

45. A surviving series by Deschamps, for example, contains three poems praising the flower for its "beauté, bonté, fresche colour," "tresprecieux odour," and "bon fruit," as well as one favoring the leaf for its verdure and longevity. See Marsh, "Sources and Analogues," 126–29. The poetic tradition persisted into the fifteenth century and beyond,

witnessed in two *balades* by Charles d'Orleans and the pseudo-Chaucerian "The Floure and the Leafe," first printed in 1598 and ascribed to Chaucer until its decanonization in the late nineteenth century. See Marsh, "Sources and Analogues," 122–24 for a synopsis of "Floure and Leafe" and 131–34 for the Charles d'Orleans poems, 121 n. 4, for sources debunking Chaucer's authorship; Pearsall, ed., *Floure and Leafe*, esp. 22–29.

46. On this passage as Chaucer's working through of his relationship to poetic "tradition," see Payne, *Key of Remembrance*, 94–96; Kiser, *Telling Classical Tales*, 34, 49; Delany, *Naked Text*, 56–58, 86–87. For discussions of how it specifically alludes to a French poetic idiom, see Wimsatt, *Chaucer and His French Contemporaries*, 167, and Copeland, *Rhetoric, Hermeneutics*, 191.

47. As Robertson, *Laborer's Two Bodies*, 58–64, has shown, Chaucer's defense of his poetic "werk" in the prologue emerges not only from literary convention but also from particular social pressures to justify labor of all kinds in later fourteenth-century England.

48. For a full discussion of these sources, see Lowes, "Prologue to the *Legend*," 618–26. Frank, *Chaucer and the* Legend, 22–23, reads the conventional love language of this passage as evidence of Chaucer's comic intention: "The hyperbolic language and postures are typical for devotion to ladies, but comic for devotion to daisies" (22).

49. Lowes, "Prologue to the *Legend*," 621; Young, "Dit de la harpe."

50. Young, "Dit de la harpe," 14–19.

51. Young, "Dit de la harpe," 4, lines 25–29.

52. Huot, *From Song to Book*, 290; Holsinger, *Music, Body, and Desire*, 325.

53. See also Delany, *Naked Text*, 57–58, and Robertson, *Laborer's Two Bodies*, 60–61, on this passage as an example of Chaucer's sense of thralldom to the authority the daisy represents. Like Delany's, my reading sees the metaphor as enabling as much as it constrains.

54. On medieval praise-poetry and its roots in epideictic rhetoric, see Curtius, *European Literature*, 155–59; Burrow, *Poetry of Praise*, esp. 6–28.

55. See Wimsatt, *Chaucer and His French Contemporaries*, 181–84; Paien's version was probably known to Chaucer by its inclusion in Machaut's *balades notées*, where it appears as a double *balade* with Machaut's own version.

56. Machaut, *Poésies lyriques*, 560–61, translation mine.

57. Machaut, *Poésies lyriques*, 561–62, translation mine.

58. Froissart, *Lyric Poems*, 209, translation mine.

59. *MED*, "disteinen," 2b.

60. *AND*, "desteindre."

61. Fradenburg, *Sacrifice Your Love*, 192.

62. In the G Prologue, the refrain becomes, "Alceste is here, that al this may disteyne." This alteration even more directly conflates Alceste's lyric and exemplary qualities; her name invokes her as an *imago virtutis* while the assertion that she is "here" puts her in the lyric present.

63. Curtius, *European Literature*, 162–65, to which the discussion in this paragraph is indebted.

64. Chaucer, *Legend of Good Women*, F.549–50.

65. Alceste has been read elsewhere as a figure for poetry; see Kiser, *Telling Classical Tales*, 132–41.

66. Frank, *Chaucer and the* Legend, 173–75.

67. Delany, *Naked Text*, 70.

68. Fradenburg, *Sacrifice Your Love*, 183, and see 183–87.

69. Frank, *Chaucer and the* Legend, 43–44.

70. Dronke, *Medieval Latin*, 1.75.

71. See, e.g., Fyler, *Chaucer and Ovid*, 105; Kiser, *Telling Classical Tales*, 118–21.

72. This point is developed in Fyler, *Chaucer and Ovid*, 114–15, although I disagree with his reading of the passage as comic.

73. On these features of lyric, see Culler, *Theory of Lyric*; Frye, "Approaching the Lyric"; Dubrow, *Challenges of Orpheus*, 26–31.

74. Although claiming both Virgil and Ovid as sources in the opening ("In thyn Eneyde and Naso wol I take / The tenor," 928–29), this legend more often follows the *Heroides*. For a more extensive discussion of the relationship between this tale and its sources, see Shannon, *Chaucer and the Roman Poets*, 196–208; Fyler, *Chaucer and Ovid*, 111–15; Kiser, *Telling Classical Tales*, 123–31.

75. On Jason's centrality to this legend, see Frank, *Chaucer and the* Legend, 79–92.

76. Ovid, *Heroides*, 12.11–12 (trans. Showerman).

77. Shannon, *Chaucer and the Roman Poets*, 219.

78. Frank, *Chaucer and the* Legend, 79–92; Fyler, *Chaucer and Ovid*, 103–4; Kiser, *Telling Classical Tales*, 100.

79. Robertson, "Medieval Materialism," 112–13.

80. Aristotle, *Physics*, 31 (trans. Waterfield).

81. Colonne, *Historia Destructionis Troiae*, 15 (trans. Meek). See also discussions of this passage in Moses, "An Appetite for Form"; Kiser, *Telling Classical Tales*, 113 n. 27; Fyler, *Chaucer and Ovid*, 103–4; Robertson, "Medieval Materialism," 112–13.

82. On possible sources and the philosophical content of these lines, see Moses, "An Appetite for Form"; Wien, "Source of the Subtitle," 605–7; Young, "Chaucer's Appeal."

83. Boethius, *Boethius' De Topicis Differentiis*, 81 (trans. Stump).

84. Boethius, *Boethius' De Topicis Differentiis*, 145 n. 21.

85. Minnis, *Medieval Theory of Authorship*, 118. The rest of this paragraph is indebted to Minnis's discussion of the *forma tractandi* and *forma tractatus* on 118–59.

86. See, e.g., Frank, *Chaucer and the* Legend, 88–90; Fyler, *Chaucer and Ovid*, 103; Kiser, *Telling Classical Tales*, 113–15.

87. Culler, *Theory of the Lyric*, 186–243.

CONCLUSION

1. See Sacks, *English Elegy*, esp. 1–37; Dubrow, *Challenges of Orpheus*, 18–26.

2. Tottel et al., *Tottel's Miscellany*, 3.

3. Percy, *Reliques*, 1.xvi.

4. See, e.g., Donatelli, "Percy Folio," 114; I have been unable to find the original source for this anecdote.

5. For Latin medieval poems in which Orpheus saves Eurydice, and the classical origins of this version, see Dronke, "Return of Eurydice."

6. All citations from Laskaya and Salisbury, eds., *Middle English Breton Lays*; line numbers given.

7. Holsinger, *Music, Body, and Desire*, 295–343.

8. See Woolf, *English Religious Lyric*, 67–113, on the *ubi sunt* topos in death lyrics, and my discussion in Chapter 4.

9. Kendall, "Family, Familia, and the Uncanny."

10. Lerer, "Artifice and Artistry in *Sir Orfeo*."

11. Dronke, "Return of Eurydice," 205–6.

12. Dubrow, *Challenges of Orpheus*, 6–10.

13. De Grazia, "Anachronism," quot. 30.

14. Luria and Hoffman, *Middle English Lyrics*, 147.

15. On the *felix culpa* and *vinculum amoris* in this poem, see Stanbury Smith, "'Adam Lay I-Bowndyn.'"

16. Wakelin, "Carol in Writing," 26.

17. Wyatt, *Complete Poems*, 77.

18. Petrarch, *Canzoniere*, 281 (trans. Musa).

19. *OED*, "alas," *int.* and *n.* and "helas," *int.*

20. Brigden, *Thomas Wyatt*, 159.

21. Brigden, *Thomas Wyatt*, 157.

22. Stamatakis, *Sir Thomas Wyatt*, 14, and see 1–15.

23. Harrier, *Canon of Sir Thomas Wyatt*, 3–5, 104–5; Powell, "Thomas Wyatt's Poetry," esp. 270, 275.

24. Harrier, *Canon of Sir Thomas Wyatt*, 3.

25. Harrier, *Canon of Sir Thomas Wyatt*, 11, 104–5.

26. Harrier, *Canon of Sir Thomas Wyatt*, 12, 104–5.

27. Stamatakis, *Sir Thomas Wyatt*, 6–34.

BIBLIOGRAPHY

MANUSCRIPTS

London, British Library MS Additional 46919
London, British Library MS Harley 2253
London, British Library MS Sloane 2593
Oxford, Bodleian Library MS Douce 139

PRINTED SOURCES

Abrams, M. H. "Structure and Style in the Greater Romantic Lyric." In *From Sensibility to Romanticism: Essays Presented to Frederick A. Pottle*, edited by Frederick W. Hilles and Harold Bloom, 527–60. Oxford: Oxford University Press, 1965.

Adorno, Theodor. "Lyric Poetry and Society." Translated by Bruce Mayo. *Telos* 20 (1974): 52–71.

Aers, David. "A Whisper in the Ear of Early Modernists; Or, Reflections on Literary Critics Writing the 'History of the Subject.'" In *Culture and History, 1350–1600: Essays on English Communities, Identities, and Writing*, edited by David Aers, 177–202. Detroit, Mich.: Wayne State University Press, 1992.

Allen, Elizabeth. *False Fables and Exemplary Truth in Later Middle English Literature*. New York: Palgrave Macmillan, 2005.

Allen, Judson Boyce. "Grammar, Poetic Form, and the Lyric Ego: A Medieval *A Priori*." In *Vernacular Poetics in the Middle Ages*, edited by Lois Ebin, 199–226. Kalamazoo, Mich.: Medieval Institute Publications, 1984.

Andrews, Bruce, and Charles Bernstein. "Repossessing the Word." In *The L=A=N=G=U=A=G=E Book*, edited by Bruce Andrews and Charles Bernstein, ix–xi. Carbondale: Southern Illinois University Press, 1984.

Aquinas, Thomas. *A Commentary on Aristotle's* De Anima. Translated by Robert Pasnau. New Haven, Conn.: Yale University Press, 1999.

Aristotle. *Metaphysics.* Translated by Hugh Lawson-Tancred. New York: Penguin, 1998.

———. *Physics.* Edited by David Bostock. Translated by Robin Waterfield. Oxford: Oxford University Press, 1996.

Auden, W. H. *Collected Poems.* Edited by Edward Mendelson. New York: Random House, 1976.

Augustine of Hippo. *Confessions.* Translated by Henry Chadwick. Oxford: Oxford University Press, 2008.

Bakhtin, M. M. "Discourse in the Novel." In *The Dialogic Imagination: Four Essays,* edited by Michael Holquist, 259–422. Austin: University of Texas Press, 1981.

Barley, Nigel. "A Structural Approach to the Proverb and Maxim with Special Reference to the Anglo-Saxon Corpus." *Proverbium* 20 (1972): 737–50.

Baswell, Christopher, Christopher Cannon, Jocelyn Wogan-Browne, and Kathryn Kerby-Fulton. "Competing Archives, Competing Histories: French and Its Cultural Locations in Late-Medieval England." *Speculum* 90 (2015): 635–700.

Bede, Venerable. *Bede's Ecclesiastical History of the English People.* Edited by Bertram Colgrave and R. A. B. Mynors. Oxford: Clarendon Press, 1969.

Berlant, Lauren. "On the Case." *Critical Inquiry* 33 (2007): 663–72.

Bernstein, Charles. "The Academy in Peril: William Carlos Williams Meets the MLA." In *Content's Dream: Essays, 1975–1984,* 244–51. Los Angeles: Sun & Moon Press, 1986.

Birkholz, Daniel. "Harley Lyrics and Hereford Clerics: The Implications of Mobility, c. 1300–1351." *Studies in the Age of Chaucer* 31 (2009): 175–230.

Blake, E. O., ed. *Liber Eliensis.* London: Offices of the Royal Historical Society, 1962.

Bliss, Alan, ed. *Sir Orfeo.* 2nd ed. Oxford: Clarendon, 1966.

Boethius. *Boethius's De Topicis Differentiis.* Translated by Eleonore Stump. Ithaca, N.Y.: Cornell University Press, 1978.

Boffey, Julia. "Forms of Standardization in Terms for Middle English Lyrics in the Fourteenth Century." In *The Beginnings of Standardization: Language and Culture in Fourteenth-Century England,* edited by Ursula Schaefer, Andrew James Johnston, and Claudia Lange, 61–70. Frankfurt, Germany: Peter Lang, 2006.

———. *Manuscripts of English Courtly Love Lyrics in the Later Middle Ages.* Cambridge: D. S. Brewer, 1985.

———. "Middle English Lyrics and Manuscripts." In *A Companion to the Middle English Lyric,* edited by Thomas G. Duncan, 1–18. Cambridge: D. S. Brewer, 2005.

Boffey, Julia, and A. S. G. Edwards, eds. *A Companion to Fifteenth-Century English Poetry.* Cambridge: D. S. Brewer, 2013.

Boitani, Piero. "Petrarch and the '*barbari Britanni*.'" In *Petrarch in Britain: Interpreters, Imitators, and Translators over 700 Years,* edited by M. L. McLaughlin, Letizia Panizza, and Peter Hainsworth, 9–25. Oxford: Oxford University Press, 2007.

Boklund-Lagopoulou, Karin. *I Have a Yong Suster: Popular Song and the Middle English Lyric.* Dublin, Ireland: Four Courts Press, 2002.

Borthwick, Sister Mary Charlotte. "Antigone's Song as 'Mirour' in Chaucer's *Troilus and Criseyde*." *Modern Language Quarterly* 22 (1961): 227–35.

Boulton, Maureen Barry McCann. *The Song in the Story: Lyric Insertions in French Narrative Fiction, 1200–1400*. Philadelphia: University of Pennsylvania Press, 1993.

Bradbury, Nancy Mason. "Proverb Tradition as a Soft Source for the Canterbury Tales." *Studies in the Age of Chaucer* 28 (2006): 237–42.

———. "Transforming Experience into Tradition: Two Theories of Proverb Use and Chaucer's Practice." *Oral Tradition* 17 (2002): 261–89.

Brantley, Jessica. *Reading in the Wilderness: Private Devotion and Public Performance in Late Medieval England*. Chicago: University of Chicago Press, 2007.

Brigden, Susan. *Thomas Wyatt: The Heart's Forest*. London: Faber and Faber, 2012.

Bright, J. W. "Chaucer and Lollius." *PMLA* 18 (1903): xxii–xxiii.

British Library. *Catalogue of Additions to the Manuscripts: 1946–51, Pt. 1*. London: British Library, 1979.

Brook, G. L. *The Harley Lyrics: The Middle English Lyrics of MS. Harley 2253*. Manchester: Manchester University Press, 1968.

Brooks, Cleanth. *The Well Wrought Urn: Studies in the Structure of Poetry*. New York: Harcourt, Brace, Jovanovich, 1975.

Brown, Carleton. *English Lyrics of the XIIIth Century*. Oxford: Clarendon Press, 1932.

———. *Religious Lyrics of the XIVth Century*. Oxford: Clarendon Press, 1952.

———. *Religious Lyrics of the XVth Century*. Oxford: Clarendon Press, 1939.

Buchanan, Ian. "Introduction: Other People: Ethnography and Social Practice." In *The Certeau Reader*, edited by Graham Ward, 97–100. Malden, Mass.: Blackwell, 2000.

Burnley, David, and Alison Wiggins. "The Auchinleck Manuscript," 2004. http://auchinleck.nls.uk/.

Burrow, J. A. *The Poetry of Praise*. Cambridge: Cambridge University Press, 2008.

———. *Ricardian Poetry: Chaucer, Gower, Langland and the "Gawain" Poet*. New Haven, Conn.: Yale University Press, 1971.

Butterfield, Ardis. "Afterwords: Forms of Death." *Exemplaria* 27 (2015): 167–82.

———. "The Construction of Textual Form: Cross-Lingual Citation in the Medieval Insular Lyric." In *Citation, Intertextuality and Memory in the Middle Ages and Renaissance: Vol. 1: Text, Music and Image from Machaut to Ariosto*, edited by Yolanda Plumley, Giuliano Di Bacco, and Stefano Jossa, 41–57. Exeter: University of Exeter Press, 2011.

———. *The Familiar Enemy: Chaucer, Language and Nation in the Hundred Years War*. Oxford: Oxford University Press, 2009.

———. "Interpolated Lyric in Medieval Narrative Poetry." Ph.D. diss., University of Cambridge, 1987.

———. *Poetry and Music in Medieval France: From Jean Renart to Guillaume de Machaut*. Cambridge: Cambridge University Press, 2002.

———. "Why Medieval Lyric?" *English Literary History* 82 (2015): 319–43.

Bynum, Caroline Walker. Docere Verbo et Exemplo: *An Aspect of Twelfth-Century Spirituality*. Harvard Theological Studies 31. Missoula, Mont.: Scholars Press, 1979.

———. *Jesus as Mother: Studies in the Spirituality of the High Middle Ages*. Berkeley: University of California Press, 1982.

Camargo, Martin. "Latin Composition Textbooks and Ad Herennium Glossing." In *The Rhetoric of Cicero in Its Medieval and Early Renaissance Commentary Tradition*, edited by Virginia Cox and John O. Ward, 267–88. Leiden: Brill, 2006.

———. "*Tria Sunt*: The Long and the Short of Geoffrey of Vinsauf's *Documentum de Modo et Arte Dictandi et Versificandi*." *Speculum* 74 (1999): 935–55.

Camargo, Martin, and Marjorie Curry Woods. "Writing Instruction in Late Medieval Europe." In *A Short History of Writing Instruction: From Ancient Greece to Contemporary America*, edited by James J. Murphy, 114–47. New York: Routledge, 2012.

Cameron, Sharon. *Lyric Time: Dickinson and the Limits of Genre*. Baltimore: Johns Hopkins University Press, 1979.

Cannon, Christopher. *The Grounds of English Literature*. Oxford: Oxford University Press, 2004.

Carruthers, Mary. "On Affliction and Reading, Weeping and Argument: Chaucer's Lachrymose Troilus in Context." *Representations* 93 (2006): 1–21.

Certeau, Michel de. *The Practice of Everyday Life*. Translated by Steven Rendall. Berkeley: University of California Press, 1984.

Cervone, Cristina Maria. *Poetics of the Incarnation: Middle English Writing and the Leap of Love*. Philadelphia: University of Pennsylvania Press, 2012.

Chaganti, Seeta. "Choreographing Mouvance: The Case of the English Carol." *Philological Quarterly* 87 (2008): 77–103.

———. "Dance in a Haunted Space: Genre, and Form in the Middle English Carol." *Exemplaria* 27 (2015): 129–49.

———. *The Medieval Poetics of the Reliquary: Enshrinement, Inscription, Performance*. New York: Palgrave Macmillan, 2008.

Chambers, E. K. *The Mediaeval Stage*. London: Oxford University Press, 1967.

———. "Some Aspects of Mediaeval Lyrics." In *Early English Lyrics: Amorous, Divine, Moral and Trivial*, edited by Frank Sidgwick and E. K. Chambers, 257–96. London: Sidgwick & Jackson, 1966.

Charland, Thomas Marie, ed. *Artes praedicandi: Contribution à l'histoire de la rhétorique au Moyen Age*. Paris: J. Vrin, 1936.

Chaucer, Geoffrey. *The Riverside Chaucer*. Edited by Larry Dean Benson. 3rd ed. Oxford: Oxford University Press, 2008.

———. *Troilus and Criseyde, with Facing-Page Il Filostrato*. Edited by Stephen A. Barney. New York: W. W. Norton, 2005.

Chavannes-Mazel, Claudine A. "Expanding Rubrics for the Sake of a Layout: Mise-En-Page as Evidence for a Particular Scribe?" In *Medieval Book Production: Assessing the Evidence*, edited by Linda L. Brownrigg, 118–24. Los Altos Hills, Calif.: Red Gull Press, 1990.

Chickering, Howell D. "'Foweles in the Frith': A Religious Art-Song." *Philological Quarterly* 50 (1971): 115–20.

Cicero, Marcus Tullius. *De Inventione: De Optimo Genere Oratorum. Topica.* Edited and translated by Harry Hubbell. Cambridge, Mass.: Harvard University Press, 1949.

Cicero, Marcus Tullius [pseudo]. *Rhetorica ad Herennium.* Translated by Harry Caplan. Cambridge, Mass.: Harvard University Press, 1999.

Clanchy, M. T. *From Memory to Written Record, England 1066–1307.* 2nd ed. Oxford: Blackwell, 1993.

Coleman, Joyce. *Public Reading and the Reading Public in Late Medieval England and France.* Cambridge: Cambridge University Press, 1996.

Collette, Carolyn P. *Rethinking Chaucer's* Legend of Good Women. Woodbridge: Boydell & Brewer, 2014.

Colonne, Guido delle. *Historia Destructionis Troiae.* Edited by Nathaniel Edward Griffin. Cambridge, Mass: Mediaeval Academy of America, 1936.

———. *Historia Destructionis Troiae.* Translated by Mary Elizabeth Meek. Bloomington: Indiana University Press, 1974.

Conrad of Hirsau. "Dialogue on the Authors: Extracts." In *Medieval Literary Theory and Criticism, c. 1100–c. 1375: The Commentary-Tradition,* edited by A. J. Minnis and A. Brian Scott, 39–64. Oxford: Clarendon Press, 1988.

Copeland, Rita. *Rhetoric, Hermeneutics, and Translation in the Middle Ages: Academic Traditions and Vernacular Texts.* Cambridge: Cambridge University Press, 1991.

Copeland, Rita, and Ineke Sluiter, eds. *Medieval Grammar and Rhetoric: Language Arts and Literary Theory, AD 300–1475.* Oxford: Oxford University Press, 2009.

Crane, Susan. "Anglo-Norman Cultures in England, 1066–1460." In *The Cambridge History of Medieval English Literature,* edited by David Wallace, 35–60. Cambridge: Cambridge University Press, 2002.

Culler, Jonathan. "Changes in the Study of the Lyric." In *Lyric Poetry: Beyond New Criticism,* edited by Chaviva Hošek and Patricia A. Parker, 38–54. Ithaca, N.Y.: Cornell University Press, 1985.

———. *Theory of the Lyric.* Cambridge, Mass.: Harvard University Press, 2015.

———. "Why Lyric?" *PMLA* 123 (2008): 201–6.

Curtius, Ernst Robert. *European Literature and the Latin Middle Ages.* Translated by Willard R. Trask. Princeton, N.J.: Princeton University Press, 1973.

Daniel, Hermann Adalbert, ed. *Thesaurus Hymnologicus Sive Hymnorum, Canticorum, Sequentiarum Circa Annum MD Usitatarum Collectio Amplissima.* 3 vols. Leipzig: J. T. Loeschke, 1855.

Dante Alighieri. *De Vulgari Eloquentia.* Translated by Steven Botterill. Cambridge: Cambridge University Press, 1996.

———. *The Divine Comedy.* Translated by Robin Kirkpatrick. New York: Penguin, 2006.

Davenport, W. A. *Chaucer: Complaint and Narrative.* Woodbridge: D. S. Brewer, 1988.

Dean, Ruth J., and Maureen Boulton. *Anglo-Norman Literature: A Guide to Texts and Manuscripts.* London: Anglo-Norman Text Society, 1999.

De Grazia, Margareta. "Anachronism." In *Cultural Reformations: Medieval and Renaissance in Literary History,* edited by Brian Cummings and James Simpson, 13–32. Oxford: Oxford University Press, 2010.

Delany, Sheila. *The Naked Text: Chaucer's* Legend of Good Women. Berkeley: University of California Press, 1994.

De Man, Paul. "Anthropomorphism and the Trope in Lyric." In *The Rhetoric of Romanticism*, 239–62. New York: Columbia University Press, 1984.

———. "Autobiography as De-Facement." In *The Rhetoric of Romanticism*, 67–81. New York: Columbia University Press, 1984.

Derrida, Jacques. *Voice and Phenomenon: Introduction to the Problem of the Sign in Husserl's Phenomenology.* Translated by Leonard Lawlor. Evanston, Ill.: Northwestern University Press, 2011.

Deschamps, Eustache. *L'Art de Dictier.* Translated by Deborah M. Sinnreich-Levi. East Lansing, Mich.: Colleagues Press, 1994.

Dillon, Emma. "Unwriting Medieval Song." *New Literary History* 46 (2015): 595–622.

Dinshaw, Carolyn. *Chaucer's Sexual Poetics.* Madison: University of Wisconsin Press, 1989.

Dobson, E. J., and Frank L. Harrison. *Medieval English Songs.* Cambridge: Cambridge University Press, 1979.

Donatelli, Joseph. "The Percy Folio Manuscript: A Seventeenth-Century Context for Medieval Poetry." In *English Manuscript Studies: 1100–1700*, edited by Peter Beal and Jeremy Griffiths, 4:114–33. Oxford: Blackwell, 1993.

Dronke, Peter. *Medieval Latin and the Rise of European Love-Lyric.* Oxford: Clarendon Press, 1965.

———. *The Medieval Lyric.* 3rd ed. Woodbridge: D. S. Brewer, 1996.

———. *Poetic Individuality in the Middle Ages: New Departures in Poetry, 1000–1150.* Oxford: Clarendon Press, 1970.

———. "The Rawlinson Lyrics." *Notes & Queries* 206 (1961): 245–46.

———. "The Return of Eurydice." *Classica et Mediaevalia* 23 (1962): 198–215.

Dryden, John. "Preface to Fables Ancient and Modern." In *Selected Poetry and Prose of John Dryden*, edited by Earl Roy Miner, 515–41. New York: Modern Library, 1985.

Dubrow, Heather. *The Challenges of Orpheus: Lyric Poetry and Early Modern England.* Baltimore: Johns Hopkins University Press, 2008.

———. *Echoes of Desire: English Petrarchism and Its Counterdiscourses.* Ithaca, N.Y.: Cornell University Press, 1995.

———. *A Happier Eden: The Politics of Marriage in the Stuart Epithalamium.* Ithaca, N.Y.: Cornell University Press, 1990.

Duncan, Thomas G., ed. *A Companion to the Middle English Lyric.* Woodbridge: Brewer, 2005.

———. "Introduction." In *A Companion to the Middle English Lyric*, edited by Thomas G. Duncan, xiii–xxv. Cambridge: D. S. Brewer, 2005.

Durand, Guillaume. *Rationale, Book Four: On the Mass and Each Action Pertaining to It.* Translated by T. M. Thibodeau. Turnhout: Brepols, 2013.

Durling, Nancy Vine. "British Library MS Harley 2253: A New Reading of the Passion Lyrics in Their Manuscript Context." *Viator: Medieval and Renaissance Studies* 40 (2009): 271–307.

Eliot, Thomas Stearns. *Three Voices of Poetry*. Cambridge: Cambridge University Press, 1954.

Enders, Jody. *Rhetoric and the Origins of Medieval Drama*. Ithaca, N.Y.: Cornell University Press, 1992.

Fairweather, Janet, trans. *Liber Eliensis: A History of the Isle of Ely from the Seventh Century to the Twelfth*. Woodbridge: Boydell Press, 2005.

Fein, Susanna. "Compilation and Purpose in MS Harley 2253." In *Essays in Manuscript Geography: Vernacular Manuscripts of the English West Midlands from the Conquest to the Sixteenth Century*, edited by Wendy Scase, 67–94. Turnhout, Belgium: Brepols, 2007.

———, ed. *Moral Love Songs and Laments*. Kalamazoo, Mich.: Medieval Institute Publications, 1998.

———. "A Saint 'Geynest Under Gore': Marina and the Love Lyrics of the Seventh Quire." In *Studies in the Harley Manuscript: The Scribes, Contents, and Social Contexts of British Library MS Harley 2253*, edited by Susanna Fein, 351–76. Kalamazoo, Mich.: Medieval Institute Publications, 2000.

———, ed. *Studies in the Harley Manuscript: The Scribes, Contents, and Social Contexts of British Library MS Harley 2253*. Kalamazoo, Mich.: Medieval Institute Publications, 2000.

Fein, Susanna, and David B. Raybin, eds., with Jan M. Ziolkowski. *The Complete Harley 2253 Manuscript*. 3 vols. Kalamazoo, Mich.: Medieval Institute Publications, 2014.

Finke, Laurie, Martin Shichtman, and Kathleen Coyne Kelly, eds. "Medieval Mobilities." *postmedieval* 4 (2013): 125–237.

Fisher, Matthew. *Scribal Authorship and the Writing of History in Medieval England*. Columbus: Ohio State University Press, 2012.

Flanigan, C. Clifford, Kathleen Ashley, and Pamela Sheingorn. "Liturgy as Social Performance: Expanding the Definitions." In *The Liturgy of the Medieval Church*, edited by Thomas J. Heffernan and E. Ann Matter, 695–714. Kalamazoo, Mich.: Medieval Institute Publications, 2001.

Förster, Max. "Kleinere Mittelenglische Texte." *Anglia* 42 (1918): 142–224.

Fradenburg, L. O. Aranye. *Sacrifice Your Love: Psychoanalysis, Historicism, Chaucer*. Minneapolis: University of Minnesota Press, 2002.

Frank, Robert Worth. *Chaucer and the Legend of Good Women*. Cambridge, Mass.: Harvard University Press, 1972.

Frere, Walter Howard, and Langton E. G. Brown, eds. *The Hereford Breviary*. London: Henry Bradshaw Society, 1904.

Froissart, Jean. *The Lyric Poems of Jehan Froissart: A Critical Edition*. Edited by Rob Roy McGregor. Chapel Hill, N.C.: U.N.C. Dept. of Romance Languages, 1975.

Frye, Northrop. *Anatomy of Criticism: Four Essays*. Princeton, N.J.: Princeton University Press, 1957.

———. "Approaching the Lyric." In *Lyric Poetry: Beyond New Criticism*, edited by Chaviva Hošek and Patricia A. Parker, 31–37. Ithaca, N.Y.: Cornell University Press, 1985.

Fulton, Alice. *Feeling as a Foreign Language: The Good Strangeness of Poetry.* St. Paul, Minn.: Graywolf Press, 1999.

Fumo, Jamie Claire. *The Legacy of Apollo: Antiquity, Authority and Chaucerian Poetics.* Toronto: University of Toronto Press, 2010.

Fyler, John M. *Chaucer and Ovid.* New Haven, Conn.: Yale University Press, 1979.

Galvez, Marisa. *Songbook: How Lyrics Became Poetry in Medieval Europe.* Chicago: University of Chicago Press, 2012.

Gaunt, Simon. "Orality and Writing: The Text of the Troubadour Poem." In *The Troubadours: An Introduction*, edited by Simon Gaunt and Sarah Kay, 228–45. Cambridge: Cambridge University Press, 1999.

Gautier de Coinci. *Les miracles de Nostre Dame.* Edited by V. Frederic Koenig. 4 vols. Geneva: Droz, 1955.

Genette, Gérard. *The Architext: An Introduction.* Translated by Jane E. Lewin. Berkeley: University of California Press, 1992.

Geoffrey of Vinsauf. *Poetria Nova of Geoffrey of Vinsauf.* Translated by Margaret F. Nims. Toronto: Pontifical Institute of Mediaeval Studies, 1967.

Gerald of Wales. *The Jewel of the Church.* Translated by John J. Hagen. Leiden: Brill, 1979.

Giancarlo, Matthew. *Parliament and Literature in Late Medieval England.* Cambridge: Cambridge University Press, 2007.

Ginsberg, Warren. *Chaucer's Italian Tradition.* Ann Arbor: University of Michigan Press, 2002.

Gneuss, Helmut. "Latin Hymns in Medieval England: Future Research." In *Chaucer and Middle English Studies in Honour of Rossell Hope Robbins*, edited by Lloyd A. Duchemin, 407–24. London: Allen & Unwin, 1974.

Gray, Douglas. *Themes and Images in the Medieval English Religious Lyric.* London: Routledge and Kegan Paul, 1972.

Green, Richard Firth. *A Crisis of Truth: Literature and Law in Ricardian England.* Philadelphia: University of Pennsylvania Press, 1999.

———. "The Two 'Litel Wot Hit Any Mon' Lyrics in Harley 2253." *Mediaeval Studies* 51 (1989): 304–12.

Greene, Richard Leighton. *The Early English Carols.* 2nd ed. Oxford: Clarendon Press, 1977.

Greene, Roland. *Post-Petrarchism: Origins and Innovations of the Western Lyric Sequence.* Princeton, N.J.: Princeton University Press, 1991.

Greentree, Rosemary. *The Middle English Lyric and Short Poem.* Woodbridge: D. S. Brewer, 2001.

Gummere, Francis Barton. *The Beginnings of Poetry.* New York: Macmillan, 1901.

Hahn, Thomas. "Early Middle English." In *The Cambridge History of Medieval English Literature*, edited by David Wallace, 61–91. Cambridge: Cambridge University Press, 1999.

Harrier, Richard C. *The Canon of Sir Thomas Wyatt's Poetry.* Cambridge, Mass.: Harvard University Press, 1975.

Hegel, Georg Wilhelm Friedrich. *Aesthetics: Lectures on Fine Art*. Translated by T. M. Knox. 2 vols. Oxford: Clarendon Press, 1974.

Herebert, William. *The Works of William Herebert, OFM*. Edited by Stephen R. Reimer. Toronto: Pontifical Institute of Mediaeval Studies, 1987.

Hollander, John. "Breaking into Song: Some Notes on Refrain." In *Lyric Poetry: Beyond New Criticism*, edited by Chavia Hošek and Patricia Parker, 73–89. Ithaca, N.Y.: Cornell University Press, 1985.

Holsinger, Bruce. "Analytical Survey 6: Medieval Literature and Cultures of Performance." *New Medieval Literatures* 6 (2003): 271–311.

———. "Liturgy." In *Middle English*, edited by Paul Strohm, 295–314. Oxford: Oxford University Press, 2007.

———. "Lyrics and Short Poems." In *The Yale Companion to Chaucer*, edited by Seth Lerer, 179–212. New Haven, Conn.: Yale University Press, 2006.

———. *Music, Body, and Desire in Medieval Culture: Hildegard of Bingen to Chaucer*. Stanford, Calif.: Stanford University Press, 2001.

———. "The Parable of Caedmon's Hymn: Liturgical Invention and Literary Tradition." *Journal of English and Germanic Philology* 106 (2007): 149–75.

———. "Vernacular Legality: The English Jurisdictions of The Owl and the Nightingale." In *The Letter of the Law: Legal Practice and Literary Production in Medieval England*, edited by Emily Steiner and Candace Barrington, 154–84. Ithaca, N.Y.: Cornell University Press, 2002.

Holt, Robert, and Robert Meadows White, eds. *The Ormulum: With the Notes and Glossary of Dr. R. M. White*. 2 vols. Oxford: Clarendon Press, 1878.

Horace. "Ars Poetica." In *Satires, Epistles, and Ars Poetica*, edited and translated by H. Rushton Fairclough, 442–89. Cambridge, Mass.: Harvard University Press, 1955.

Hornstein, Lillian Herlands. "Petrarch's Laelius, Chaucer's Lollius?" *PMLA* 63 (1948): 64–84.

Hošek, Chaviva, and Patricia A. Parker, eds. *Lyric Poetry: Beyond New Criticism*. Ithaca, N.Y.: Cornell University Press, 1985.

Hsy, Jonathan. *Trading Tongues: Merchants, Multilingualism, and Medieval Literature*. Columbus: Ohio State University Press, 2013.

Hughes, H. V., and H. E. Wooldridge, eds. *Early English Harmony from the 10th to the 15th Century*. 2 vols. London: B. Quaritch and The Plainsong and Medieval Music Society, 1897.

Hunt, Tony. "*Deliciae Clericorum*: Intellectual and Scientific Pursuits in Two Dorset Monasteries." *Medium Aevum* 56 (1987): 159–82.

———. *Miraculous Rhymes: The Writing of Gautier De Coinci*. Cambridge: D. S. Brewer, 2007.

———. *Teaching and Learning Latin in Thirteenth-Century England*. Cambridge: D. S. Brewer, 1991.

———. "Wordplay Before the 'Rhétoriqueurs'?" In *De Sens Rassis: Essays in Honor of Rupert T. Pickens*, edited by Keith Busby, Bernard Guidot, and Logan E. Whalen, 283–96. Amsterdam: Rodopi, 2005.

Huot, Sylvia. *From Song to Book: The Poetics of Writing in Old French Lyric and Lyrical Narrative Poetry*. Ithaca, N.Y.: Cornell University Press, 1987.

Hutson, Lorna. "Ethopoeia, Source-Study and Legal History." In *Post-Theory: New Directions in Criticism*, edited by Martin McQuillan, 139–60. Edinburgh: Edinburgh University Press, 1999.

Ingham, Patricia Clare. "Chaucer's Haunted Aesthetics: Mimesis and Trauma in *Troilus and Criseyde*." *College English* 72 (2010): 226–47.

Isidore of Seville. *The Etymologies of Isidore of Seville*. Translated by Stephen A. Barney, W. J. Lewis, J. A. Beach, and Oliver Berghof. Cambridge: Cambridge University Press, 2006.

Jackson, Virginia. *Dickinson's Misery: A Theory of Lyric Reading*. Princeton, N.J.: Princeton University Press, 2005.

———, ed. "Theories and Methodologies: The New Lyric Studies." *PMLA* 123 (2008): 181–234.

Jackson, Virginia, and Yopie Prins, eds. *The Lyric Theory Reader: A Critical Anthology*. Baltimore: Johns Hopkins University Press, 2013.

James, M. R. *The Western Manuscripts in the Library of Trinity College, Cambridge: A Descriptive Catalogue*. 4 vols. Cambridge: Cambridge University Press, 1900.

Jameson, Fredric. *The Political Unconscious: Narrative as a Socially Symbolic Act*. Ithaca, N.Y.: Cornell University Press, 1981.

Jeffrey, David L., and Brian J. Levy, eds. *The Anglo-Norman Lyric: An Anthology*. Toronto: Pontifical Institute of Mediaeval Studies, 1990.

Jeffreys, Mark. "Ideologies of Lyric: A Problem of Genre in Contemporary Anglophone Poetics." *PMLA* 110 (1995): 196–205.

Jerome, St. *Liber De Optimo Genere Interpretandi (Epistula 57)*. Edited by G. J. M. Bartelink. Leiden: Brill, 1980.

John of Garland. *The Parisiana Poetria of John of Garland*. Edited and translated by Traugott Lawler. New Haven, Conn.: Yale University Press, 1974.

John of Grimestone. *A Descriptive Index of the English Lyrics in John of Grimestone's Preaching Book*. Edited by Edward Wilson. Oxford: Blackwell, 1973.

John of Salisbury. *The Metalogicon: A Twelfth-Century Defense of the Verbal and Logical Arts of the Trivium*. Translated by Daniel D. McGarry. Berkeley: University of California Press, 1955.

Johnson, Eleanor. *Practicing Literary Theory in the Middle Ages: Ethics and the Mixed Form in Chaucer, Gower, Usk, and Hoccleve*. Chicago: University of Chicago Press, 2013.

Jonsen, Albert R., and Stephen Edelston Toulmin. *The Abuse of Casuistry: A History of Moral Reasoning*. Berkeley: University of California Press, 1988.

Jotischky, Andrew. "Herbert, William (d. 1333/1337?)." In *Oxford Dictionary of National Biography*. Oxford: Oxford University Press, 2004. http://www.oxforddnb.com/view/article/13052.

Joyce, James. *A Portrait of the Artist as a Young Man*. Edited by John Paul Riquelme. Norton Critical Edition. New York: Norton, 2007.

Julian, John. *A Dictionary of Hymnology, Setting Forth the Origin and History of Christian Hymns of All Ages and Nations.* 2 vols. New York: Dover Publications, 1957.

Kaufman, Robert. "Lyric Commodity Critique, Benjamin Adorno Marx, Baudelaire Baudelaire Baudelaire." *PMLA* 123 (2008): 207–15.

Kay, Sarah. "Desire and Subjectivity." In *The Troubadours: An Introduction*, edited by Simon Gaunt and Sarah Kay, 212–27. Cambridge: Cambridge University Press, 1999.

———. *Parrots and Nightingales: Troubadour Quotations and the Development of European Poetry.* Philadelphia: University of Pennsylvania Press, 2013.

———. *Subjectivity in Troubadour Poetry.* Cambridge: Cambridge University Press, 1990.

Kemmler, Fritz. *"Exempla" in Context: A Historical and Critical Study of Robert Mannyng of Brunne's "Handlyng Synne."* Tübingen: G. Narr, 1984.

Kendall, Elliot Richard. "Family, Familia, and the Uncanny in *Sir Orfeo*." *Studies in the Age of Chaucer* 35 (2013): 289–327.

Kennedy, George Alexander, trans. *Progymnasmata: Greek Textbooks of Prose Composition and Rhetoric.* Leiden: Brill, 2003.

Ker, N. R., ed. *Facsimile of British Museum MS. Harley 2253.* Oxford: Oxford University Press, 1965.

Kieran, Kevin. "Reading Caedmon's 'Hymn' with Someone Else's Glosses." *Representations* 32 (1990): 151–74.

Kinney, Clare Regan. "'Who Made This Song?': The Engendering of Lyric Counterplots in *Troilus and Criseyde*." *Studies in Philology* 89 (1992): 272–92.

Kiser, Lisa J. *Telling Classical Tales: Chaucer and the* Legend of Good Women. Ithaca, N.Y.: Cornell University Press, 1983.

Kittredge, George Lyman. "Antigone's Song of Love." *Modern Language Notes* 25 (1910): 158.

———. "Chaucer's Lollius." *Harvard Studies in Classical Philology* 28 (1917): 47–133.

Kittsteiner, H.-D. "Kant and Casuistry." In *Conscience and Casuistry in Early Modern Europe*, edited by Edmund Leites, 185–213. Cambridge: Cambridge University Press, 1988.

Kuczynski, Michael P. "An 'Electric Stream': The Religious Contents." In *Studies in the Harley Manuscript: The Scribes, Contents, and Social Contexts of British Library MS Harley 2253*, edited by Susanna Fein, 123–61. Kalamazoo, Mich.: Medieval Institute Publications, 2000.

Lakoff, George. "The Neural Theory of Metaphor." In *The Cambridge Handbook of Metaphor and Thought*, edited by Raymond W. Gibbs, 17–38. Cambridge: Cambridge University Press, 2008.

Lanham, Carol Dana. "Writing Instruction from Late Antiquity to the Twelfth Century." In *A Short History of Writing Instruction: From Ancient Greece to Contemporary America*, edited by James J. Murphy, 77–113. New York: Routledge, 2012.

Laskaya, Anne, and Eve Salisbury, eds. *The Middle English Breton Lays.* Kalamazoo, Mich.: Medieval Institute Publications, 1995.

Lawton, David. "Voice and Public Interiorities: Chaucer, Orpheus, Machaut." In *Answerable Style: The Idea of the Literary in Medieval England*, edited by Frank Grady and Andrew Galloway, 284–306. Columbus: Ohio State University Press, 2013.

Leach, Elizabeth Eva. *Sung Birds: Music, Nature, and Poetry in the Later Middle Ages*. Ithaca, N.Y.: Cornell University Press, 2007.

Le Goff, Jacques. *Medieval Civilization 400–1500*. Translated by Julia Barrow. Oxford: Blackwell, 1988.

Lerer, Seth. "Artifice and Artistry in *Sir Orfeo*." *Speculum* 60 (1985): 92–109.

———. "The Endurance of Formalism in Middle English Studies." *Literature Compass* 1 (2004): 1–15.

———. "Medieval English Literature and the Idea of the Anthology." *PMLA* 118 (2003): 1251–67.

Levine, Caroline. *Forms: Whole, Rhythm, Hierarchy, Network*. Princeton, N.J.: Princeton University Press, 2015.

Levinson, Marjorie. "What Is New Formalism?" *PMLA* 122 (2007): 558–69.

Lewis, C. S. *The Allegory of Love: A Study in Medieval Tradition*. Oxford: Oxford University Press, 1958.

———. "What Chaucer Really Did to *Il Filostrato*." *Essays and Studies* 17 (1932): 56–75.

Little, A. G. *The Grey Friars in Oxford*. Oxford: Clarendon Press, 1892.

Lossing, Marian. "The Prologue to the *Legend of Good Women* and the *Lai de Franchise*." *Studies in Philology* 39 (1942): 15–35.

Lowes, J. L. "The Prologue to the *Legend of Good Women* as Related to the French Marguerite Poems and the *Filostrato*." *PMLA* 19 (1904): 593–683.

Luria, Maxwell, and Richard Lester Hoffman, eds. *Middle English Lyrics*. New York: Norton, 1974.

Lynch, Kathryn L. *Chaucer's Philosophical Visions*. Cambridge: Brewer, 2000.

Machan, Tim William. "Editing, Orality, and Late Middle English Texts." In *Vox Intexta: Orality and Textuality in the Middle Ages*, edited by Alger Nicolaus Doane and Carol Braun Pasternack, 229–45. Madison: University of Wisconsin Press, 1991.

———. *Textual Criticism and Middle English Texts*. Charlottesville: University Press of Virginia, 1994.

Machaut, Guillaume de. *Le livre dou voir dit (The Book of the True Poem)*. Edited by Daniel Leech-Wilkinson. Translated by R. Barton Palmer. New York: Garland Publishing, 1998.

———. *Poésies lyriques*. Edited by Vladimir Fedorovich Chichmaref. 2 vols. Geneva: Slatkine Reprints, 1973.

Mannyng, Robert. *Handlyng Synne*. Edited by Idelle Sullens. Binghamton, N.Y.: Medieval & Renaissance Texts & Studies, 1983.

Marsh, George L. "Sources and Analogues of The Flower and the Leaf Part I." *Modern Philology* 4 (1906): 121–67.

Matonis, A. T. E. "An Investigation of Celtic Influences on Harley 2253." *Modern Philology* 70 (1972): 91–108.

———. "The Harley Lyrics: English and Welsh Convergences." *Modern Philology* 86 (1988): 1–21.

Matthew of Vendôme. *Ars Versificatoria: The Art of the Versemaker*. Translated by Roger P. Parr. Milwaukee, Wisc.: Marquette University Press, 1981.

Matthews, David. *Writing to the King: Nation, Kingship, and Literature in England, 1250–1350*. Cambridge: Cambridge University Press, 2010.

Mayhew, A. L., ed. *The Promptorium Parvulorum. The First English-Latin Dictionary*. EETS 102. London: K. Paul, Trench, Trubner & Co., 1908.

McCall, John P., and George Rudisill. "The Parliament of 1386 and Chaucer's Trojan Parliament." *Journal of English and Germanic Philology* 58 (1959): 276–88.

McNamer, Sarah. *Affective Meditation and the Invention of Medieval Compassion*. Philadelphia: University of Pennsylvania Press, 2010.

McSparran, Frances, gen. ed. *Middle English Dictionary*. Ann Arbor: University of Michigan, 2001. http://quod.lib.umich.edu/m/med/.

Middleton, Anne. "The Idea of Public Poetry in the Reign of Richard II." *Speculum* 53 (1978): 94–114.

Mill, John Stuart. *Essays on Poetry*. Edited by F. Parvin Sharpless. Columbia: University of South Carolina Press, 1976.

Miller, Mark. "Displaced Souls, Idle Talk, Spectacular Scenes: *Handlyng Synne* and the Perspective of Agency." *Speculum* 71 (1996): 606–32.

Millett, Bella. "Chaucer, Lollius, and the Medieval Theory of Authorship." *Studies in the Age of Chaucer: Proceedings* 1 (1984): 93–103.

Minnis, Alastair J. *Medieval Theory of Authorship: Scholastic Literary Attitudes in the Later Middle Ages*. 2nd ed. Philadelphia: University of Pennsylvania Press, 1988.

———. "Quadruplex Sensus, Multiplex Modus: Scriptural Sense and Mode in Medieval Scholastic Exegesis." In *Interpretation and Allegory: Antiquity to the Modern Period*, edited by Jon Whitman, 231–58. Leiden: Brill, 2000.

Minnis, Alastair J., and A. Brian Scott, eds. *Medieval Literary Theory and Criticism, c. 1100–c. 1375: The Commentary-Tradition*. Oxford: Clarendon Press, 1988.

Mitchell, J. Allan. *Ethics and Exemplary Narrative in Chaucer and Gower*. Cambridge: D. S. Brewer, 2004.

Mooney, Linne, Daniel W. Mosser, and Elizabeth Solopova. *The Digital Index of Middle English Verse (DIMEV)*. http://dimev.net.

Morison, Benjamin. *On Location: Aristotle's Concept of Place*. Oxford: Oxford University Press, 2002.

Morris, Colin. *The Discovery of the Individual, 1050–1200*. London: S.P.C.K. for the Church Historical Society, 1972.

Moser, Thomas C. "'And I Mon Waxe Wod': The Middle English 'Foweles in the Frith.'" *PMLA* 102 (1987): 326–37.

Moses, W. R. "An Appetite for Form." *Modern Language Notes* 49 (1934): 226–29.

Murphy, James, ed. *Three Medieval Rhetorical Arts*. Tempe: Arizona Center for Medieval and Renaissance Studies, 2001.

Muscatine, Charles. *Chaucer and the French Tradition: A Study in Style and Meaning.* Berkeley: University of California Press, 1957.

Nelson, Ingrid. "The Performance of Power in Medieval English Households: The Case of the Harrowing of Hell." *Journal of English and Germanic Philology* 112 (2013): 48–69.

———. "Premodern Media and Networks of Transmission in the Man of Law's Tale." *Exemplaria* 25 (2013): 211–30.

Nelson, Ingrid, and Shannon Gayk. "Introduction: Genre as Form-of-Life." *Exemplaria* 27 (2015): 3–17.

Newman, Barbara. *Medieval Crossover: Reading the Secular Against the Sacred.* Notre Dame, Ind.: University of Notre Dame Press, 2013.

Nichols, Stephen G. "'Art' and 'Nature': Looking for (Medieval) Principles of Order in Occitan Chansonnier N (Morgan 819)." In *The Whole Book: Cultural Perspectives on the Medieval Miscellany*, edited by Stephen G. Nichols and Siegfried Wenzel, 83–121. Ann Arbor: University of Michigan Press, 1996.

Nichols, Stephen J. "Introduction: Philology in a Manuscript Culture." *Speculum* 65 (1990): 1–10.

O'Keeffe, Katherine O'Brien. "Orality and the Developing Text of Caedmon's Hymn." *Speculum* 62 (1987): 1–20.

Ong, Walter J. *Orality and Literacy: The Technologizing of the Word.* 5th ed. New York: Routledge, 2002.

Orme, Nicholas. *Medieval Schools: From Roman Britain to Renaissance England.* New Haven, Conn.: Yale University Press, 2006.

Ovid. *Heroides and Amores.* Translated by Grant Showerman. Cambridge, Mass.: Harvard University Press, 1921.

Owst, G. R. *Literature and Pulpit in Medieval England; a Neglected Chapter in the History of English Letters & of the English People.* Cambridge: Cambridge University Press, 1933.

Oxford English Dictionary. Oxford: Oxford University Press, 2016. http://www.oed.com.

Page, Christopher. *The Owl and the Nightingale: Musical Life and Ideas in France, 1100–1300.* Berkeley: University of California Press, 1990.

Parker, Patricia A. "Introduction." In *Lyric Poetry: Beyond New Criticism*, edited by Chaviva Hošek and Patricia A. Parker. Ithaca, N.Y.: Cornell University Press, 1985.

Patterson, Lee. *Chaucer and the Subject of History.* Madison: University of Wisconsin Press, 1991.

———. *Negotiating the Past: The Historical Understanding of Medieval Literature.* Madison: University of Wisconsin Press, 1987.

———. *Temporal Circumstances: Form and History in the Canterbury Tales.* New York: Palgrave Macmillan, 2006.

———. "Writing Amourous Wrongs: Chaucer and the Order of Complaint." In *The Idea of Medieval Literature: New Essays on Chaucer and Medieval Culture in Honor of Donald R. Howard*, edited by James M. Dean and Christian Zacher, 55–71. Newark: University of Delaware Press, 1992.

Payne, Robert O. *The Key of Remembrance: A Study of Chaucer's Poetics*. New Haven, Conn.: Yale University Press, 1963.

Pearsall, Derek, ed. *The Floure and the Leafe; And, The Assembly of Ladies*. Manchester: Manchester University Press, 1980.

———. *The Life of Geoffrey Chaucer: A Critical Biography*. Oxford: Blackwell, 1992.

———. "Medieval Anthologies, Compilations, Miscellanies: The Rage for Order." Lowrie J. Daly, S.J., Memorial Lecture on Manuscript Studies, presented at the Fortieth Annual St. Louis Conference on Manuscript Studies, St. Louis, Mo., October 12, 2013.

———. *Old English and Middle English Poetry*. London: Routledge & K. Paul, 1977.

Pepin, Ronald E., trans. *An English Translation of Auctores Octo, a Medieval Reader*. Lewiston, N.Y.: Edwin Mellen Press, 1999.

Peraino, Judith A. *Giving Voice to Love: Song and Self-Expression from the Troubadours to Guillaume de Machaut*. Oxford: Oxford University Press, 2011.

Percy, Thomas. *Reliques of Ancient English Poetry. Consisting of Old Heroic Ballads, Songs, and Other Pieces of Our Earlier Poets, Together with Some Few of Later Date*. 4th ed. 3 vols. London: F. and C. Rivington, 1794.

Perloff, Marjorie. "Can(n)on to the Right of Us, Can(n)on to the Left of Us: A Plea for Difference." *New Literary History* 18 (1987): 633–56.

Petrarch, Francis. *The Canzoniere, Or, Rerum Vulgarium Fragmenta*. Translated by Mark Musa. Bloomington: Indiana University Press, 1996.

———. *Letters of Old Age: Rerum Senilium Libri, I–XVIII*. Translated by Aldo S. Bernardo, Saul Levin, and Reta A. Bernardo. 2 vols. Baltimore: Johns Hopkins University Press, 1992.

———. *The Life of Solitude*. Translated by Jacob Zeitlin. Urbana: University of Illinois Press, 1924.

Pezzini, Domenico. " 'Velut Gemma Carbunculus': Le Versioni Del Francescano William Herebert." *Contributi dell'Istituto Di Filologia Moderna: Serie Inglese* 1 (1974): 3–38.

———. "Versions of Latin Hymns in Medieval England: William Herebert and the English Hymnal." *Mediaevistik* 4 (1991): 297–315.

Pound, Ezra. *ABC of Reading*. New York: J. Laughlin, 1960.

Powell, Jason. "Thomas Wyatt's Poetry in Embassy: Egerton 2711 and the Production of Literary Manuscripts Abroad." *Huntington Library Quarterly* 67 (2004): 261–82.

Powicke, F. M., and C. R. Cheney. *Councils & Synods, with Other Documents Relating to the English Church*. Edited by D. Whitelock, M. Brett, and C. N. L. Brooke. 2 vols. Oxford: Clarendon Press, 1964.

Pratt, Robert Armstrong. "A Note on Chaucer's Lollius." *Modern Language Notes* 65 (1950): 183–87.

Priscian. "Fundamentals Adapted from Hermogenes." In *Readings in Medieval Rhetoric*, edited by Joseph M. Miller, Michael H. Prosser, and Thomas W. Benson, translated by Joseph M. Miller, 52–68. Bloomington: Indiana University Press, 1973.

Puttenham, George. *The Art of English Poesy*. Edited by John Lumley, Frank Whigham, and Wayne A. Rebhorn. Ithaca, N.Y.: Cornell University Press, 2007.

Quintilian. *The Institutio Oratoria of Quintilian.* Translated by H. E. Butler. 4 vols. Cambridge, Mass.: Harvard University Press, 1979.

Raby, F. J. E. *A History of Secular Latin Poetry in the Middle Ages.* 2 vols. Oxford: Clarendon Press, 1934.

———, ed. *The Oxford Book of Medieval Latin Verse.* Oxford: Clarendon Press, 1959.

Rancière, Jacques. *The Politics of Aesthetics: The Distribution of the Sensible.* Translated by Gabriel Rockhill. New York: Continuum, 2004.

Ready, Kathryn J. "The Marian Lyrics of Jacopone Da Todi and Friar William Herebert: The Life and the Letter." *Franciscan Studies* 55 (1998): 221–38.

Reeves, Andrew. "Teaching the Creed and Articles of Faith in England: 1215–1281." In *A Companion to Pastoral Care in the Late Middle Ages (1200–1500)*, edited by Ronald J. Stansbury, 41–72. Leiden: Brill, 2010.

Revard, Carter. "Gilote et Johane: An Interlude in B. L. MS. Harley 2253." *Studies in Philology* 79 (1982): 122–46.

———. "Oppositional Thematics and Metanarrative in MS Harley 2253, Quires 1–6." In *Essays in Manuscript Geography: Vernacular Manuscripts of the English West Midlands from the Conquest to the Sixteenth Century*, edited by Wendy Scase, 95–112. Turnhout, Belgium: Brepols, 2007.

———. "Scribe and Provenance." In *Studies in the Harley Manuscript: The Scribes, Contents, and Social Contexts of British Library MS Harley 2253*, edited by Susanna Fein, 21–109. Kalamazoo, Mich.: Medieval Institute Publications, 2000.

Richards, I. A. *Principles of Literary Criticism.* Edited by John Constable. London: Routledge, 2001.

Robbins, Rossell Hope. "Friar Herebert and the Carol." *Anglia* 75 (1957): 194–98.

———. *Secular Lyrics of the XIVth and XVth Centuries.* Oxford: Clarendon Press, 1952.

Robertson, Kellie. *The Laborer's Two Bodies: Literary and Legal Productions in Britain, 1350–1500.* New York: Palgrave Macmillan, 2006.

———. "Medieval Materialism: A Manifesto." *Exemplaria* 22 (2010): 99–118.

Rossiter, William T. *Chaucer and Petrarch.* Cambridge: D. S. Brewer, 2010.

Rothenberg, David J. *The Flower of Paradise: Marian Devotion and Secular Song in Medieval and Renaissance Music.* Oxford: Oxford University Press, 2011.

Rothwell, William, gen. ed. *The Anglo-Norman Dictionary Online.* Aberystwyth University and Swansea University, 2001. http://www.anglo-norman.net/.

———. "Introduction to the On-Line AND: Section 1: Anglo-French and the AND." *Anglo-Norman Online Hub.* http://www.anglo-norman.net/sitedocs/main-intro .shtml.

Rouse, Richard H., and Mary A. Rouse. *Preachers, Florilegia and Sermons: Studies on the Manipulus Florum of Thomas of Ireland.* Toronto: Pontifical Institute of Mediaeval Studies, 1979.

———. "Statim Invenire: Schools, Preachers, and New Attitudes to the Page." In *Authentic Witnesses: Approaches to Medieval Texts and Manuscripts*, 191–219. Notre Dame, Ind.: University of Notre Dame Press, 1991.

Sacks, Peter M. *The English Elegy: Studies in the Genre from Spenser to Yeats*. Baltimore: Johns Hopkins University Press, 1985.

Salter, Elizabeth. *Fourteenth-Century English Poetry: Contexts and Readings*. Oxford: Oxford University Press, 1983.

Sampson, Margaret. "Laxity and Liberty in Seventeenth-Century English Political Thought." In *Conscience and Casuistry in Early Modern Europe*, edited by Edmund Leites, 72–118. Cambridge: Cambridge University Press, 1988.

Sanok, Catherine. "Criseyde, Cassandre, and the Thebaid: Women and the Theban Subtext of Chaucer's *Troilus and Criseyde*." *Studies in the Age of Chaucer* 20 (1998): 41–71.

Scanlon, Larry. *Narrative, Authority, and Power: The Medieval Exemplum and the Chaucerian Tradition*. Cambridge: Cambridge University Press, 1994.

Scase, Wendy. *Literature and Complaint in England, 1272–1553*. Oxford: Oxford University Press, 2007.

Scattergood, John. "Authority and Resistance: The Political Verse." In *Studies in the Harley Manuscript: The Scribes, Contents, and Social Contexts of British Library MS Harley 2253*, edited by Susanna Fein, 163–201. Kalamazoo, Mich.: Medieval Institute Publications, 2000.

———. "The Love Lyric before Chaucer." In *A Companion to the Middle English Lyric*, edited by Thomas G. Duncan, 39–67. Cambridge: Brewer, 2005.

Shannon, Edgar Finley. *Chaucer and the Roman Poets*. Cambridge, Mass.: Harvard University Press, 1929.

Sidney, Philip. "The Defence of Poesy." In *Sidney's "The Defence of Poesy" and Select Renaissance Literary Criticism*, edited by Gavin Alexander, 1–54. New York: Penguin, 2004.

Silliman, Ron. "Disappearance of the Word, Appearance of the Word." In *The L=A=N=G=U=A=G=E Book*, edited by Bruce Andrews and Charles Bernstein, 121–32. Carbondale: Southern Illinois University Press, 1984.

Simpson, James. "Ethics and Interpretation: Reading Wills in Chaucer's *Legend of Good Women*." *Studies in the Age of Chaucer* 20 (1998): 73–100.

———. *Reform and Cultural Revolution: 1350–1547*. Vol. 2. Oxford English Literary History. Oxford: Oxford University Press, 2002.

Smalley, Beryl. *English Friars and Antiquity in the Early Fourteenth Century*. Oxford: B. Blackwell, 1960.

Smith, D. Vance. *Book of the Incipit*. Minneapolis: University of Minnesota Press, 2001.

Spearing, A. C. *Medieval Autographies: The "I" of the Text*. Notre Dame, Ind.: University of Notre Dame Press, 2012.

———. *Textual Subjectivity: The Encoding of Subjectivity in Medieval Narratives and Lyrics*. Oxford: Oxford University Press, 2005.

Specht, Henrik. " 'Ethopoeia' or Impersonation: A Neglected Species of Medieval Characterization." *Chaucer Review* 21 (1986): 1–15.

Spitzer, Leo. "Note on the Poetic and Empirical 'I' in Mediaeval Authors." *Traditio* 4 (1946): 414–22.

Stamatakis, Chris. *Sir Thomas Wyatt and the Rhetoric of Rewriting: "Turning the Word."* Oxford: Oxford University Press, 2012.

Stanbury Smith, Sarah. " 'Adam Lay I-Bowndyn' and the Vinculum Amoris." *English Language Notes* 15 (1977–78): 98–101.

Statius, P. Papinius. *Thebaid: A Song of Thebes.* Translated by Jane Wilson Joyce. Ithaca, N.Y.: Cornell University Press, 2008.

Steiner, Emily. "Authority." In *Middle English,* edited by Paul Strohm, 142–59. Oxford: Oxford University Press, 2007.

———. *Documentary Culture and the Making of Medieval English Literature.* Cambridge: Cambridge University Press, 2003.

Stemmler, Theo. "Miscellany or Anthology? The Structure of Medieval Manuscripts: MS Harley 2253, for Example." In *Studies in the Harley Manuscript: The Scribes, Contents, and Social Contexts of British Library MS Harley 2253,* edited by Susanna Fein, 111–21. Kalamazoo, Mich.: Medieval Institute Publications, 2000.

Stillinger, Thomas C. *The Song of Troilus: Lyric Authority in the Medieval Book.* Philadelphia: University of Pennsylvania Press, 1992.

Stock, Brian. *The Implications of Literacy: Written Language and Models of Interpretation in the Eleventh and Twelfth Centuries.* Princeton, N.J.: Princeton University Press, 1983.

Stubbs, Charles W. *Historical Memorials of Ely Cathedral: In Two Lectures Delivered in Cambridge in the Summer of 1896.* London: J. M. Dent & Co., 1897.

Summerfield, Thea. "The Political Songs in the Chronicles of Pierre de Langtoft and Robert Mannyng." In *The Court and Cultural Diversity,* edited by Evelyn Mullally and John Thompson, 139–48. Woodbridge: D. S. Brewer, 1997.

Sutherland, Donald W. Quo Warranto *Proceedings in the Reign of Edward I, 1278–1294.* Oxford: Clarendon Press, 1963.

Switten, Margaret. "Borrowing, Citation, and Authorship in Gautier de Coinci's *Miracles de Nostre Dame.*" In *The Medieval Author in Medieval French Literature,* edited by Virginie Greene, 29–59. New York: Palgrave Macmillan, 2006.

Symes, Carol. *A Common Stage: Theater and Public Life in Medieval Arras.* Ithaca, N.Y.: Cornell University Press, 2007.

Taylor, Andrew. "The Myth of the Minstrel Manuscript." *Speculum* 66 (1991): 43–73.

———. *Textual Situations: Three Medieval Manuscripts and Their Readers.* Philadelphia: University of Pennsylvania Press, 2002.

Taylor, Karla. "Proverbs and the Authentication of Convention in *Troilus and Criseyde.*" In *Chaucer's Troilus: Essays in Criticism,* edited by Stephen A. Barney, 277–96. Hamden, Conn.: Archon Books, 1980.

Terada, Rei. "After the Critique of Lyric." *PMLA* 123 (2008): 195–200.

Tottel, Richard, Amanda Holton, and Tom MacFaul, eds. *Tottel's Miscellany: Songs and Sonnets of Henry Howard, Earl of Surrey, Sir Thomas Wyatt and Others.* London: Penguin, 2011.

Turville-Petre, Thorlac. *England the Nation: Language, Literature, and National Identity, 1290–1340.* Oxford: Clarendon Press, 1996.

van Dijk, Conrad. *John Gower and the Limits of the Law*. Cambridge: D. S. Brewer, 2013.

Vance, Eugene. *Mervelous Signals: Poetics and Sign Theory in the Middle Ages*. Lincoln: University of Nebraska Press, 1986.

Vendler, Helen. *Soul Says: On Recent Poetry*. Cambridge, Mass.: Harvard University Press, 1995.

Vickers, Nancy J. "Diana Described: Scattered Woman and Scattered Rhyme." *Critical Inquiry* 8 (1981): 265–79.

Vidal, Raimon. *The Razos de Trobar of Raimon Vidal and Associated Texts*. Edited by J. H. Marshall. Oxford: Oxford University Press, 1972.

von Düringsfeld, Ida, and Otto von Reinsberg-Düringsfeld. *Sprichwörter der Germanischen und Romanischen Sprachen Vergleichend*. 2 vols. Leipzig: H. Fries, 1872.

Wakelin, Daniel. "The Carol in Writing: Three Anthologies from Fifteenth-Century Norfolk." *Journal of the Early Book Society for the Study of Manuscripts and Printing History* 9 (2006): 25–49.

Wallace, David. *Chaucerian Polity: Absolutist Lineages and Associational Forms in England and Italy*. Stanford, Calif.: Stanford University Press, 1997.

———. "Europe: A Literary History, 1348–1418." http://www.english.upenn.edu/~dwallace/europe/index.html.

———. "Problematics of European Literary History, 1348–1400." In *The Construction of Textual Identity in Medieval and Early Modern Literature*, edited by Indira Ghose and Denis Renevey, 83–109. Tübingen: Narr, 2009.

Walter de Bibbesworth. *Le Tretiz*. Edited by William Rothwell. London: Anglo-Norman Text Society, 1990.

Walther, Hans, ed. *Proverbia Sententiaeque Latinitatis Medii Aevi: Lateinische Sprichwörter Und Sentenzen Des Mittelalters in Alphabetischer Anordnung*. 6 vols. Göttingen: Vandenhoeck & Ruprecht, 1963.

Ward, John O. *Ciceronian Rhetoric in Treatise, Scholion and Commentary*. Typologie des sources du Moyen Age occidental, fasc. 58. Turnhout: Brepols, 1995.

Warren, Michelle R. "Introduction: Relating Philology, Practicing Humanism." *PMLA* 125 (2010): 283–88.

Waters, Claire M. *Angels and Earthly Creatures: Preaching, Performance, and Gender in the Later Middle Ages*. Philadelphia: University of Pennsylvania Press, 2004.

Watson, Nicholas. *Richard Rolle and the Invention of Authority*. Cambridge: Cambridge University Press, 1991.

Webbe, William. "From a Discourse of English Poetry." In *Sidney's "The Defence of Poesy" and Select Renaissance Literary Criticism*, edited by Gavin Alexander, 254–59. New York: Penguin, 2004.

Wenzel, Siegfried. *Latin Sermon Collections from Later Medieval England: Orthodox Preaching in the Age of Wyclif*. Cambridge: Cambridge University Press, 2005.

———. *Preachers, Poets, and the Early English Lyric*. Princeton, N.J.: Princeton University Press, 1986.

———. *Verses in Sermons: Fasciculus Morum and Its Middle English Poems*. Cambridge, Mass.: Medieval Academy of America, 1978.

Wetherbee, Winthrop. *Chaucer and the Poets: An Essay on* Troilus and Criseyde. Ithaca, N.Y.: Cornell University Press, 1984.

Whiting, Bartlett Jere. *Chaucer's Use of Proverbs*. Cambridge, Mass.: Harvard University Press, 1934.

———. *Proverbs, Sentences, and Proverbial Phrases; from English Writings Mainly Before 1500*. Cambridge, Mass.: Belknap Press of Harvard University Press, 1968.

Wien, Clementine E. "The Source of the Subtitle to Chaucer's Tale of Philomela." *Modern Language Notes* 58 (1943): 605–7.

Wilson, Richard M. *The Lost Literature of Medieval England*. 2nd ed. London: Methuen, 1970.

Wimsatt, James I. *Chaucer and His French Contemporaries: Natural Music in the Fourteenth Century*. Toronto: University of Toronto Press, 1991.

———. *Chaucer and the Poems of "Ch" in University of Pennsylvania MS French 15*. Totowa, N.J.: Rowman & Littlefield, 1982.

———. "The French Lyric Element in *Troilus and Criseyde*." *Yearbook of English Studies* 15 (1985): 18–32.

———. "Guillaume de Machaut and Chaucer's *Troilus and Criseyde*." *Medium Aevum* 45 (1976): 277–93.

Wimsatt, William K., and Monroe Beardsley. *The Verbal Icon: Studies in the Meaning of Poetry*. Lexington: University of Kentucky Press, 1954.

Windeatt, B. A. *Troilus and Criseyde*. Oxford Guides to Chaucer. Oxford: Clarendon Press, 1992.

Wise, Jennifer. *Dionysus Writes: The Invention of Theatre in Ancient Greece*. Ithaca, N.Y.: Cornell University Press, 1998.

Wogan-Browne, Jocelyn. "General Introduction: What's in a Name: The 'French' of 'England.'" In *Language and Culture in Medieval Britain: The French of England c. 1100–c. 1500*, edited by Jocelyn Wogan-Browne, Carolyn Collette, Maryanne Kowaleski, Linne Mooney, Ad Putter, and David Trotter, 1–13. Woodbridge: York Medieval, 2009.

Wogan-Browne, Jocelyn, Carolyn Collette, Maryanne Kowaleski, Linne Mooney, Ad Putter, and David Trotter, eds. *Language and Culture in Medieval Britain: The French of England c. 1100–c. 1500*. Woodbridge: York Medieval, 2009.

Wogan-Browne, Jocelyn, Nicholas Watson, Andrew Taylor, and Ruth Evans, eds. *The Idea of the Vernacular: An Anthology of Middle English Literary Theory, 1280–1520*. University Park: Pennsylvania State University Press, 1999.

Woods, Marjorie Curry. "Rhetoric, Gender, and the Literary Arts: Classical Speeches in the Schoolroom." *New Medieval Literatures* 11 (2009): 113–32.

———. "Weeping for Dido: Epilogue on a Premodern Rhetorical Exercise in the Postmodern Classroom." In *Latin Grammar and Rhetoric: From Classical Theory to Medieval Practice*, edited by Carol Dana Lanham, 284–94. New York: Continuum, 2002.

Wooldridge, H. E. *Oxford History of Music, Vol. 1: The Polyphonic Period*. 2nd ed., rev. Percy C. Buck. London: Humphrey Milford, 1929.

Woolf, Rosemary. *The English Religious Lyric in the Middle Ages*. Oxford: Clarendon Press, 1968.

Wright, Thomas. *Specimens of Lyric Poetry, Composed in England in the Reign of Edward the First*. London: T. Richards, 1842.

Wright, Thomas, and J. O. Halliwell-Phillipps, eds. *Reliquiae Antiquae: Scraps from Ancient Manuscripts, Illustrating Chiefly Early English Literature and the English Language*. 2 vols. London: J. R. Smith, 1845.

Wyatt, Thomas. *The Complete Poems*. Edited by R. A. Rebholz. New Haven, Conn.: Yale University Press, 1981.

Young, Karl. "Chaucer's Appeal to the Platonic Deity." *Speculum* 19 (1944): 1–13.

———. "The Dit de la harpe of Guillaume de Machaut." In *Essays in Honor of Albert Feuillerat*, edited by Henri Peyre, 1–20. New Haven, Conn.: Yale University Press, 1943.

Zeeman, Nicolette. "The Gender of Song in Chaucer." *Studies in the Age of Chaucer* 29 (2007): 141–82.

———. "Imaginative Theory." In *Middle English*, edited by Paul Strohm, 222–40. Oxford: Oxford University Press, 2007.

———. "The Theory of Passionate Song." In *Medieval Latin and Middle English Literature: Essays in Honour of Jill Mann*, edited by Christopher Cannon and Maura Nolan, 231–51. Woodbridge: D. S. Brewer, 2011.

Zieman, Katherine. "Chaucer's Voys." *Representations* 60 (1997): 70.

———. *Singing the New Song: Literacy and Liturgy in Late Medieval England*. Philadelphia: University of Pennsylvania Press, 2008.

Zink, Michel. *The Invention of Literary Subjectivity*. Translated by David Sices. Baltimore: Johns Hopkins University Press, 1999.

Zumthor, Paul. *Toward a Medieval Poetics*. Translated by Philip Bennett. Minneapolis: University of Minnesota Press, 1992.

INDEX OF LYRICS BY FIRST LINE

ACKNOWLEDGMENTS

This book has evolved tactically, as a too-often ad hoc and improvisatory set of responses to the generous engagement of others. And just as lyric tactics, as this book seeks to demonstrate, emerge socially, so too has this project owed its development to the encouragement, support, and interlocutions of many friends, family members, and colleagues.

Bruce Holsinger and Elizabeth "Beth" Robertson fostered and sustained my earliest ventures in medieval literary criticism at the University of Colorado, Boulder. As I explored the possibility of changing professions over a decade ago, their friendship, encouragement, and professional guidance lent me the confidence to venture onto the path of scholarship. I am grateful every day for their unwavering and continuous support that made it seem plausible to abandon the comfort and job security of a career in computer programming for the sometimes uncertain but always fulfilling life of a professional scholar and teacher.

Many others contributed to the development of this project with intellectual, emotional, and moral support. James Simpson and Nicholas Watson were instrumental in shaping this project in its early stages. Peter Sacks helped expand my understanding of the relationship between medieval poetry and the larger field of lyric poetics. Emily Steiner, Ardis Butterfield, Paul Strohm, Virginia Jackson, Jessica Brantley, Julie Orlemanski, and Jennifer Jahner all provided astute and timely responses to portions of this project, along with the encouragement necessary to sustain any long endeavor. The two anonymous readers for the University of Pennsylvania Press offered engaged and incisive comments on an earlier version of the manuscript that strengthened and clarified its argument and structure. I am grateful for the patience and encouragement of my editor at the press, Jerome Singerman, as he has shepherded this project toward publication.

The members of the Radcliffe seminar titled "What Kind of Thing Is a Middle English Lyric?" offered many helpful responses to my presentation of this work; Cristina Cervone, Andrew Galloway, Stephen Burt, Andrew Albin, and Ian Cornelius merit particular mention. My colleagues in FORMER: The Working Group on Medieval Form and Poetics have earned my enduring gratitude: Shannon Gayk, Eleanor Johnson, Arthur Bahr, Rebecca Davis, Seeta Chaganti, Marisa Libbon, Sarah Novacich, and Jennifer Sisk have provided extraordinarily attentive readings and commentary on previous drafts of this project. Patrick Pritchett has been a dedicated, indefatigable interlocutor and friend throughout the duration of this project. His intellectual and personal generosity has helped to expand my understanding and love of both lyric and assertively nonlyrical poetry.

My colleagues at Amherst College and in the Five-College Consortium have engaged enthusiastically with this work, even when it fell outside of their respective fields. Jenny Adams at the University of Massachusetts, Amherst, and Nancy Bradbury at Smith College have both responded to portions of this project with great insight and fostered a community of medievalists in the Pioneer Valley that I have been privileged to join. At Amherst College, Geoffrey Sanborn, Amelie Hastie, and Judith Frank have read and responded to portions of this work with intelligence and grace. Christopher van den Berg and Paul Rockwell have provided assistance with my Latin and French translations, respectively. My undergraduate research assistants— Terence Cullen, Elizabeth Ballinger-Dix, Dan Kim, and Cassandra Hradil— have cheerfully taken up numerous clerical tasks related to the completion and presentation of this work. Amherst College librarians have tirelessly tracked down numerous obscure sources. The manuscript librarians at the British Library, the Cambridge libraries, and the Oxford Bodleian library have all provided invaluable assistance during the course of my research.

I gratefully acknowledge the financial support for this project provided by Harvard University's Presidential Fellowship and Dexter Term-Time and Summer Fellowships, as well as Amherst College's Trustee Faculty Fellowship and Gregory S. Call Academic Intern Awards.

I am thankful for the love and support of my parents and sister throughout the long process of developing this project. Chris Thompson has been a steady source of support, laughter, and companionship in the final stages of bringing this book to fruition. This book is dedicated to the memory of my grandmother, Lillian Brooker, whose unconditional love has been a sustaining force in my life and work.